DRAMA IN EDUCATION 2

The Annual Survey

Edited by

John Hodgson and
Martin Banham

Pitman Publishing

wY

First published 1973

SIR ISAAC PITMAN AND SONS LTD.
Pitman House, Parker Street, Kingsway, London WC2B 5PB
P.O. Box 46038, Portal Street, Nairobi, Kenya

SIR ISAAC PITMAN (AUST.) PTY. LTD.
Pitman House, 158 Bouverie Street, Carlton, Victoria 3053, Australia

PITMAN PUBLISHING COMPANY S.A. LTD.
P.O. Box 11231, Johannesburg, South Africa

PITMAN PUBLISHING CORPORATION
6 East 43rd Street, New York, N.Y. 10017, U.S.A.

SIR ISAAC PITMAN (CANADA) LTD.
495 Wellington Street West, Toronto 135, Canada

THE COPP CLARK PUBLISHING COMPANY
517 Wellington Street West, Toronto 135, Canada

Printed by photolithography and bound in Great Britain at
The Pitman Press, Bath
G3—(G.3522:13)

Editorial

DRAMA IN EDUCATION 1 was concerned with putting our subject into perspective — historically, educationally, and philosophically. With the present and future editions of The Annual Survey we shall focus upon those issues that we feel to be most in need of attention and discussion at the time. In DRAMA IN EDUCATION 2 we discuss the factors of 'Play' and 'The School Play', and in addition we look at the politics of our subject and the range of international activity in the field.

Our contributors to the main theme are examining three basic questions:

a) What is Play? What has it got to do with Education? What has it got to do with Drama?

b) What is the link of **The** Play with Play?

c) What are the current attitudes towards The School Play?

These are the realistic concerns of drama teachers, and we hope that the ideas raised in this issue will challenge and stimulate work at all levels.

We should also be aware, at this time, of the opportunity that is offered to drama in education by two developments in secondary education. They are the extra year at school, consequent upon the raising of the school leaving age, and the rapid growth of Comprehensive education. In the first case, the extra year leaves a gap that **has** to be filled with purposeful activity designed to lead the student towards adult life and to bridge the gap between school and the outside world. Here drama surely has a special responsibility and a special chance, as Lord Boyle implies in his discussion with DRAMA IN EDUCATION. Drama teachers in the secondary schools must, **now**, be asserting their right to work centrally in this area. For once we can be working free of the traditional boundaries of timetabling and examination commitments. The opportunity of drama based project work must be accepted by drama teachers in the secondary schools as their special and unique contribution towards making this extra year not one of boredom and frustrated time-serving, but one of adventure, exploration, excitement, stimulus, and **relevance**.

On the point of Comprehensive education we, as drama teachers, should again be aggressive. Comprehensivization means coordination. Drama is the logical core subject, the clear and natural centre of humane studies. This is not mere sloganizing — it can be argued clearly and cogently and is so by contributors to the DRAMA IN EDUCATION Forum, which, be it noted, included not only drama specialists but a critical and sensitive educational scientist.

What we sometimes lack is not the strength of argument, it is the courage to argue. We have to stop being content with the nice things people say about our work — we have to make them match their words with action. And we have to be sure that we deserve the nice words.

Acknowledgments

Patrick Meredith's article, a lecture given in 1968 to the British Children's Theatre Association Conference, was first published in 'Greater London Arts'.

Youngson Simukoko's article is abridged from 'Chikwakwa 1971: a Review of Theatre Events at the University of Zambia'.

The editors would like to thank Nesta Macdonald for permission to use the photographs which appear throughout this issue. The photograph of Charles Gardiner and his pupils which appears on pages 134 and 135 is reproduced by permission of the 'Daily Mirror'.

The Index was compiled by Kate Banham.

Finally, grateful thanks are due to Dorothy Clark for secretarial assistance.

Contents

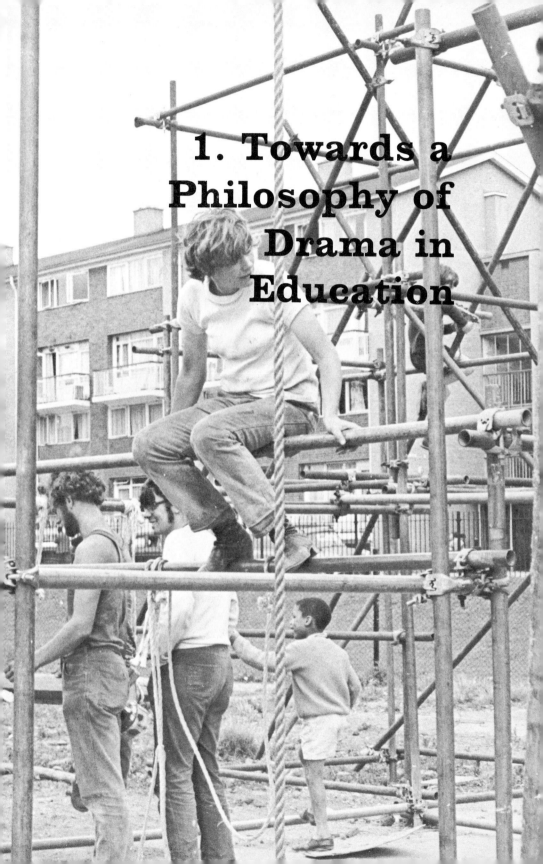

1. Towards a Philosophy of Drama in Education

Point Counterpoint

A symposium of ideas and experiences about drama teaching

Earlier this year, 'Drama in Education' invited four teachers concerned with various aspects of education to discuss their philosophy of drama in the teaching situation. They were Christabel Burniston, Director of the English Speaking Board, Alyn Davies, Principal of Bretton Hall College of Education, a scientist, and a former HMI, Peter Thomson, Lecturer in English at University College, Swansea and formerly Lecturer in the Drama Department at Manchester University, and Russell Whiteley, Head of the Drama Department at Knottingley High School, and Secretary of the BCTA.

DRAMA IN EDUCATION: Can we put the verb to teach in front of the word drama?

ALYN DAVIES: I for one don't think so. The reason I think it's non-sense, whether grammatically or in terms of its actual meaning, is that the word 'teach' predicates certain things happening in the learner which are part and parcel of the process of grasping and ordering knowledge, skills, certain kinds of insights, and nothing that I know about drama, using the word in the broadest sense, can possibly be described — certainly not defined and contained within any particular set of insights, any particular set of skills or any particular body of knowledge. I'd much rather think the word could be used in a context such as learning through drama, because I see drama as an experience rather than a subject.

PETER THOMSON: It is a kind of historical experience for me. When
I went to teach drama at Manchester there was, when I arrived, a
learning situation. Over the years there developed a teaching situation, and I felt the more drama that was taught the less drama was
learnt. And I can't explain that: it is a positive experience.   It
began to be a 'subject'. Instead of leaving the teacher and the
student in a similar situation we began to separate off the teacher
from the student, putting the teacher at a point where he had something to say and the student had to listen. I was interested by something Russ was saying earlier, and I wonder whether this doesn't
apply very vividly at the schools as well. The drama lesson stands
away from the English lesson, away from the physics lesson, history
lesson or whatever, because the drama teacher removes himself
from the position of teaching a particular skill, a particular discipline, and says "Look, I'm not quite sure what's going to happen.
Now let's see."

RUSSELL WHITELEY: I would have thought that the only teaching that
was involved, if teaching is the right word, is in helping children to
organize ideas and the expression of ideas. That is really as far as
you can go. You can't teach this. All you can do is give them to a
certain extent, in the initial stages, an organization round which to
work, or a structure, a skeleton around which they can hang flesh
in order to communicate their ideas to each other or to the rest of
the group.

CHRISTABEL BURNISTON: You have to give them a set of disciplines
though, haven't you? Awareness must be sharpened through their
senses and reported observation. It can't be taught, because you
are hoping to induce them to come to terms with their varying personalities, and if you're making them come to terms with their
varying personalities so must the teacher. The teacher is learning
while doing this. Therefore she or he is in the learning situation as
much as the children.

PETER THOMSON: There is a very simple way of demonstrating this.
If as a teacher I decide there are three things that should be known
about Marlowe my job as a teacher becomes — in order to help my
students to pass their examination — to tell them those three things.
We can only teach what we believe has to be known. If you start
with a certain series of dramatic formulae which you think should

be known you can, I suppose, set up a teaching situation and you can discipline your class, whether it's a school class or an extra-mural class or whatever, to receive those formulae.

CHRISTABEL BURNISTON: Yes, you can teach if your experience has been **more** than the children's. I just wonder in some cases whether the teacher's experience **has** been, or if it's as vicarious as the children's experience.

PETER THOMSON: I don't possess the three things I want to tell them! That's my problem.

CHRISTABEL BURNISTON: If, for instance, in drama we are concerned with a conflict of personality against personality, the teacher should have experience of those conflicts and is hardly likely to have done so. But with a few years added on at least the teacher has got a perspective on those conflicts. The children themselves must learn through contending with meeting those different personalities and the different situations. The teacher's job is to give the probing question and **listen** to their answers.

RUSSELL WHITELEY: I think that in the Drama situation the teacher acts very largely as a catalyst rather than an implanter of a body of information.

DRAMA IN EDUCATION: Why do you have this narrow view of what teaching is?

RUSSELL WHITELEY: I would have thought that the whole point of teaching was to draw out rather than to put in.

CHRISTABEL BURNISTON: To learn how to learn. This applies to every subject whether it's drama, science or history. The pupil must **question** what he is being taught.

ALYN DAVIES: There are other words in the language, like 'educating'. You choose the word because of what it means, and you don't choose the word 'teach' unless it's saying something about the process you are talking about which is helpful to the person who is reading the word or listening to it. The word 'educate' has dimensions greater than the word teach.

5

DRAMA IN EDUCATION: But all words accumulate different meanings and 'teach' has accumulated different meanings. This discussion is amazing because it seems to us that we have gone past 'instruct'. You are thinking of teachers being the instructor, the lecturer or the teller of truths. Whereas surely the teacher has always been the catalyst, has been the person who can set up a situation in which discoveries can be made.

PETER THOMSON: 'Teach' is a transitive verb, and education a largely intransitive activity. That's the problem.

RUSSELL WHITELEY: In a school situation you come up against this all the time. As I said, I see myself as a catalyst and, because of this, children coming into my room talk to me and express themselves without any fear. Then I have trouble from the science department or maths department because a child will get up in these lessons and challenge what members of staff are saying. This I think is vitally important because I see one of my jobs as teaching children to challenge ideas and to think for themselves, and once this happens — once you create this sort of situation — it spreads over into other subjects. So you are constantly getting a member of staff coming flying at you and saying, "One of your drama kids actually had the audacity to stand up and say 'I don't believe that' or 'Why should I do that?' ". I am trying to encourage children to think, whereas a lot of teachers think the verb to teach purely and simply means standing and dropping pearls of wisdom which children will accept.

CHRISTABEL BURNISTON: If on the other hand we can't use the word 'teach', there is an awful danger — and I've seen this so often with young teachers — of thinking they'll abdicate. They leave children to wallow in self-indulgence and to go on experimenting, and do not give them any target or encourage true observation or criticism. This is the danger if we remove the word 'teaching' completely. Children need trained muscles, trained minds and language in order to have true 'self-expression'.

ALYN DAVIES: Well, I don't like the idea of the drama teacher as Messiah. I think any good teacher's business is to encourage children to be critical or to be aware of what is happening, in whatever the subject. The material you are concerned with doesn't necessarily predicate certain relationships at all. The point about drama and to teach is that drama is more than something which can adequately be put at the end of the word teach. The reason I put it in this way is because it has something to say about a whole range of human experiences, a whole range of knowledge. It has an existence outside any terms you might choose to describe normally associated with it. In other words it has dimensions which go beyond those of a body of knowledge and all the other things I mentioned before.

DRAMA IN EDUCATION: How do you see the relationship of drama, in a secondary school for instance, to other subjects which work basically on information which is gained and stored and worked upon by the students?

ALYN DAVIES: I'm not willing to agree that they work basically on information gained and so stored. Science does it. None of the sciences, even taken in a very narrow sense, are simply operating on a basis of information received and stored. They are operating on a way of looking. They select certain kinds of problem or question proper to their investigation and then investigate them according to certain procedures. In one sense traditional procedures, in that they can be recognized as having historical roots, but in a far more important way, methodological procedures. In the case of drama, what I see it having to offer is a certain kind of experience of examining and analyzing, responding to a whole range of experience, ideas, information. What's particular about it is the way it will set up a situation for examination, analysis, etc.

DRAMA IN EDUCATION: Don't you think it might encourage children to be arrogant as opposed to being informed?

CHRISTABEL BURNISTON: Not if they are guided towards imaginative awareness. They should have that sensibility about all people and be able to 'get into the shoes' of other people and thus develop compassion.

ALYN DAVIES: I absolutely agree with you. Without sensitivity to the ways relationships develop in a group you're getting nowhere.

CHRISTABEL BURNISTON: And their science is going to be terribly dangerous if they haven't the imaginative awareness to know what's

going to happen with the things they invent and the things they help
to make.

PETER THOMSON: There is a very interesting thing emerging. Alyn
and Christabel are both raising an objection to a notion of drama as
something separate from other disciplines. I'm glad of it, but there
is a quality in most of us who teach drama which I might call missionary. The missionary tends to have to do two things: he tends to have
to convert and in order to convert he has to recognize the opposition.
The opposition is probably there in the real missionary situation.
But we may force ourselves into being missionaries. We may find
ourselves creating the opposition in the school, in the college, in
the other kinds of discipline. We oppose ourselves as drama teachers
against science teachers. Science teachers, we say, merely feed in
information. Drama teachers have to create. What I want to say is
that inside the schools or educational institutions in general there is
a danger that the drama teacher will feel himself to be a lone missionary. I think all the teachers I know who teach drama in big
comprehensive schools do feel some of this sense of the missionary.
In Universities, drama departments tend to feel like isolated missionaries.

RUSSELL WHITELEY: Could we look at this from the children's point
of view? In the drama lesson they are not going to be expected to
pick up a pen and put it to paper. They are not going to be given an
examination. They feel a certain freedom, and because this tends
to be different from the other lessons, then they look upon the drama
lesson as something special. They have a sense of security in a
drama lesson, particularly with the less able, less intelligent child,
which they don't have in the other lessons, because they always have
the fear that somebody is going to ask them something, where the
answer is either right or wrong. Now in drama this is not necessarily so, because they can argue, they can justify, they can talk
about what they are doing, they can work it out either by themselves,
or with other people. This I think is something they miss in the
formal type of lesson.

CHRISTABEL BURNISTON: I would take you up, Russell, on your 'less
able'. You mean less 'academic'. I feel that there are all sorts of
areas of intelligence that we simply do not measure in our science
and maths and so on. In drama we are able to develop qualities to

do with people and creativity which are immeasurable in terms of facts, and right or wrong answers. They are a probing and a finding; therefore you can't, in a sense, teach it, but you must have drama teachers with ethical standards, a vision of excellence and all sorts of super qualities because so many things are at stake. I have heard teachers taking drama classes with too little language themselves for either cognitive or imaginative thought or expression of feelings.

ALYN DAVIES: I'd want those in science or mathematics or the study of English.

RUSSELL WHITELEY: Perhaps it's easier to measure these missionary qualities in a drama teacher than in a science or maths teacher from a child's point of view?

ALYN DAVIES: It's audible, for a start! But I know children of well below your average academic ability who respond quite miraculously to certain kinds of work in science. What I'm trying to say, I think, is, it's no good living in a cosy world where drama has the messianic tag and to be a missionary is all. We have got past that stage.

DRAMA IN EDUCATION: Isn't there a fairly reasonable parallel to be drawn between the approach to the learning of a science subject and the approach of the drama teacher in the terms of the measuring of what one sees in actuality or in practice or in theory?

ALYN DAVIES: I think you are right about a parallel, but it is more than this. In the process of learning in a scientific mode, what you are trying to do is build mental pictures, patterns, which enable you to understand that which you have observed, and enable you to predict that you can understand other things, therefore, and extrapolate from your present stage of understanding. Now I should imagine that in the drama what we are talking about are kinds of experience that enable you to arrive at certain **temporary** (as they are in science) understandings, but to feel competent enough to launch from these to **new** understandings. To that extent both have an on-going developmental aspect. I think most learning of any real value has this quality. After all, from a learner's point of view, if it isn't the beginning of a stage in a developing process then we are talking about conditioning, not talking about learning.

DRAMA IN EDUCATION: Is something that Russell is saying exemplified by the fact that a head master, a few weeks ago, rang us up and told us that drama was the most dangerous subject on the curriculum?

CHRISTABEL BURNISTON: Of course it's dangerous! So is Living!

ALYN DAVIES: Absolutely! This is where we are on good ground, I think. It is dangerous because of the kind of dynamite it's playing with. We've got used to the kind of dynamite science played with. What happened to Thomas Huxley and company against Bishop Berkeley? All hell broke loose in the nineteenth century, but we digested it. But the kind of dynamite you people are playing with now, which is going off all over the place, hasn't been digested by education and society as it were, the people involved or the children and the parents, all the rest of it. That's your problem, God help you.

CHRISTABEL BURNISTON: If you've developed a responsible imaginative attitude to science so that you bring your dramatic element to bear on 'what am I inventing?', 'what am I making?' and 'what will the effect of this be on human beings?' then you have this amalgam of science and drama which in itself is wholly productive and creative.

RUSSELL WHITELEY: This brings me back to the first point I made, that drama has not been digested by educationalists in general and it certainly hasn't been digested by the schools. And this is why you will always get or you will get for the next five or ten years your rigid teachers of (I'm sorry, but I've only come across these) maths and science, who will come to you and say "one of your kids has challenged what I said." And they are not used to this.

CHRISTABEL BURNISTON: But when I met the Nuffield science researchers who were examining science **orally**, they said the thrill was that the boys were saying "Yes, but when I did this .... when I found this .... Your theory paper was wrong, it was out of date!" I call that 'drama in science'.

DRAMA IN EDUCATION: To switch the direction: Peter, you taught drama in the University of Manchester for a number of years. We've been talking about younger students, we've been talking about schools. You've been teaching drama to young adults. **Why,** in

10

terms of your own raison d'être as a teacher, and in terms of their concepts of what they were doing as students?

PETER THOMSON: There's a negative answer. The alternative, teaching English to young adults, was terrifying. I mean by that, that there is a great danger that universities will reverse the process which the best schools are starting. Universities tend to endorse an old-fashioned kind of instruction, and in English departments it has always terrified me that there is an over-insistence on the instructive element in the role of the teacher. He can help his students through their examinations. There are certain definable areas in which he can give the right kind of jargon advice, the right kind of direction, and a wise student will follow him.

   In drama departments, I found I was no longer as easily able to define the areas in which I could give this kind of instruction. Anyway the student didn't want it. And that was very exciting − to meet students who actually wanted my direct response, provided me with theirs and went on from there. The tendency, in fact, is to say "This is no good, we can't sit in this room and talk about this any more, we've got to go and see." And I go with them. I don't say "You come with me." I say "Let's go," or they say "Let's go." I'm worried genuinely by this, because I think lots of universities are retrograde, much more retrograde than colleges of education as I see them — much more retrograde than schools. I think I could talk about that for far too long!

CHRISTABEL BURNISTON: They are bound by their academic disciplines, and are unwilling to accept drama as a practical subject. In most universities drama is a literary exercise.

DRAMA IN EDUCATION: But what are the disciplines of drama teaching in the university?

PETER THOMSON: The disciplines of drama teaching in universities should be defined to an extent by the departments themselves, and defined only so far. I think Exeter is the university that has come closest, so far, to setting up its own dramatic discipline. You're looking at me!

ALYN DAVIES: I'm laughing! I'm thinking of Japanese No Theatre. If you want to start defining disciplines and establishing a body of

11

knowledge in certain traditional skills, that's the direction you are going into — this land of traditional drama. That is to say, drama which is essentially a vehicle for the transmission of traditional culture. At the moment drama as I understand the term, and as I've heard it used, is certainly not used as signifying transmission of a received culture. That is why drama in the universities is very different from history or what have you. Drama at the moment exists in terms of its future, not in terms of its past.

PETER THOMSON: Universities can establish very easily certain areas like theatre history and the study of plays that can be left to drama departments. The next area comes with what's been sepa-rated off, unfortunately, as practical theatre. And what happens when you get to work on practical theatre is that all hell is let loose in a drama department, potentially. You can have a kind of demon-strative function of practical work, you can demonstrate a point that you might otherwise make by lectures: you might take Elizabethan stage forms and demonstrate them by presenting them. It would be a legitimate function for practical work in a drama department. Or you might try to generate something which you couldn't initially define. Essentially you should try to avoid defining a generative kind of practical work in advance; otherwise you are not generating anything. But there's another area of practical work which is a terrifyingly tempting one, which I will call terminal, because I want to be rude about it. The work is its own end. You set up a practical project and that's where it ends. All unsupervised student work tends towards that kind of practical approach, because they want a quick result, they want to be told, immediately, "We've achieved that much, we were good." Terminal work finishes there. We can put it behind us. That kind of terminal approach to practi-cal work in drama is terrifying because it's tempting, it's easy and it has quick rewards. The devastating thing is that terminal work can always ruin other kinds of work because it's more tempting to the student and often to the teacher than progressive work.

CHRISTABEL BURNISTON: Progressive work must lead you into the **future**. I still would come back to this. So much of our teaching today doesn't make children able to grapple with the future. Now if they are going to be able to grapple with the future they've to be able to take imaginative leaps but they also need to have orderly thinking; the thrill of drama but the skill of the scientist. I think the danger with drama, as I see it done by limited teachers, is that they produce 'explosion' but without progression leading towards genuine enquiry and experience.

DRAMA IN EDUCATION: Perhaps the concept of Drama in isolation is wrong. The logic of drama is that it should be integrated with sciences, sociology, the arts. It only really works fundamentally in that context. We have a kind of arrogance that says drama is the common denominator for all things. We like to think of ourselves, as specialists in drama, as being the logical centre of all things. Clearly we are!

RUSSELL WHITELEY: There is a problem here. I went off at a great tangent about this two years ago when I felt that I was working very much on my own and I ought to relate to the other subjects on the curriculum. So I had this big thing where I just went around and said, "Do you feel that the drama department can help you in any way?" However, in a normal school timetable, the problem with this approach is a question of time and syllabus. Say, for example, I was asked to work on a project concerned with the Luddites − not only would I want to go into the historical background, but also into social conditions, personality clashes and develop the work possibly towards parallels in modern society to complete a rounded dramatic experience. Time would need to be taken over discussion and the throwing about of ideas, both factual and imaginary. However, because of the fairly rapid progression in the history work, the time would not be available and I would have to be content with perhaps dramatizing just one episode from the vast field which I feel would not be particularly satisfying for the children. Drama would become a filmstrip-type visual aid in black and white, rather than a moving picture which could contain the grey shades which a subject of this kind demands.

ALYN DAVIES: As I see it the raw material of drama is the person, the self. If this is where the drama begins, if this is the substance out of which dramatic experience (if the words are right) develops, then one of the great things drama in education can be about is a refining of experience that is already there as part of the person. At the first stage, that is the first stage of the child's understanding of happening, it is a re-living and a refining and a re-appraisal of the child's experience. Out of this comes some degree of self-awareness. Once this begins to develop in quite a young child (in the years before puberty) you've got youngsters who are very very excited about themselves. It's the R S Thomas thing about a man "Like a tree, from my topmost branches I see, the footsteps that lead up to me." This is the beginning of conscious enjoyment of drama, as opposed to the unconscious enjoyment of role playing and other things which can happen earlier on. The reason why I think it's so exciting at the higher education level is that it does not predicate a given set of mental stances, perspectives, what have you. It simply predicates a lively, sensitive awareness to my own experience that I will share with others. My prejudice is exposed with yours and, in the shock of recognition, there is a new growth and a new development. This is the kind of activity I think drama is about.

RUSSELL WHITELEY: This is why I would always say that in working with children you start from their own experience and build on this rather than throwing them into a situation which is completely alien.

CHRISTABEL BURNISTON: Then the next thing is: "How would you feel, if..... ?"

RUSSELL WHITELEY: Exactly. You must start from the known and move to the unknown.

DRAMA IN EDUCATION: Shouldn't we be doing something about training actors, training directors, training writers, training theatre technicians? Isn't that part of our responsibility?

PETER THOMSON: In my experience all people who decide they want to be actors during the course of a university education opt out of great areas of university education. They simply say "I'm not interested in that" and turn their backs on some of the things the university has to offer them. I don't blame them for it, but what I would say is that either the university must accommodate them or we must find educational facilities for these manifestly intelligent people. We must find places for them to work. If the drama schools aren't those places, I don't know where they are. But there is honestly a real problem which I speak feelingly about. The fact which isn't adequately admitted is that most people who apply for universities and get admitted to read drama want to go into professional theatre. A very high proportion of them want to act. The question is, then, what do the drama departments do for them? Two, at least, attempt to re-define the

14

wish to act, but the fact is that no drama department I know of really copes with the people who want to act.

ALYN DAVIES: We get them in a teachers' college!

RUSSELL WHITELEY: In the initial stages, in the secondary school particularly, young children are not imbued with this wonderful idea 'I want to be an actor'. Their interest in the drama lesson lies purely and simply in the fact that here is a lesson in which they have a certain amount of freedom.

PETER THOMSON: Most Arts disciplines at universities are trying to teach recent sixth formers to work by themselves. To **really** work by themselves is a new thing. Drama sets itself apart from these in trying to make people **really** for the first time work together. This creates in many students a real problem. I've seen people virtually cracking up on this problem. They don't know which they are supposed to do.

DRAMA IN EDUCATION: To bring it down to a more mundane level. We've discussed the extent to which what we do is vocational, and we seem to be agreed in general that we hope to bring to pupils, students, certain values, certain attitudes through drama work and experience. How far do we think that the work that we do results in the people we've worked with being able to approach what they've received through the public media, television, radio, film with greater discrimination? To what extent, at this very simple level, does drama in education work?

ALYN DAVIES: I think Christabel's been on to this with the word sensibility. I think that's what we ought to be talking about now.

CHRISTABEL BURNISTON: Yes, I think so. If we built this awareness into muscles, eyes, hearing and everything else; if we gave our pupils and students a vision of excellence (which I don't think is done enough) then I think they would have a more searching criticism of television and film. I think what we do (and we're all guilty of this) is give them far too much **stimulus** without enough **discrimination**. This is especially so in the kind of world we live in, but it is an openness and freedom which taxes the human resources of the individual. In most creative school drama there isn't a big enough target; too much self-indulgence, too little discipline, not enough discrimination.

15

DRAMA IN EDUCATION: So, what do you want from the drama work that you do or are associated with?

PETER THOMSON: Inside the university situation I find myself operating in this curious world where half of my job is to give people the confidence to study alone, and the other half of my job is to give people the much rarer confidence to study together. What I would really like to know is how I can improve my ability to teach them to study together, because I reckon I can just about scrape along on helping them to study alone.

RUSSELL WHITELEY: My job is first of all to make the children I work with think for themselves and be discriminating in the face of the barrage of propaganda which is thrown at them, then to make them realise that they've got to live with other people, must work with other people, and finally to try and make them responsive to other people's ideas and receptive to their thoughts — to try to make them see that there is something beyond their own little world, the world that they have been brought up in. Not to make them discontented with it but to try and help them to make their world more interesting and a better place for themselves and their children.

CHRISTABEL BURNISTON: We are all saying the same thing in different ways! I would say that one must develop one's personality to its full potential and through this work towards imaginative awareness in all experience. This would then lead on to ability as an individual to work within a group to the full strength and full stretch of individual powers, but through this to lose oneself in a corporate exercise.

ALYN DAVIES: I think it's about time teachers whose medium is drama developed a philosophy which made sense. I'd suggest as a starting point the simple conception that what is unique about drama is that the reality which each person involved in an experience of learning through drama has is one of an unfolding awareness. What's unique about the drama is that it doesn't happen **now**, it happens **during** a span of time. This is Suzanne Langer's idea of the unfolding mode. The conception of the whole is something that emerges only when the experience is completed and you look back upon it. It's a growth, a development, and it has within itself these vital seeds of reflection upon the shared experience. This sounds awfully airy-fairy. What it is essentially about, is people involved in drama in education having confidence that they can launch themselves into unknown and

16

uncharted seas and in the voyage learn things they did not know existed — about each other and themselves and about the future. If they have the confidence to cope with this complicated idea they have a very special contribution to make in education at every level. If they haven't that confidence, quite simply I think they are involved in a process of running down, here and now. I'm afraid the next generation will see the decay of drama unless the confidence in the **now** and revelation in the **now** is sustained.

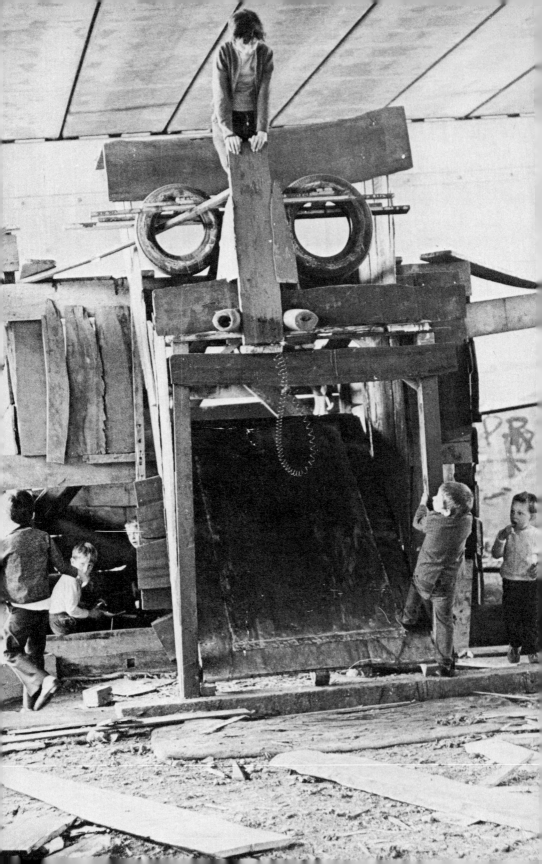

Making the Point: The Politics of a New Subject

Lord Boyle, Vice Chancellor of the University of Leeds and a former Secretary of State for Education, is a strong advocate of the role of the Arts in Education. Here he discusses some of the problems facing new subjects and gives his views on the place of drama in education

DRAMA IN EDUCATION: There seems to be an incredible delay between the acceptance of the value of a new subject and the actual appearance of the subject or an acceptance of the method in the schools. Could you talk about the politics of the development of drama in the school curriculum and how one may best approach the problems which this implies?

LORD BOYLE: Can I just say one very brief word first about the importance of drama in the school curriculum? I have no professional background in drama at all. I am not an English graduate: in fact I haven't taken part in a school play since I was about thirteen, though when young I very much enjoyed doing so. But I have felt the importance of this subject, not only from the conventional point of view that it enables a large number of boys and girls to 'discover' themselves, in a way that is true of very few other activities, but for a deeper reason. It's my impression that a growing number of intelligent sixth formers and older teenagers in schools, living in the kind of world we have today, do concern themselves a great deal with and are generally interested in, not just the conventional emotions but the wilder, untamed emotions. If you talk to a Sixth Form Conference today about pity and fear and those things, you quite rightly get rather a rough time. Many young people today have flashes of mature insight about things like religion which can be very disconcerting to their teachers. In my experience many older teenagers think about the world at a much deeper, much more uncomfortable, level than we often suppose. I think this is all the more important in the context of raising the school leaving age and the high probability of a great

19

increase in the numbers of sixth form pupils in the 1970s — possibly up to half a million — and a great increase in the whole of the fifteen-eighteen age groups, who will still be in full-time education. Now I agree with you, I think it's easy to say those things, but then one asks, "What are the schools doing about it?" I don't myself believe that, in political terms, elected representatives, either at the national level or the local level, would necessarily disagree with what I've said — that's to say that this is not a politically difficult subject in the narrow sense. But of course the problem for the schools is very real. First of all there is the problem of resources. Secondly, there is the problem of specialist advice from local authorities. One of the reasons I have been opposed to too many small local education authorities, is because I do not believe smaller authorities as a general rule can afford the full range of specialist advice that children need today. I am not making any accusations here, but I shall be surprised if some of these new metropolitan districts that are being set up as education authorities under the present local government bill, can in fact provide what Alec Clegg calls the 'marginal enriching resources' that are particularly needed in certain areas, and I think this can be especially true of drama advisers. I think specialist resources are extremely important in this context, and just one other political point does occur to me: I do think a rather more responsible, and in some ways perhaps more effective, role given to school governors could be helpful here in helping to promote experiments in drama. I think this really comes under the heading of the arts and society — this isn't just an optional extra in schools, it's one rather important aspect of school life if schools are to play their full part in bringing about mature citizens.

DRAMA IN EDUCATION: Isn't it more likely that school governors, as presently selected, would tend to be conservative in their attitude towards new subjects rather than experimental?

LORD BOYLE: Well, this is exactly why I'm not keen on having them just as at present constituted. That's to say you don't want political hacks as school governors. You need to take a few risks with your appointments. I think we are terribly bad in Britain about taking risks with appointments at the local level. I belong, although my background of politics is moderate right wing, to that school of thought which says it's a good idea that people should have their ideas and their certainties shaken up. You must always find room for the creative person who will say things we find uncomfortable and I think this ought to be true of a Board of School Governors. To take always the safe line in appointments, is really a terribly unwise policy these days.

DRAMA IN EDUCATION: Don't you think there's a possibility that in making room for the creative man who might make the uncomfortable statement, you are thereby accommodating him without giving him the full potential to develop? There are many schools which will put a drama studio in, and a drama specialist, but regard this facility or this person as a decoration, a status symbol, but not fundamental to the work of the school. It's very easy to absorb the creative arts in this way. In fact the demands of subjects like our own are really overwhelming; they encroach on other subjects and they demand time and facilities and staffing. It's really very extravagant when viewed by school governors or headmasters or other sections of the school. It's an aggressive kind of subject. Isn't this rather frightening for the authorities?

LORD BOYLE: Oh yes — you are of course quite right. It's terribly easy to make a token gesture to the nonconformist. I suppose this is what some people mean by regressive tolerance, and I hope I meant something rather more than that. That is to say, so far as the politics of this are concerned, I would like to see a society where, if a school is a good one, it should from time to time put on performances which visitors may find highly disturbing. Of course, merely because a play is disturbing, it doesn't necessarily follow that it's good. You can be a 'hack' in a radical direction as you can in any other. But I would distinguish in my mind the writer or dramatist who is creative, with ideas or insights that give us a new and disturbing sense of what life is about. For instance I still find William Blake a profoundly disturbing poet. In fact in this sense, and in their different ways, Blake in poetry, Schubert in music and Goya in painting (all died the same year, curiously enough, in 1828) are to me three major creative contributors to the cultural history of the Western world. They all straddled the old arcadian world of the pre-industrial society with the new industrial world we have inherited today. Now personally I would always want to encourage and give opportunities for the William Blakes of this world, not just out of tolerance but because I think this is connected with becoming a full human being. The difficulty, of course, comes not only when people become aggressive in the kind

21

of show they want to put on, but also over money. I think one has always got to distinguish between the problems of the kind of artistic performance one thinks is meritorious, and the amount of money you have with which to do it. I'm afraid I think that from the financial point of view there will have to be for a very long time a restraint on drama. But I do emphasize this point: while money will not be unlimited, I hope that a good many people, fairly widely spread across the political spectrum, would not want schools to be too timid about the kind of performances they put on; and just as we all change in appearance these days, so the kind of dramatic performance a school might consider appropriate will change as well.

DRAMA IN EDUCATION: Can I take you up on vocabulary? You are using the word 'performance' and the word 'show'. Do you think of drama work in the schools in this context?

LORD BOYLE: Well, fair point. I've instinctively found myself — and perhaps this is the conservative in me — I instinctively find myself using old-fashioned words like this, but of course as soon as you challenge me I see exactly what you mean. I was, for a short time, Chairman of the sort of pre-committee that set up the New Activities Committee on the Arts Council, and one of the things I learned there was the importance of artistic activities including dramatic activities that are meant to be ephemeral — where it isn't just the finished performance but it's the actual activity itself which is the raison d'être. Certainly, one musn't just think in terms of the school play, but dramatic activity going on within the school.

DRAMA IN EDUCATION: To go back to the politics of the situation. How does the civil servant come into this picture? How far is the civil servant the person one has to persuade? He, by the very nature of the civil service, may be more cautious and perhaps a rather slower moving person than one would sometimes wish. How far does one have to take him into consideration or is he really an irrelevance?

LORD BOYLE: A number of leading civil servants advising the Secretary of State do not all that frequently go inside a maintained school! To be fair they have got lots of other things to do.

DRAMA IN EDUCATION: Can we quote that?

LORD BOYLE: Certainly. I can remember the day with respect to one

22

Making the Point

senior officer of the Department, when David Eccles was Minister,
when David Eccles said to me, "I've done much better than you ever
did, I've got X actually into a maintained school." I remember that
very well. But I'm not just mocking them. One has got to remember
that they haven't all that time for school visits and of course the
Schools Territorial Offices in the Department are terribly busy with
things like the school building programme, and corresponding
and checking and drafts of letters for ministers explaining why they
can't approve a particular project. I think at the centre one is very
much dependent on the advice of the Inspectorate, and it's common
ground, I think, among many of us — I said this in that book I did
with Maurice Kogan as Tony Crosland did too — that the Inspectorate
in our time never really played as big a part in the Department as
perhaps it might have done. I think, though, one has also to remember that a good many civil servants are fairly regular theatregoers.
I mean the Arts are something very much 'in' with the British Civil
Service. We don't have in Britain a philistine civil service. I can
say that with confidence. At the local level you have got Directors
of Education, Chief Education Officers (like Alec Clegg at Wakefield)
who have always been extremely keen on this side of education. It's
fair to say that a powerful local official can do a very great deal purposefully to get things going — things like drama and the arts. And
then there is all the work of the local inspectorate too. Of course
local inspectors, and divisional inspectors, play a bigger part locally
than the HMIs at the centre.

DRAMA IN EDUCATION: You think the Inspectorate is much more effective on a regional, or local scale, than nationally?

LORD BOYLE: I think this has sometimes been true. Mind you, there
is one other thing one must say purely in political terms. I think, to
a fault myself, we don't really expect ministers to spend an awful lot
of time concerning themselves with what is actually taught in the
schools. Obviously it would be wrong if ministers started decreeing
this or that subject was taught or need not be taught, and yet I do
think myself, in Britain, our expectations of what the Secretary of
State is for, get a bit out of balance. If only just part of the time we
have spent arguing about the organization of Secondary education,
long after it's been apparent that the movement away from eleven-
plus selection isn't going to stop, had been spent interesting ourselves
in what is actually being taught in the schools! This is what I really

23

do find myself deploring sometimes. We do get this balance wrong.

DRAMA IN EDUCATION: Can a Secretary of State for Education, if he or she chooses to do so, further the interests of a particular subject very fundamentally? It may be improper, but it's possible?

LORD BOYLE: Well, there is one very easy way to do it, and I hope just occasionally I did this. Go to conferences of specialist teachers when you are asked to go, and tell them that you are with them and that you will do what you can to help. I think the morale-boosting effect of a minister can be quite considerable at times. Actually voting with your feet is always worth while: taking the trouble — when it might have been a free weekend — taking the trouble on a Saturday to go off and speak to a conference and travel there and talk to them and meet them. I think it always had a certain effect.

DRAMA IN EDUCATION: You mentioned earlier on the importance of the development of sixth form education, the raising of the school leaving age and the extension of comprehensive education. Will subjects such as drama, the more creative subjects, have a particular rôle to play in respect of the new 15-16 year old group who have to remain at school with or without their cooperation, and in the comprehensive system which makes new demands of contact and communication between groups of children of the same age? Do you think subjects like drama can serve particularly well in this context?

LORD BOYLE: I think they will become more important, and of course, there is another category that you left out just then, which is those that will now stay on voluntarily until 17 or 18. One effect of raising the school leaving age is always to encourage voluntary staying on to a later period still, and I think you will get a number of older teenagers for whom drama in educational terms, and not just drama as conventionally described in the past, will be a more important and a more worthwhile subject. Of course we have been talking hitherto mainly from the point of view of the pupils in the schools. Surely more and more good teachers trained in this subject, or even generally trained teachers with some interest in the subject, will be coming out of the colleges all the time? I would expect this from some of the married women coming back for a second spell in education, many of whom make excellent teachers. I hope a number of those who have been used to regularly going to the Theatre will take a special interest in the drama in the schools.

DRAMA IN EDUCATION: One of the difficulties facing the drama teacher in a secondary school is having sufficient time within the timetable. The children have to move out of the history lesson and into drama and out again to French, and there is a change of mood and of style implied here, which is not easy for a child to accommodate. One of the opportunities of the raising of the school leaving age is that the educational authorities seem willing to look at very new ways of filling up the year and filling up time during the day and do not assume that the traditional patterns of timetabling need to be followed. So there is a new opportunity for the drama teacher. This creates the possibility of the kind of time scale changes coming about which some of us feel are essential for effective teaching of drama. Do you think this is a pipe-dream or a possibility?

LORD BOYLE: I think it's a real possibility. I think this is quite true. There will be more time with the raising of the age. The same is true of that category I mentioned just now: the, as it were, semi-academic sixth former. You see there is a real problem for the traditional sixth former who is concerned about A-levels and is concerned — and maybe his teachers are even more concerned — about his A-level performances and his chances of getting into university. But you are going to get a growing number of sixth formers who will not want just a pre-university course, but something different.

DRAMA IN EDUCATION: Most of the things we have been saying assume that the quality of drama teaching measures up to the ideas and to the potential and obviously this is not always true. Some drama teachers are poor and lazy teachers, which in a sense brings us to James. It seems to us that one of the major needs of our subject at all levels, primary, secondary, college of education, university, is for more and better informed and more exciting teachers. How far do you think that James is going to assist the development of new ideas in education?

LORD BOYLE: Well, I think the proposals for the third cycle of James, the in-service training, could be enormously helpful here. I think this should provide a real possibility for teachers to re-tool, in the course of their working lives and this will be true of drama teachers

at least as much as any others. About the proposals for the first and
second cycles, I still have my reservations. I am nervous of teacher
training getting too far away from universities because I do believe
that what I sometimes call 'the undistributed middle' of university
teaching, by which I mean the experienced professor or senior lecturer
in an experienced university department with a long history, really has
got something very special to contribute here in cooperation with the
colleges, in bringing about the optimum kind of course. My feeling is
the first cycle, as suggested by James, may become a bit too general,
the second cycle a bit too narrowly vocational. But I think the great
hope for the drama in James are the proposals for the third cycle,
provided of course adequate money can be put behind this.

DRAMA IN EDUCATION: Yes indeed, and also — and this is a point we
have raised in 'Drama in Education 1' — that there are sufficient
teachers of quality available to teach in the colleges of education,
which in the field of drama is at the moment still rather a problem.

LORD BOYLE: Well, this is of course most important and this comes
back to another point, that surely one crucial thing in teacher training
is that the college lecturers themselves should be encouraged to do
what they want to do and do well. There are moments in James,
Chapter 4, where it seems to me that the Committee do see this
point clearly but there are other moments when you rather lose sight
of it. But I believe that this is vital. The quality of the trainers is
absolutely crucial.

DRAMA IN EDUCATION: This is an unfair question because this won't
be printed until February 1973, by which time the Secretary of State
will have made her decision. But what adjustments to the basic
James report do you think it is likely that the Secretary of State will
make? In what form do you think the report will survive?

LORD BOYLE: I wouldn't like to forecast that. I'm very ready to say,
though, what is the single recommendation I would like to see amen-
ded or refined and what I think is one of the most important decisions
we have to make arising out of James, and that is the proposal for
the BA (Ed). I would like to see a validating body being able to rule
out, as well as to approve, schemes of study designed to lead to the
award of a BA (Ed). The whole strength of the CNAA (the Council
for National Academic Awards) has been that it has had the power to

rule out certain degree courses. Two things need always to be remembered about CNAA. The first is that it grew out of the National
Council for Technological Awards, whose own Diploma overlapped
with university degree standard from the start. We have always had
the university degree as a sort of guide-post and I don't think we
ought to lose it. And secondly, from the very beginning the CNAA
had the power to rule out certain schemes of study as well as to
approve them. Now I do think it is most important that this validating
body should have that power. Where education is concerned I am
always on the side of trying to make teaching a bit more of a learned
profession than it is already. And I'm convinced that something on
the lines of what I have proposed is essential if the BA (Ed) is to have
a standing comparable with a CNAA degree, let alone a university
degree.

DRAMA IN EDUCATION: As you know, UGC policy at the moment limits
the number of drama departments in British universities to four major
departments and restricts development in this field as in other fields
in terms of what it presumably regards as the need in relation to the
subject. Despite this a large number of universities under various
guises do involve themselves in drama work. What are your views
about the role of drama at university level?

LORD BOYLE: I doubt if we shall see a major change here in UGC
policy, and with all the pressures being exerted in the UGC, I think
this would be difficult. I am certain, though, that drama does have
an important part to play, not just in terms of the English School in
the University but in terms of the University as a whole. May I say
with regret and even some feeling of shame, I don't give you personally as much support as I should in this university; and I think this
university is, and I suspect has been for a long time, rather bad
about drama. Considering the meagreness of the resources available
I think it is remarkable what is achieved in this university and I think
it is very creditable to all those concerned. But I must say I did find
myself pleased and relieved, as I think you know, at the very last
moment when we were contemplating the academic planning report,
when we were just about finally completing the exercise, that it was
in fact two professors (without mentioning them by name), one a
scientist, the other an applied scientist, who said "Look, are we really
just going to leave out the subject of drama altogether?" And it was

one of these professors who said it distressed him that this university appeared to be, as he put it "almost concrete from the neck up on this subject". Now this was a criticism of the university; of the total university community and not in any sense at all a criticism of those who are carrying this flag.

DRAMA IN EDUCATION: Do you think of it basically as a curricular or as para-curricular activity?

LORD BOYLE: I don't think you can make an absolutely sharp distinction between curricular subjects and para-curricular subjects. I think it must be both.

DRAMA IN EDUCATION: Therefore, it should serve, as it were, a cultural purpose within the university community as a whole and not simply within a Faculty of Arts?

LORD BOYLE: That's right. It's not just a Faculty of Arts subject. And as I say it's some of the other Faculties whose members are the first to say so.

DRAMA IN EDUCATION: Support for the development of drama often comes from outside the Faculty of Arts in Universities. This is a very sad state of affairs. Do you think there is any logical reason for it?

LORD BOYLE: Well, I think there can be particular reasons. I wouldn't like to speculate too much about this. One possible reason is that I think it's some of the Arts and social science disciplines who are specially affected by rising numbers in universities, because their subjects are very time-consuming ones. I always think of historians here, being a history graduate myself. But of course it is true, isn't it, that a love of the drama and a love of music often does go along with scientific or engineering interests. I mean trains and music are a very frequent combination!

DRAMA IN EDUCATION: Also we find that we speak the same language as colleagues in Faculties of Science and Applied Science and Medicine because we are concerned both with theory and with measuring that theory in practice. Both in the Drama and perhaps in Physics or whatever it may be, this is the usual process. We have the idea, and we have the laboratory to test the ideas, and this seems to be a common attitude between the scientists and the people working in the drama. We often think drama belongs in a Faculty of Science or a Faculty of Technology rather than in the Faculty of Arts.

LORD BOYLE: I think there is some truth in that. 'Theatre workshop' is not just a trendy term — it's a reality. I know this from my time on the New Activities Committee.

DRAMA IN EDUCATION: I think one of the problems is that colleagues in the Arts, traditionally, have a difficulty in accepting the manner in which we say results can be measured. They will measure and assess the quality of their students in quite a different way from the drama departments who will accept that it is possible to assess a student's practical work, and to make judgements about the contribution of a student as an actor or an interpreter in some way or another. These claims seem very suspect from the view of the traditional arts subjects.

LORD BOYLE: Yes, I think you have a point there too.

DRAMA IN EDUCATION: If you were in a position of political power today what recommendations concerning the status of drama and the creative arts would you make? Is that a question you are prepared to answer?

LORD BOYLE: Yes, I'll try. I have never known Mr Heath carry an audience with him more effectively than when he spoke at a Party Conference once about what the Promenade Concerts and their audience meant to him. It was so obvious that he not only felt and believed what he was saying but he also in Dr Leavis's expression appeared to 'enact' what he was saying. Now I believe that if he or some other Minister spoke about drama from their own experience, and enacted their feelings on this subject, and on what it can mean in terms of the exploration of what life is about, coming to learn about oneself — which seems to me one of the most important life-long adventures — then this is something that would make a contribution. And it's in that context that I would want, myself, to take every opportunity I could of proclaiming my belief in drama's importance.

Poor Relations in the Staff Room

A view of drama and learning from David Morton, Inspector of Schools (Drama) for Leeds, and Chairman of the National Association of Drama Advisers. Before taking up his present post he was Drama Adviser for Oldham where he built up an adventurous and successful Youth Theatre Workshop

Those of us responsible for the teaching of drama are often, still, regarded as the poor relations of the staff room, or, alternatively, as an out-of-reach luxury. This situation has caused us to try to define clearly our aims and objectives, no bad thing in itself, but the result has often been exaggerated and unproven claims made by us on behalf of drama in education. Recently the need for more scientific research and analysis on the role and function of drama in education has become clear and, indeed, at the time of writing the National Association of Drama Advisers is preparing the brief for such a piece of work by a University Department. This paper, while in no way representing the National Association of Drama Advisers, is concerned with the same subject. Having chosen a particular piece of work with which I was associated, I have tried to assess it as a learning situation, relate it to clearly defined global objectives of secondary education and indicate specific learning processes within it. Because of the nature of the dramatic activity, if my observations are accurate they would suggest that drama can make some contributions to the learning process that are unique to drama.

AIMS AND OBJECTIVES OF SECONDARY EDUCATION

I think the aims of secondary education, within the compulsory age limit at least, should be expressed in terms of human capacities to be developed rather than subjects or topics to be studied. Thus, the extent of the pupil's growth will be seen in his behaviour patterns which will reflect the success of the education he has received. The basic task is to help the pupil to make a model of his world that accords with his experience; there will usually be need for adjustment. As teachers, we must do two things:

a) help the pupil to appreciate, evaluate, and understand his world

b) 'arrange' experiences which will improve understanding

The peculiar nature of secondary (as distinct from primary) education is that of the self-conscious awareness of the young adult. He is using growing awareness of himself, of other people, and of his environment as a basis for decisions about the kind of person he wants to be, his relations with others, and his expectations from life generally.

Development of human capacities involves the individual becoming increasingly open to the world and to himself. The former aspect emphasizes the importance of undergoing new formative experiences and the latter that of internalizing, organizing, and integrating these experiences.

Work Through Dramatic Activity

This example is not a ready-made scheme for a school. Any activity is one facet of the overall climate of the school and cannot be used in isolation. Nor is it suggested that a method of approach which might work for one teacher is necessarily suitable for others whose talents may be different.

Drama involves the development of certain attitudes, skills, and techniques which pupils can use not only for interpreting scripted and unscripted material, but also for exploring aspects of life in which they are directly involved. As they increase their control over the skills and techniques, they are able to explore increasingly complex human situations. The example set out below could only be attempted, therefore, after several years of serious education through drama.

The forty boys and girls involved in this activity were fourth and fifth formers who had 'opted' for drama for one afternoon per week. They represented the whole ability range. All had taken part in drama lessons in school over the previous three to four years. The school is situated on a large housing estate. Standard dress used for all drama sessions was sweat shirts and jeans. There were two tutors to the group.

These pupils had taken part previous to this in work linking human sounds with movement and speech. To place the following work in course context, it was followed by half a term's work in Victorian melodrama. The final session of the movement and sound work finished with time to spare. During a 'fill-in' discussion one boy was telling some others about a girl he had 'fallen for'. Despite much teasing and scepticism from the others he maintained that this was the 'real thing'.

Discussion then developed around the question asked by one boy "What is love anyway?". After much argument it was suggested by the tutors that the whole group might embark on some exploratory work in the drama course on the nature of love. The tutors felt that such work would have value since the climate of the school, staff/pupil relationship in general, and relationships between themselves and this group were such that the youngsters could freely discuss in a serious manner sensitive subjects of moral import. The group was also sufficiently experienced and proficient in dramatic work to use these skills in helping to express and clarify their complex emotions on this subject.

Sub-groups of five or six were formed, and they were given a choice of tasks which included searching for plays, poems, pop music, lighter classical music concerned with love, and also newspaper articles concerning love which had 'gone wrong'. Group discussions had thrown up these areas of research, but the two tutors suggested specific examples to look at, such as 'Billy Liar', 'A Kind of Loving', 'The Knack', 'A Taste of Honey', Donne's 'Love Sonnets', D H Lawrence's poems, 'Troilus and Cressida' and 'Antony and Cleopatra'. From the studio's records one group chose Tchaikovsky's 'Romeo and Juliet' because it was provocative of dramatic activity.

Subsequent development by the groups for the next three weeks (some nine hours) was concerned with interpreting in dramatic form — eg music, movement, dance, improvisation, and script interpretation — the various stimuli selected. The final stage of polishing each activity was followed by the presentation of work to each other within the group.

Discussion led by the tutors then followed on their achievements in dramatic terms, and whether they were any nearer discovering the true meaning of love. The group's conclusions were well put by one who said "If this is love, I am very disappointed".

The tutors then asked them if, although their enquiries had not satisfied their intuitive concept of love, they had clarified in any way their ideas about what love is. The group still felt that they had made little progress. However, from this general feeling of dissatisfaction there developed a free discussion based on the idea that, although they could not say what love was, they had some strong ideas about certain forms of human relationships which they considered to be far removed from real love. Although the group had been dealing with aspects of love for several sessions, it was quite clear that these ideas were acquired from direct and indirect experience of the world outside the school. The group discussed these and from them developed the dramatic activities set out below.

It should be emphasized at this point that the tutors were faced with the situation of having to deal with points arising spontaneously from discussion. The ideas came from the children, and to have played down or neglected any of them might have been dangerous. The tutors therefore decided to deal with each one in an honest yet sensitive manner. Thus, in no way did they give the impression that they, as representatives of the adult world, had anything to hide.

Small groups then studied the possibilities of the following topics as outlined:

i)   The group discussed many ways in which the essence of loveless sex could be portrayed in a dramatic form within the bounds of human dignity. They realized that it would be very difficult to achieve this. However, after careful thought they considered it possible to overcome this difficulty by portraying it symbolically in dance. The whole concept was expressed in an abstract of patterns and shapes. To have omitted this facet of unsatisfactory love from the enquiry would have been dishonest, and moreover would have incurred the very real danger of so investing sex with the mystery and appeal of a taboo that the youngsters would have instinctively rejected the spiritual aspects of love dealt with later in the work, as incomplete and unsatisfactory.

ii) Petrarchan love poetry was investigated for some expression of idolization in shallow terms. Some Elizabethan sonnets were offered to this group and they chose the King of Navarre's sonnet in 'Love's Labour's Lost'. This then found expression with one boy reading the sonnet, a girl on a pedestal, and a boy improvising movement.

iii) **Self-love**: based on an idea from previous experience of clowning exercises was expressed in mime by a boy dressing himself, for a date, in front of a mirror. Further development was introduced by a second boy who was keen on playing drums, wanting to use his skill in producing a series of percussive sound patterns to point the mime. Subsequent practice enhanced both roles and led to a high level of sensitivity between the two performers.

iv) **Jealousy**: this theme was taken up by a group which also wanted to do comic work, so they decided to use silent film techniques, ie high-speed movement as in silent film comedies. The idea of a duel with pistols was taken, the group interpreting a 45 rpm record (Max Harris's 'Hat and Cane') played at 78 rpm.

v) **Infatuation**: using the type of love expressed in women's magazine love stories, a group of girls did a speech improvisation set in the clubhouse of a tennis club, where they discussed experiences they had had with 'E-type Romeos'. This scene became a continuous improvization with neither plot nor climax — it was, in fact, a typical conversation. One interesting aspect of this activity was that the girls' speech became sufficiently flexible to characterize people outside their own social situation.

vi) **Male-ego love**: this was a parallel speech improvisation by a group of boys set in a coffee-bar, engaged in the ego-building, often fictitious love stories exchanged by men. Again, there was neither plot nor climax, it was a typical conversation.

Several sessions were now spent on exploring, expanding, and refining these and other similar situations — and eventually polishing into dramatic shape. Finally one session was devoted to the groups sharing their work with each other in private performance.

This was followed by a discussion of their achievements in dramatic terms, and further consideration was given to whether they had now discovered, by a process of elimination, the true meaning of love. The class was still dissatisfied. They considered that they were not any nearer to the solution of their problem. Incidentally, by this time the boy who had sparked off this whole theme had 'finished' with the girl with whom he had thought he was in love!

By chance, the school assemblies of that week were on the theme 'God is Love' and one of the group asked if this could help them. This led to a reading in the AV and the New English Bible of 1 Corinthians, Ch. 13, which had been used one morning. The group decided that although they were not completely satisfied (probably because of the biblical source of the material) they could not improve on St Paul's definition of love (partly because they were becoming weary of the theme and were ready to move on to something else).

From the tutors' point of view there were now three possibilities:

i) To end this theme and to move on to something else
ii) To introduce outside speakers for further exploration —
eg Marriage Guidance Counsellors, Christians, newly-weds etc
iii) To develop the work for production to an outside audience.

The last course was decided upon collectively because a non-competitive drama festival was pending, the group liked to perform from time to time, the tutors felt that this sort of pressure might clarify some of the group's findings and also the tutors assessed that

the group was sufficiently developed for public performance not to pros-
titute the curriculum work.

Having decided to develop the work into a polished improvisation for
an outside audience, the tutors then presented the group with the problem of linking six separate pieces of work into one whole, which would
be an effective form of theatre. The group needed to consider aspects
of dramatic form — situation, plot/theme, climax. In one two-hour
session, therefore, the group discussed these problems and experi-
mented with possible solutions, rejecting eventually five of the six tried.
The one guiding factor was the decision of the group to present the work
theatrically, yet with the precise aim of having an emotional impact upon
an audience through the content as well as the performance.

They finally decided that the situation should be a group of youngsters interested in theatre, who stroll in and 'find themselves' in an
acting area surrounded on four sides by an audience. One of its numbers
would be sitting in the audience, not being with them since he was with
the girl he 'loves' on a theatre visit! On seeing him amongst the audience
some of the group feel they must question his ability to be certain of
real love, and finally the natural leader of the group decides to 'produce'
them in a play designed to examine the meaning of love. This 'producer',
therefore, becomes a 'camp' theatrical type and summons the electrician to 'throw down a pool of purple light' into one section of the acting
area. Into this the 'producer' puts some of the group and asks them to
'conceive a scene about sex'! The electrician is then asked to provide
further pools of light until all of the six items noted in the pre-production
work have their own 'space'. The 'producer' then tells them all (and
this includes the audience) that the boy and girl left in the middle are
about to embark on a searching journey for real love.

All lights dim to black-out, and in the gloom one girl reads a piece
of her own creative writing to set the theme. The boy and girl in the
centre, in movement to the music of 'Somewhere' from 'West Side Story',
not knowing each other, break out from the circle of light that has
warmed around them and proceed to 'search' for love among the activities of each of the groups, which are lit in turn as either the boy or girl
approaches. Thus the six items take place in the order set out above,
but are linked by the search, in movement, of the couple. It will be
noted that the six items embrace all the essential areas of drama in
education's tools — from mime to work with script.

As the group had been unsuccessful in finding a better definition of
real love than St Paul's Epistle to the Corinthians, after the last item
(ie the male-ego improvisation) a movement sequence to 'Satisfaction'

by the Rolling Stones was inserted, ending in a grotesque grouping depicting their despair and dissatisfaction. In the heavy silence at this point, from the edge of the acting area, unlit, St Paul's words were spoken, and as each group item's weakness was mentioned by St Paul the members of the relevant group melted away into the darkness at the edge of the acting area until only the boy and the girl, who had begun the search remain. The recognition of love between them was then expressed in a sensitive movement sequence by the two of them to 'One Hand, One Heart' from 'West Side Story'.

At first the group felt this to be a suitable point at which to end the production. But in their discussion, it later emerged that some felt that since they had had difficulty in finding the true meaning of love themselves, the ending was too easy. They decided that they wished to show that real love is very precious and easily lost, and so sought a means of expressing this in dramatic form. In an earlier session one boy had written a poem about a road accident which had been suggested to him by David Holbrook's 'Unholy Marriage' in which the girl friend is killed. The boy called his poem 'The Accident':

> "Earth to Earth"
> Your words mean nothing to me, Father.
> My life has entered the dust,
> The mud and worm-infested ground —
> The hole of nothingness
> Dark and depressing.
> How can I live with her dead?
>
> "Ashes to Ashes"
> If only my blood had dissolved with hers
> On the wet motorway.
> My darling
> Dead and bleeding —
> What an unholy marriage is this!
> Enjoy your ritual, Father —
> Stand in your divine preaching box —
> Chant your mystic incantations —
> Gesticulate and pontificate —
> But you can't return my love;
> Prematurely stolen by Death.
>
> Pray for her, Father.
> Pray for me.

The group felt that a simple, stylised scene to illustrate this poem, set at the graveside, and performed as the poem was being read, would be a symbolic way of expressing the precious quality that they felt essential to real love. Therefore, immediately after St Paul's words there was a blackout, sound effects of a crowd were heard, and cold, dim lights then came up on this graveside scene, the production ending as the mourners left the boy, who had searched and finally recognized love, standing above his girl's grave, as the lights slowly dimmed.

This final framework for the production was finally arrived at six days before the performance of it was due. An interesting piece of background information to the ending is the fact that two days later, on a Friday night, the boy playing the part of the searcher whose girl friend had died, broke off a friendship with his own girl friend. On the Saturday, therefore, they did not go together to a local beat-club. The girl went out with her parents instead and the family car was in a crash in which the girl was killed. This gave the tutors, and, it should be noted, the class, much concern at the possible harm to the boy that the ending to the production might cause if it was performed as planned. After much thought and careful discussion between the tutors and the boy it was decided to keep the ending but to remove the emotional pressure from the boy by getting him to leave with the mourners. It was decided that the priest should stay at the graveside as the lights faded.

Although it was an awful thing to happen, the tutors felt that the real-life incident had forced a deeper awareness of the theme of the activity upon the minds of all those involved with it. And it would seem that this extraordinarily deep involvement of the youngsters had caused the work to have an unusually forceful impact upon the audience. There was no emotional wallowing, simply an honesty of work typical of that of which young people are capable.

GENERAL OBJECTIVES

The above account of a piece of work in educational drama is simply an account. It includes consideration of the attitudes of the tutors, but no account of their assessment of it in educational terms. This can come more accurately at this later stage when it is possible, through detachment, to be more objective.

There are, perhaps, four areas within which the adolescent attempts to establish his identity. Each may be illustrated by several examples from the account of that dramatic activity.

i) The adolescent is concerned with himself as a person, with his powers and their limitations. Youngsters exploring their own capacities might be asking themselves, "Can I — communicate through mime, — attract the opposite sex, — express my feelings effectively through verse?" Or, "Can I understand my own hopes, fears, ambitions?". Growth in this dimension involves the pupil in acquiring a healthy awareness of his present position.

ii) The adolescent is concerned with the acceptance of himself in his relationship to a group. One recognizes that one is sometimes a leader, sometimes a follower: "Can I match my drumming to his miming?" "Can I play a supporting role in a movement sequence?"

iii) A third area of adolescent study concerns the surprising range of individual differences among other human beings. The adolescent has an awakening criticism of himself and of his relationship to groups. An example of the teaching-learning situation is 'Some people have undergone profound emotional experiences' or 'Why did he make it with that girl when I didn't?' or 'I don't seem to fit in this group'.

iv) Acceptance of others in relation to oneself: 'To evolve an improvised scene requires the give and take of the group' and 'sexual relationships demand personal responsibility'.

It is suggested that this type of drama work leads towards greater awareness of the adolescent himself as a social being. It helps him to enter the world of ideas, to use powers of reason and to acquire the beginnings of good judgement, especially if the teacher does not take the critical decisions out of the hands of his pupils. Whilst drama pupils are becoming increasingly aware through creative improvisation of the nature of love it is defeating this objective to redirect this effort to wards a stage production aimed at pleasing an audience. However, a similar production staged a few weeks later may well reinforce the same pupils' learning, by confirming for them that they have grasped the idea of love well enough to communicate it effectively to an audience.

Understanding involves both comprehension and appreciation. Education must be concerned with the emotional and social aspects of understanding. Direct involvement, as in dramatic activity, can induce the pupil to try to improve his understanding of the scheme of things and of his place in it, so that he may adjust appropriately to it.

PUPIL GROWTH

If education should primarily be concerned with human capacities to be developed rather than with subjects or topics to be studied, the usual patterns of teacher assessments through, for example, marking, cannot be applied. This has always been true of drama in education and, hence, the constant concern over 'standards' and a sense of direction and development. It is, therefore, necessary to try to trace the stages of pupil growth, both emotionally and intellectually, in order that as teachers we continually present the appropriate challenges to our pupils. Starting at its lowest levels and moving to its highest levels pupil growth might be tabulated as follows:

COGNITIVE (Intellectual):   i) knowledge; ii) comprehension;
iii) application; iv) synthesis;
v) evaluation.

AFFECTIVE (Emotional):   i) attending; ii) responding;
iii) valuing; iv) organization of values;
v) characterization.

All learning/teaching situations contain elements of both the cognitive and affective domains, and the example of dramatic activity that has been given can be used to illustrate this — to illustrate pupil growth, or the development of human capacities from the lowest levels to the highest levels in both domains.

AFFECTIVE DOMAIN

Attending The affective domain contains objectives expressed as interests, attitudes, appreciation, and values. Clearly, then, the lowest rung on the ladder must be the pupil's willingness to attend to the dramatic activity towards which an attitude is to be developed — awareness without discrimination, a willingness to tolerate a stimulus rather than to avoid it.

Pupil behaviour illustrative of this:

i)   Expresses exhilaration after a physically demanding movement sequence.

ii)   Recognizes that other people may respond to a stimulus (eg music) differently to himself.

iii) Listens for descriptive words in the verse accompanying the movement sequence.

Responding Responses which go beyond the level of merely attending to the dramatic activity. The pupil is sufficiently motivated to be actively attending — acquiescence in responding, willingness to respond, and satisfaction in response:

i)   Willingness to force himself to participate in a dramatic improvisation which has little interest for him.

ii)   Voluntarily looks for books dealing with the nature of love because he is interested in the dramatic activity.

iii) Finds pleasure in sharing the results of his work through performance to others in the class.

Valuing The activity is seen by the pupil to have worth, and displays this behaviour consistently enough in appropriate situations for him to be perceived as holding the value — deepening degrees of internalization become apparent in such valuation:

i)   Continuing desire to express his feelings effectively in speech, writing, or dramatic activity.

ii) Initiates group action in order to find out more about the reasons for failure of the love relationship.

iii) Faith in the precious nature of real love accompanied by the wish to convince others through a dramatic presentation.

Organization As the learner successfully internalizes values, he encounters situations for which more than one value is relevant. Thus, the necessity arises for organizing the values, for determining the interrelationships among them and for establishing the dominant and pervasive ones. As the pupil goes out of his way to argue and verbally to defend his point of view he is building his value into a concept. This is a necessary pre-requisite to organizing it as part of a value system, whose parts are in ordered relationship with one another:

i) Attempts to identify the characteristics of love.

ii) Takes into account human characteristics that have impaired a love relationship and is tolerant of them.

Characterization At this level the individual acts consistently in accordance with the values he has internalized. That is, the experience through dramatic activity directly transfers itself positively to the individual's own life.

This will normally come later in the pupil's adult life, rather than in the relatively immature state of the youngster at school.

COGNITIVE DOMAIN

Knowledge In the cognitive domain the unifying principle is the pupil's capacity to apply information and skills previously acquired to new problems and situations.

The process of judging and relating is involved:

i) Knowledge of stage lighting components is necessary to put it to use.

ii) Knowledge of the rules of the game we call 'drama' — ie lack of 'blocking' in the make-believe situation.

iii) Recall of the priorities of pointing, shape, climax etc when performing to an audience.

Comprehension This represents the lowest level of understanding — translation from one form of communication to another, the re-ordering of a set of ideas in terms of their interrelations or relative importance, extrapolation involving the extension of trends beyond the given data to determine effects:

i) Ability to work a lighting cue sheet.

ii) Ability to interpret a written scene in dramatic action.

iii) Ability to estimate or predict the consequences of various forms of personal relationship, each called 'love'.

Application The pupil, given a new problem, must apply the appropriate abstraction without having to be prompted as to which abstraction is correct or having to be shown how to use it in that situation. For example:

Skill in applying principles of dramatic technique to particular problems — eg to discover as much as possible about 'love'.

Analysis The breakdown of material into its constituent parts, and the detection of the relationship between the parts. At the lowest level the pupil is expected to identify the elements in the material. At the second he is required to make explicit the relationships among these elements. The third level involves recognizing the organizing principles, the structure which holds together the material:

i) Ability to distinguish dominant from subordinate themes or ideas in a play text.

ii) Ability in any of the discussion situations to realize which of the assumptions (eg that real love is precious) are essential to the main thesis.

iii) Ability to infer the author's purpose, point of view, or traits of thought and feeling as exhibited in the dramatic literature, such as 'Taste of Honey'.

Synthesis The putting together of elements or parts so as to form a pattern or structure not clearly seen before. Combining experience with new material, the whole being reconstructed into a new, more or less well integrated unit — communication of ideas and experience to others, development of a plan of work which satisfies the requirements of a particular task, the development of a set of abstract relations to clarify or to explain particular facts:

i) Skill in improvising speech, involving good organization of ideas accumulated in any experiences.

ii) Ability to work out an effective structure for a dramatic improvisation.

iii) Ability to perceive in abstract terms the relationships between parents and boy friend both 'loving' a girl.

Evaluation The making of judgements about the value, for some purpose, of ideas, works, solutions, methods, materials etc. It involves the use of criteria as well as standards for appraising the extent to which particular aspects under review are accurate. Evaluation represents not only an end process in dealing in the cognitive behaviour, but also a

major link with affective behaviour, since values and feelings play an
important part in the judgements made:

i)   The ability to indicate logical fallacies in arguments propounded in
     any of the discussions.

ii) Ability to apply self-developed aesthetic standards to the choice and
     use of material for a dramatic activity.

CONCLUSIONS AND IMPLICATIONS

Thus, human growth is continuous. Teachers will be attaining a measure
of success whenever the pupil moves to a higher level of behaviour and
is conscious of his growth. Whenever pupils enjoy this experience with
some regularity teachers of drama may reasonably hope that the pupils
concerned have reached the stage of continuing contributions to their own
education, which will remain with them into adult life. Within the terms
of this assessment of the function of the educational process, it can be
seen that the value of producing a piece of dramatic work is not to be
measured by the quality of the finished product, important as this can
be. The crucial test is the often internalized personal and group struggle
towards such a finished product — that is, we are concerned with the process, not the artefact of the outward display. The success of the educational process should be measured in terms of pupil growth, not in
bodies of knowledge acquired.

The piece of work described took place seven years ago. Educational
ideas have developed since then, and one hopes this is also true of the
writer. Although drama in education is still regarded as a 'new' subject
by many, it is true to say that many of the value judgements made by
teachers of drama, even in the early days of Caldwell Cook and Peter
Slade, were ahead of their time and in advance of similar judgements
being made in other areas of the curriculum. There are now many educationists concerned with the humanities and the other creative arts who
would now accept the nature of the assessments in terms of pupil growth
in relation to their own work, who would less easily have done so ten
years ago. We see this change reflected in thematic approaches to learning, in team-teaching and block time-tabling, in the work of inter-
disciplinary-enquiry (IDE) pioneered by the Goldsmith's Curriculum
Laboratory. So that now we should no longer ask for separate timetable provision for drama, but look for ways in which the teacher of
drama can contribute in a team of teachers working in the humanities
and/or the creative arts. The piece of work would have been much
more meaningful and relevant in terms of the process, in terms of pupil
growth had it been part of the work of a team of teachers covering the
traditional subject areas of RI, social and environmental studies, science,
visual education and music.

43

NOTES

i) Detailed information on the classification of pupil growth can be found in:

'Taxonomy of Educational Objectives: 1. Cognitive Domain'.
B S Bloom. Longmans, London
'Taxonomy of Educational Objectives: 2. Affective Domain'.
D R Krathwohl. Longmans, London

ii) Broom Field School, Havant is where this dramatic activity took place. The second tutor was Sheila Dubut, now at a College of Education in the Midlands.

David Morton

In My Innocence

A personal view of the place of drama in education by Michael Duane, former Headmaster of Risinghill Comprehensive School

For many decades, certainly from long before the last war, opinion about the nature, function and value of drama in education has tended to polarize between on the one hand, a rejection of the study of plays for public presentation in favour of children's spontaneous and undirected dramatization of their own experiences or of stories to which they had responded well; and on the other hand, the specific study of scripts and of the techniques necessary to 'project' to an audience, as a method of getting closer to the intention of the author through the combined disciplines of speech and precisely expressed bodily movement.

Caldwell Cook's 'The Play Way' and Stanislavsky's 'An Actor Prepares' were, each in its own way, an attempt to resolve the differences between these two points of view. Cook is to be credited with having helped to break down the old, dreary textual study that probably did more than anything else to give pupils a permanent distaste for Shakespeare and to deprive them, at least until the advent of cinema and television adaptations, of their common heritage. Stanislavsky gave rise to the post-war 'Method' school of acting that added a new dimension to dramatic communication.

But neither book provided a basis of critical thought about what constituted education and why drama is an essential and continuing part of every form of culture with its roots in the spontaneous play of children, as well as in religious and social ritual. Until such an attempt is made, the debate about drama in education will continue to revolve around personal taste or to be determined by prevailing fashion, so that the teacher will have no adequate criteria for assessing the value of what is being done in the name of 'drama'.

What Is 'Education'?

It is common for lecturers in Philosophy or Principles of Education in
training colleges to reject as non-educational the training of children
for specific forms of adult work, or the training or conditioning of
children to have certain specific attitudes or valuations held to be important by the family, the social group or the society as a whole. Conditioning is held to occur when influence is brought to bear on the child
in such a way that he has no choice but to accept that influence, or when
he is unaware of the influence, and when the results of that influence
limit his choice of action in the future. The superficiality of this type
of 'philosophy' is easily exposed when one analyses the effects of, for
example, bringing up a child in one particular culture rather than
another.

The philosophical definition of education is as difficult as the definition of love, another portmanteau word. Like love, it is a process
and an activity, a state of mind and a relationship. As John Dewey
writes, "What nutrition and reproduction are to physiological life,
education is to social life". It is common to all men and has been seen
in action at all times, though the activities and the states agreed to be
subsumed under the heading of 'education' are as diverse as the cultures
in which it takes place.

Even to refer to education as 'it' tends to create the assumption
that there is a content, that there are bounds, definable processes to
be observed and an objective to be reached that somehow endow the
concept with tangible reality; and this sense of education as a concrete
reality is reinforced by our habit of dismissing any form of education,
not associated with schools or colleges, books, teachers and, above all,
certificates, diplomas or degrees to 'prove' that education has occurred.
I remember an occasion a few years ago when I was discussing what I
should do after the closure of Risinghill with the Chief Inspector of
Schools. In my innocence I had suggested that I might be used in the
training of teachers, as I had taught in a variety of schools, both as
assistant and as head, had trained graduates for teaching, and had been
writing about education for a number of years. "But you have no qualifications! You have no degree in psychology or philosophy!" said the
Chief Inspector, as though I had made an improper suggestion.

We can now see that to try and pin down a definition of what we
mean by 'education' in a couple of sentences is unrealistic, or that,
where such an attempt is made, the result is not much better than what
Milton wrote to Samuel Hartlieb in 1644, "I call, therefore, a complete
and generous education that which fits a man to perform justly, skilfully

47

and magnanimously, all the offices, both private and public, of peace
and war" — a truly comprehensive, but frustratingly unhelpful statement. It is the tension between the large sweep of the concept and the
need for pragmatic solutions to the here and now problems of the home
and the school that gives rise to the feeling among many students and
teachers that philosophy has little of practical value to offer in the training of teachers. To say that education starts at or even before birth
and ends only with death; that it includes all the interactions between
the individual and his environment that foster growth; that it is the
totality of all those forces which change the human infant from a bundle
of reflex mechanisms into an adult — sensitive, cooperative and actively
engaged with his fellows in furthering the purposes of the human community — hardly helps the young teacher to know how to help the child who
cannot read or the child shocked by his home experience into near-
autistic non-communication. To begin with, such a definition begs so
many questions. What do we mean by 'interactions'? How do we define
an 'individual'? What is included in his 'environment'? What is 'growth'?

From Darwin onwards we have learned that man's 'divine spirit'
has little to do with differences of physical structures from his brothers
the vertebrates. The intuitive responses of St Francis are borne out by
the researches of Tinbergen and Lorenz. 'Culture' is a continuum,
with its tentative beginnings in the individual communication of the ritual
love dance of the woodcock or the species protective communication of
the dawn chorus and the dance of the bees. In man culture is equally
the result of pressures to survive, though it may be difficult to trace
the specific ritual of the missa cantata or the Queen's opening of
Parliament back to the magic of the cave paintings.

Communication — The Essence of Our Humanity

Individually man is a puny weakling in comparison with many vertebrates. Collectively he can protect himself against tigers, poisonous
snakes and even bacteria, through his power to communicate. However
well taught, even chimpanzees and dolphins respond to, and with, only
the most rudimentary elements of human communication. They appear
to be quite unable to 'take off' into the creative development of these
elements in the way a human child does. Up to the point when the
human infant extends his response to speech by himself using words,
both human and chimpanzee babies display similar 'intelligence' (a
grossly misused word that should be replaced by 'linguistic skills' or,
in the case of animals 'capacity to respond to symbols'). From that
point onwards the human child pulls away at an accelerating rate so

48

that, within weeks, he shows capacities of reason and insight not matched by even mature chimpanzees.

Now this capacity for reason and insight is closely correlated with linguistic ability so if this ability is not developed in the child by, above all, the parents in the first three years of life, the child will remain at or near the animal level of capacity for thought. The more his linguistic capacity is fostered the more fully human he will become — 'linguistic capacity' meaning the ability to deal with symbols to convey meaning, whether intellectual or emotional. So linguistic ability embraces the capacity to handle not only words or sounds, but mathematical, scientific, musical, visual, plastic, kinaesthetic or any other system of symbols that have been developed in human culture.

But the particular forms of this linguistic capacity that will be developed in particular children will depend on the total culture of the society in which he grows. This, in turn, will arise as a result of the particular techniques evolved by that culture to feed, clothe and protect its members in the specific geographical conditions of the region in which they have lived for some time. The linguistic capacities will also be affected by whether they have a predominantly oral tradition and rely on word of mouth and memory to preserve collective experience, or whether they have found other ways to record that experience.

Within a given society different linguistic skills will develop according to the degree to which the forms of work are differentiated among sub-groups of the culture. In modern Britain, for example, the middle classes, by reason of the work they do, which tends to concentrate on those skills in language that enable them to control the environment — observation, analysis, discovery and application of cause/effect relationships, forecasting or extrapolation from given data, coordination of discrete experiences — and to convey their findings and decisions to others in language, mathematical forms, scientific formulae or visual forms such as film, blueprints, models etc, develop skills in communication suited to the control of complex machines, systems, processes and organizations without the need for forms of meaning conveyed through body tensions, emphasis, tone, volume or gesture.

Similarly the working classes, and in particular the semi-skilled and unskilled sections of our population, having, through the historical development of mass-production, become virtual appendages to machines, requiring a minimum of language, judgement, initiative to perform the mechanical and routine operations that time-and-motion studies have simplified to the point of inanity, have similarly developed forms of language usage that are perfectly apt for the range of experiences normal to their lives. They do not have, however, the facility in verbalizing forms of experience outside that range such as can be seen in the 'elaborated code' of the middle class. In particular, for example, middle class work roles more often require the ability to reflect not only about cause/effect relationships, as between material events or processes, but about human relationships in work, leisure and education. Their children are socialized through language to a much greater degree than are the children of the lower social classes. They are taught to examine the consequences of what they do at an early age and so they develop a low 'threshold of guilt' which, among other things, inhibits the need to 'act out' their feelings.

The capacity for internal reflection is essential to any appreciation of artistic forms. It is hardly surprising, then, to see that it is the middle classes that form the bulk of the audiences at poetry recitals, symphony concerts, picture galleries and exhibitions of sculpture, just as it is those with similar linguistic skills who buy books of poetry, philosophy, sociology and political analysis. For the same reason the upper middle classes, a tiny minority of the total population, are linguistically equipped to maintain their position of dominance over the rest of the people. Their capacity to analyze situations and motives, to use the organs of mass communication for stating their own case and for demolishing or holding up to ridicule that of their opponents, gives them a class cohesion disproportionate to their numbers.

But, our industrial and commercial activity being what it is, the central drive for profitability compels even the middle classes to concentrate on those linguistic skills that are essential to mass-production, and at the expense of linguistic skills concerned with artistic, social or psychological development. So, while we have produced outstanding poets, dramatists and artists, the familial and educative experience of the working classes does not enable them to participate fully in what should be a national culture, while the culture that **does** arise among the working classes is too often held in contempt by their superiors. How then can we create a common culture?

The 'short' answer is, of course, to bring about a political and economic revolution that will sweep away the existing social classes, the existing forms of gross disparity between the rich and the poor and, what gives rise to these differences, the whole system of sub-divided labour that is closely associated with high levels of social reward for those who control, regulate and organize our society — the professional classes and the property owners — and subsistence levels of reward for those whose labour, however 'humble' is of more immediate importance for the survival of the community; and to reorganize the production of goods and services and the control of all institutions on more democratic lines so that all workers share the burdens and the rewards of making the decisions that affect their own lives as well as the wealth that their skills and energy produce. Such a change would change the linguistic skills of those with restricted ranges of experience under current forms of living.

However desirable such a change is, and the mounting rate of crime, delinquency and mental illness bears urgent witness to the destructive inhumanity of our present 'system', the teacher is faced, here and now, with the need to increase and broaden the sensitivity and the linguistic skills of the children in his care. Generations of his predecessors have been similarly concerned for their charges and have pinned their faith in education to bring about the results they hoped for. Against the in-human requirements of mass-production for machine-minders they have been, after a hundred years of state education, conspicuously unsuccess-ful, and for the reason that, given over-large classes; separated in effect from the community to which the children belong; separated cul-turally from those children; and trained to behave as missionaries for middle-class culture, they have had to fall back on book-learning and a work-oriented curriculum. The governing bodies of schools have been dominated by employers and those who have administered education have been, and are still, largely saturated by narrow concepts of 'efficiency' derived from the factory floor. The effectiveness of education at all levels is measured by its 'cost-effectiveness' in terms of material return, not in terms of human happiness. Symptomatic of the material-istic criteria applied to education has been the slow growth of art, music and drama within the school and university curricula. The resistance to the introduction of these subjects has always been more intense in schools for older children. Nursery and infant schools have long accep-ted them and have more recently begun to accept play and more freedom for their children. Even so, quite recently, the headmistress of an infant school rebuked one of my students for encouraging a class of five-year-olds to play with water. "These children are here to work, not to play. The rest of their lives will be spent in work and the sooner they realize that the better!" The fates of Chris Searle in London and R D Gregory in Market Drayton are typical of what happens to those who take poetry and drama seriously for working-class children.

The Importance of Drama
Book-learning is not only useless, it is positively destructive to perso-nal integrity, unless it rests on a foundation of sensory and social

experience to give it meaning. For that reason all good teachers have sought to associate the written word with practical experience or with reflection on practical experience. In the infant school the teacher knows that she has to build up, through the activities she provides for the children, as rich a reservoir of sensory and social experience as she can contrive, and, above all, to do this in association with language since that is the only way in which intelligence is created. She also knows that she has at hand the whole range of songs, nursery rhymes, games, puzzles, stories that the collective wisdom of the ordinary people has evolved to educate their children pleasurably. If one studies this rich repertoire and observes those stories, rhymes and activities that are most popular with children of different ages one begins to detect that they contain the seeds of skills and concepts that will later blossom into their adult and sophisticated forms. "One, two, buckle my shoe.." teaches the small child to count. "Round and round the garden", for which infants will call time and time again, is one of the many forms of repetitive action that enables the child to anticipate future consequences and leads on through such songs as "The grand old Duke of York" or the story of the three little pigs, to stories that require longer and longer anticipation of the dénouement.

In all these activities the children are encouraged to use their bodies, limbs and facial expressions in appropriate ways so as more deeply to enter into the meaning of the story, and the teacher uses tone, facial expression, body posture and tension, pace, pause and volume to realize as fully as possible the intention of the story. Quite naturally the children enact these stories and undertake the roles and portray the characters. In this they are learning sympathetically to enter imaginatively into characters and situations outside their direct experience. At this stage play and drama are indistinguishable and will remain so for many years.

Right up to the age of puberty this identity of drama and play is seen in the rapidity with which children will seize on an idea and act it out; in the fluidity with which they pass from one idea to another or, in imagination, from one place to another. That the drive to play comes from within is seen in their ability to use the sketchiest of 'props' or to use the same 'prop', within minutes, for a variety of purposes. Here the art of the teacher lies not only in allowing the fullest possible play for the children's invention, but in seeking to make as fully available to them as possible in words, the events, the states of mind and the personal and social consequences of their creations — and to do this while maintaining the pace and the vigour of their invention. In a recent and

interesting book, 'Education and Children's Emotions', Geoffrey Yarlott
writes:

"Drama lessons offer another excellent means of influencing
emotional attitudes. Through drama a child can enter into
situations which he would not normally come across, and in
doing so he can begin to perceive the complexity of human
situations and the endless variety of emotional responses.
One of the great merits of role-playing is that, as well as
encouraging a pupil to explore other people's attitudes, it
enables him, under the safe protection of a mask or adopted
persona, to try out his own attitudes and feelings in safety.
Here again, the teacher can never know the full impact which
the activity is having upon any individual pupil, although, if
he follows up the drama lesson with informal discussion,
pointers will usually emerge. He can encourage children to
talk about what they felt while they were acting and, in the
calmer atmosphere of the classroom, invite them to comment
upon and evaluate their dramatic resolutions of human situations. Was that the only possible resolution? Was that how
they would have wanted the situation to work out in real life?"

And later in the same chapter:

"By all means let pupils experiment with crude, violent
behaviour, in order that they can see where this leads, but
when they have done with improvising and acting on impulse,
let them reflect upon the social and ethical implications of
their actions."

During the pre-pubertal period the task of the teacher is to provide
as wide a range of situations as possible so that the children enter
imaginatively into as many situations and characters as possible. They
should not be inflicted with problems of 'projection' to an audience. The
informal 'audience' of their classmates, themselves flowing into and
out of the action according to their own inclinations and the need of the
play, itself provides a critique. They will be more likely to complain
that the actions of a particular character are inappropriate than that
his enunciation is poor; that he is 'hogging' the scene or that he has
not entered into the spirit of the action, rather than that his movements
lack precision.

Puberty brings with it a new power of self awareness, of introspection: the place of drama becomes of supreme importance in helping the
emerging adult to discover himself. From this time on he is able and
anxious to put himself into the shoes of characters in ancient or modern
plays and to learn many of the multitudes of ways in which his new,
struggling desires, impulses and feelings may be directed. The girl who
has taken into herself the words and the situation of Antigone, Beatrice,
Joan of Arc or Janice of 'Family Life' has created for herself a new
frame of reference, to which she can refer her own strivings and begin
to articulate them.

Drama in Education

Further, the discussions that will arise, about the characters and
the situations and about the precise forms in which these may be interpreted, will be of supreme importance in helping the young persons to
express their own uncertainties, anxieties and aspirations without having
to reveal, except to the sensitive and sympathetic classmate or teacher,
that these are also deeply personal problems.

It will be at about this time that technical problems of 'projection'
can arise if the class feels that it would like to produce a play for the rest
of the school or the parents to see. Obviously such technical problems
must be subsidiary to the central purposes of producing the play — the
deeper exploration of character and character-interaction that is more
clearly necessary in production than in simply reading a play; and when
they arise they can be seen, not as a body of 'tricks of the trade' but as a
means of ensuring that meaning carries across to the audience, now at a
greater distance than in the more intimate situation of the classroom.

Drama is the one activity in education that can give a creative outlet to every single child through the medium that is both his own most
intimate possession and the instrument he uses more skilfully than any
other — language and the movement of his own body. It is in the co-
ordinated blending of the two that consists human communication in its
most everyday form. To the extent that this blending is not the conscious
adjustment of one to the other, but the intuitive and unconscious harmony
powered by the need to 'get across' to the other person, to that extent
will each child steadily find himself and others at depths to which only
the most sensitively nurtured now attain.

Michael Duane

Some useful books

An Actor Prepares	Stanislavsky (Bles)
The Play Way	Caldwell Cook
Teacher	Sylvia Ashton-Warner (Penguin)
Dibs in Search of Self	Virginia Axeline (Gollancz)
Class, Codes and Control	Basil Bernstein (Routledge)
Language and Learning	James Britton (Allen Lane)
The Education of Young Children	Dorothy Gardner (Methuen)
Intellectual Growth in Young Children	Susan Isaacs (Routledge)
Social Development in Young Children	Susan Isaacs (Routledge)
Drama in the English Classroom	Douglas Barnes (Nat. Council of Teachers of English, Illinois)
Education Survey 2. Drama	HMSO
The Role of Speech in the Regulation of Normal and Abnormal Behaviour	A R Luria (Pergamon)
The Lore and Language of School-children	I and P Opie (OUP)
Say	Simon Stuart (Nelson)
Thought and Language	L Vygotsky (MIT Press)
Revolution in Learning	Maya Pines (Allen Lane)

In My Experience

A survey of drama in education and the philosophies upon which it is based in Britain, Australia, the United States and Canada

The biggest blow to my pride came when I first visited Canada in 1966. I was a British drama teacher with many years of experience, and I had held a senior post in teacher-training for nine years. But in the Summer of 1966 in Halifax, Nova Scotia, teachers asked questions which seemed nonsensical to me. They were normal, intelligent people, but I just could not understand the point of their questions. It was then that I realized that my basic British assumptions were not necessarily those of my Canadian audiences. Although we both spoke English, the language that we were using was not necessarily the same. That was my first and biggest exposure to 'culture shock', but it was not my last.

The basic philosophic assumptions upon which language is based differ as between Canada and Britain. In my five years of permanent teaching in Canadian universities, I have been amazed at the number of influences upon drama in education: the British, from 'child drama' to 'speech training'; the French, with their emphasis upon technique and 'le mime' in schools; the United States, with drama based on story-telling as well as behavioural approaches; whole sub-cultures of Ukranians, Russians, Poles, Germans, Italians, and other Europeans, who bring their own assumptions with them; the massive influx of teachers from Australia and New Zealand, attracted to the West of Canada by the higher standard of living, as well as teachers from India, the West Indies, South Africa, and elsewhere. My subsequent visits to the United States, Australia and Asia were still shocks, but none of them have the variety of influences that occur in Canada. In adjacent schools in Vancouver, for example, you will find teachers doing different things: 'child drama' with teenagers, or old-fashioned theatre skills with nine-year-olds, or Laban movement education with girls, or asking

"What is the behavioural objective of the first Billygoat Gruff when he comes to the bridge?" of ten-year olds! In Britain, some might seem appropriate, others not. But in Canada, with its variety of peoples, tongues, and attitudes, there is some validity in each of them.

Canada is a melting-pot of approaches, and the philosophies upon which these practices are based, and this in itself leads to excitement. But it also leads to the question: what are the different approaches between countries? And upon what philosophies are they based?

ENGLAND AND WALES

It is only when you stand back from the English drama situation that you can realize the enormous advances that have been made. Drama in the classroom, however inadequate we believe it is while we are teaching within it, is far in advance of any other country I have visited. Why?

Much is due to the situation in which the teacher works. The independence of the drama teacher in England is in marked contrast to his counterpart in the States or Australia (and to a lesser extent in Canada) who often has to follow a syllabus, pretty exactly, as laid down by a State, or some other authority. Even those United States 'course guides' which seem the most liberal cover a basic assumption that someone, somewhere, knows WHAT and HOW to teach the child better than the individual teacher. As a drama teacher in British schools, I was never subjected to such a 'big brother' attitude (except from one particular headmaster — and him I'll never forget!) and I was always treated as a responsible individual. And alongside this teacher independence, there is the system of national excellence brought about by the Department of Education and Science — a system strictly absent from other English-speaking countries. The HMI system, with one or more responsible for drama, provides a reasonable lower level at which drama teachers in England can operate (or they are fired), and a constant inter-change of ideas between various parts of the country and different levels of the educational system. In contrast, drama teachers in Adelaide could be on a different planet from those in Melbourne, while a drama teacher from the Prairies may not be qualified to teach in British Columbia! As I conducted workshops in Canada, the States, and Australia, I have often wished for the door to open and the Drama HMI (whether C A Alington or John Allen) to walk in.

The basic premise behind British education and the drama within it is, of course, empiricism. Traditionally, British thought has been empirical from Locke and Berkeley to G E Moore's 'Proofs of an External World' (1939) [1] when he showed the audience his two hands and had,

ipso facto, proved the existence of the external world. The whole tenor
of modern British thought and language (as we know from Austin, Russell,
Ayer, and others) is against excessive idealism, and works towards the
practical everyday use of ideas. It is not pragmatic, like Dewey in the
States, but is more rigidly logical, and demands a high degree of literacy from its practitioners. This intellectually tough empiricism leads,
in practical fields such as drama, to considerable differences between
individuals — as between Peter Slade and E J Burton, or between Brian
Way and Dorothy Heathcote[2] — yet these very differences, arising out
of the same empiricism, provide an enrichment through the very variety.
No one way is 'right' and no way is 'wrong'. Each difference feeds the
rest. All are acceptable, provided they stand the test of the tough
empiricism inherent in the educational system.

In North America, British education is often thought of as some
wierd mixture of 'Tom Brown's Schooldays' and 'The Guinea Pig'. The
eighteenth century scholastic methods which this picture evokes have
not completely died, of course. There are still headmasters (fewer
each year) who consider that children should be seen and not heard,
and that education is regurgitating facts. Superimposed upon this scholastic tradition, and increasingly taking over from it, is paedocentric
education — 'child-centred' teaching, or education from the child's
point of view.[3] "Start from where you are," says Brian Way, and that
means from where the child is. (In addition, it also means from where
the teacher is — and that is often ignored.) Drama work in the English
classroom almost always attempts to start from the child's individual
needs, subject to empirical results. This is at the heart of John Allen's
important 1968 Report.[4]

Yet some qualities of the scholastic approach have been retained,
even if the 'rod rule' methods have been jettisoned. Despite the paedocentric nature of the 1968 Report, which contains such statements as,
"Improvisation lies at the heart of school drama," and "Teachers will
use improvisation at a level appropriate to the children to help them to
express themselves in dramatic form and in so doing to reveal a kind
of inner life which on the whole we tend to suppress," it also has constant reminders from the scholastic tradition — "But a great deal of
improvisation is shapeless and without clear purpose. Its aims are in
urgent need of clarification," and elsewhere emphasis is placed "on
the importance of the word, written and spoken, as a means of clarifying
the inner image and establishing exact means of thought and communication in certain areas of experience." It is this kind of double-barrelled
approach which provides an inherent strength to the paedocentric empi-

ricism of British educational drama. The methods that result change slowly. Individual experiments continue, often affecting other areas merely by a process of osmosis. In contrast, Governor Ronald Reagan's administrator responsible for education in California (Mr Rafferty) decided that the Dewey method of 'learning by doing' was producing too many disaffected youths and he attempted to sweep it all away in one fell swoop.

There are many day-to-day problems, of course, which affect too many drama teachers: large classes, few specifically designed spaces, out-dated methods of teacher-training, minimal equipment, lack of in-service courses so that mental atrophy can result, and conservatism can on occasion be seen as a virtue. But the fact remains that drama in education is constantly improving — slowly, of course, as always in England — but nevertheless improving. And the empiricism upon which it is based develops one key factor which encourages this improvement: the demand for flexibility in the drama teacher. It is not merely that I required different approaches and methods when teaching in the country-side of Suffolk and the conurbation of London — I needed the same flexibility of approach when moving from Leeds to Huddersfield! In contrast, I have talked to a number of teachers in the States who were fired from their jobs because their approach was different from the prescribed State method. In Britain, the drama teacher who does not retain an inherent flexibility day-to-day, class-to-class, is going to fail. He proceeds empirically from step to step with no idealistic position which has to be maintained. It may provide uncertainty, but it breeds flexible teaching.

This flexibility is reflected in the use of a syllabus. As a drama teacher in Britain, I could start from improvisation, or script, or dramatic movement, or spontaneous speech and sound; or from play with young children, or from theatre with older students. I could alter the emphasis from day to day, as I viewed the needs of the children. If necessary, whole areas might be omitted. The results were self-evident (like Moore's proof of the external world), empirically successful or not depending on my sensitivity to the needs of the children. The contrast with certain approaches elsewhere in the English-speaking world is considerable.

AUSTRALIA

Drama teachers in Australia are isolated: not merely from the rest of the world, but from drama teachers in other states. In 1970, I attended a seminar in Canberra for the Australian government[5] where were

gathered drama teachers from all the Australian states. It was the first
such gathering since John Allen had attended a similar seminar in 1959.
Many teachers spent most of the recent seminar talking to their counterparts in other states in order to discover what had happened elsewhere
during the intervening eleven years.

The origins of Australian drama teaching are British. Most Commonwealth countries, including Australia, suffer from their colonial inheri-
tance. Nineteenth century administrators in London set up detailed
syllabuses in each state or province, and woe betide the teacher who did
not follow it. It is not so many moons ago (and rumour tells me that
there are still traces of the practice) that at 9.30 am on Monday, April
23rd, an administrator in Sydney would know that exactly the same lesson was being taught throughout all the schools in New South Wales. The
1904 Morant Act and its ramifications in Britain destroyed such practices; but they continued in the old Empire, and their remnants are still
to be found in the Commonwealth.

These two facts alone (state isolation, and administrative rigidity)
make for differences between drama teaching in Britain and Australia.
Old methods, for example, have a much longer life in Australia. Many
of the questions put to me when I addressed the NSW Speech Teachers'
Association at Sydney in 1970, could have been echoes of similar gather-
ings in Britain during the days of Elsie Fogerty or Clifford Turner.
There is less chance of new approaches spreading — whether within the
state, or inter-state. Teachers return with high qualifications from the
UK, the USA, or Canada, only to find themselves frustrated beyond
measure.

Also on the black side is the inherent 'Anzac conservatism' of
Australian popular life. To the ordinary man in the street, theatre and
drama smack of homosexuality and prostitution. It's still 'a man's life'
in the outback and this affects every walk of life. I heard from bus
drivers and bank clerks that if a man was in the theatre there 'must be
something wrong with him'. Things are changing it is true (witness the
renaissance in Australian arts) but drama teachers told me that there
was still strong parental resistance in some areas to drama in schools.

These factors mitigate against adequate development of drama in
education. And when they are added to the huge class sizes in conurba-
tions like Sydney, the wonder is that there has been any progression at
all.

But there has.

The general pattern is two-fold: older teachers trained in older
British drama methods, and younger teachers, immigrating from

Britain, bringing newer approaches with them. In addition, a few (a very few) Australians returning with their graduate degrees from North America have been appointed to senior university or administrative positions.

The greatest advances, however, have been the result of strong and determined men, often working in isolation. As a result, there are pockets of brilliant work surrounded by vast areas of mediocrity. Two examples will serve. First, the drama teacher-training in Melbourne which is of the highest calibre compared to anywhere in the world. Ron Danielson at Melbourne Teachers' College, John Ellis at Monash Teachers' College, and Graham Scott at La Trobe University, all lead exciting, empirical, and progressive programmes. That of MTC is a full, separate programme of teacher training in 'The Creative Arts' (drama, music, crafts, painting, etc) in its own building and producing drama teachers who can relate their work across all artistic fields. These three programmes are led by three men, all of whom know each other well and, on occasion, work together building three disparate but complementary programmes. The second example is from Perth, itself isolated thousands of miles away on the Indian Ocean. The drama adviser for Western Australia, John Bottomley, was about to retire when I visited there. He had spent most of his working life encouraging and developing basic British drama approaches in the educational system, and with considerable success. At the Canberra Conference, he and Dr Mossenson (the senior educational administrator for WA) had met for the first time with the concepts of 'actor-teachers' and the 'Theatre in Education team'. During my subsequent visit to Perth, many of their questions were directed to these ideas, and they were planning how best to build such work into their state. By this time, they may well have done so.

There could be countless other examples of strong and determined men, working empirically on British bases, to bring drama in Australian education into the last quarter of this century.

THE UNITED STATES

Any remarks about drama in American education must be prefaced with the fact that there are vast differences in drama practice. This is the case from state to state, and from city to city. In the slums of New York or Detroit there are conditions that even teachers in the London docks or the back streets of Smethwick would find hair-raising: "Don't turn your back on the kids," is the first rule — you could be raped or mutilated. A school principal in California told me that over 80% of his secondary students were on drugs, over half of them on hard drugs. On the other hand, only 50 miles from Portland, Oregon, a teacher could find himself in 'a little red schoolhouse' and there are still teenagers in parts of New England that could come straight out of 'Our Town'.

But if there are differences in practice, there appear to be certain philosophic assumptions that are common to drama in American education. They can best be seen in historical perspective.

For well over half of the twentieth century, the main approach was John Dewey's pragmatism. This was a 'liberal' education approach, based on 'learning by doing'. [6] It was shattered by Sputnik — the Americans suddenly discovered that the Russians had beaten them in the space race. They immediately blamed their educational system (based on Dewey): the Russian method of education had to be superior, they argued; Russian education was based on behaviourism (from Pavlov), so they turned to their own behaviourists (from Watson to Skinner) and up-graded them quickly in the educational system. As a result today, although there is still a minor Dewey influence, Skinner's behaviourism holds sway. [7]

The Dewey influence upon drama in education came, philosophically, through Hughes Mearns' 'Creative Power': a beautifully written, idealistic book which was written to encourage the inherent goodness he saw in all human beings. [8] This was paralleled later by Harold Rugg's 'Imagination', a book of more intellectual fibre but, as became an old friend of Dewey, one that espoused liberal and pragmatic results. [9] Out of this philosophic climate came two practical giants: Winifred Ward [10] and Charlotte Chorpenning. [11]

Ward's main work was in creative dramatics which she based on story-telling (the old stories, the tried-and-true) which the children then acted. Her main effect was upon the teaching of younger children (up to thirteen-year-olds) when, in most American schools even today, 'Theatre Arts' took over. Chorpenning was a writer and director of children's theatre: performances often based on fairy-tales with mixed adult-child, professional-amateur actors, singers and dancers, to audiences composed of both children and adults. The objectives of this work were defined as (1) to provide worthwhile and appropriate entertainment for young audiences, and (2) to promote individual and social growth through experience in the dramatic arts. [12] Many teachers from England, exposed to this approach for the first time, feel that it is old-fashioned because it reminds them of their own childhood: lessons based on Rodney Bennett's books for the classroom, [13] or watching 'Peter Pan' with Russell Thorndike as Smee. But such initial assumptions by British teachers come from different philosophical predictions.

The British approaches of years ago were part of an empirical growth, and most of them are long since gone. But the Ward approach did not die — in fact, it is very much alive. It is the basis of most American work, including the famous book of Geraldine Brain Siks, [14] and it still continues. The reason for its longevity is that it matches the idealisms inherent in American life. The basic objectives (as given above) were defined within an idealistic philosophy that is still inherent in the United States. Let us look at the objectives again: (1) emphasizes 'entertainment' — and that which is 'worthwhile and appropriate' indicates that adults, in their wisdom, know automatically what is worthwhile and appropriate (? a moral judgement) for children and they should, therefore, provide them with it; (2) considers that individual and social growth (a Dewey-like phrase) can be promoted through experience in the dramatic 'arts' — note this is not 'processes' as implied by Slade, Way, Heathcote et al, but 'arts' which implies 'forms' (and even the sub-title of the Siks' book is 'An Art for Children'). The whole tenor of the Ward-Chorpenning approach is objective rather than subjective, ideal rather than empirical, and based on forms ('arts', skills) rather than processes (developmental needs).

It was no wonder that when the behaviourists came into their own they found that their inherent idealism could match with some elements of the older drama approaches. Yet Skinner's approach, in one sense, is the reverse of Dewey. For Dewey and Mearns, man was inherently good. Skinner trains people out of their inherently evil nature into acceptable (and therefore 'good') behaviour. People ARE their behaviour. Inner processes, like emotion and imagination, have less importance in the Skinnerian system than the forms these processes take — behaviours. 'What is the behavioural objective of the first Billygoat Gruff when he comes to the bridge?" asked of ten-year-olds, means that the children must 'verbalize' first (establish the form in a cognitive way) before acting (behaviour). This is the reverse of the main empirical approach which is to 'do' something first and only later talk about it for analytic purposes.

The common factor in the two American idealisms is that form has primacy over process. British approaches, on the other hand, place prime importance upon process; form is inherent, however, in the background of literacy and scholasticism, but the drama teacher in England normally considers that the child's individual needs (process) are of more importance than appropriate and worthwhile behaviours (skills, or the forms that the processes take). It is a question of emphasis, but the differences are basic and breed different languages.

To illustrate this, let us take three modern American examples based on these idealisms, one from education as a whole and two from drama. Jerome Bruner's work is justifiably famous throughout the world, yet his educational approach is based upon cognition and its forms, and virtually ignores the internal life, such as emotion and imagination; as a result, he gives drama the most cursory treatment.[15] The second example is based on Bloom's Taxonomy[16] which was an attempt to establish a system of hierarchies for educational forms. Recently, Ann Shaw has delineated[17] such a taxonomy for creative dramatics (based on the written works of Ward and her co-workers). Graham Scott has shown[18] that Shaw's approach is basically idealist, based on objective forms rather than process, and ignoring what he calls 'the mind style' of the individual. As an Australian researching in Canada, and therefore working within a different philosophical tradition, he calls for other ways to examine dramatic activity which are less form-oriented. Thirdly, at all levels of education from thirteen year-olds in America (secondary, teacher-training, university) there is a common tendency to put all dramatic activity into one classification: 'Theatre Arts'.[19] Thus all activity after thirteen years is seen as oriented towards stage production, and that which is based on known values — the 'big' show, often with an orchestra, singers, and dancers. Ward's creative dramatics has made little inroad upon education after the age of thirteen. But, in addition, this emphasis upon 'Theatre Arts' comes to influence work with younger children. For example, in a co-ordinated syllabus within one state, all school drama can be classified as 'Theatre Arts' whether it be for six-year-olds or for teenagers; as a result, the overall behavioural objectives are conceived within the framework of 'Theatre Arts' and this directly influences the teacher of the very youngest children.

Outside this tradition is the professional theatre. In America, there is a clear distinction between 'Educational Theatre' and the profession, but it is the latter which has generated most excitement in recent years. The Paper-Bag Players, and The Bread and Puppet Theatre, for example, have radically altered concepts of children's theatre in the USA: both start from the needs of the children in their audience but do not remain static; rather, they alter their forms of theatre when new needs are acknowleged. Alongside this type of work can be placed the Story Theatre of Paul Sills which has taken the 'story approach' of Chorpenning and brought it more into line with the present day: one actor narrates the story while the characters mingle mime and speech with the simplest of properties and settings.

In these days of modern travel, there has been some resultant mingling of traditional American approaches with empiricism. The most recent California curriculum guide [20] reads to a non-American like a curious mixture of Ward, Slade, Way, and Theatre Arts with smatterings of theatre history — all set in a framework that requires behavioural objectives at each point. More interesting, perhaps, will be the forthcoming printing of Barbara Salisbury's 'Oregon project' that was funded by the federal government. [21] Each step in this coordinated programme was tried out with participating Language Arts (called 'English' in Britain) teachers in Oregon and empirically tested. Another fascinating item should be mentioned. Several times, while I was at the University of Victoria in British Columbia, I took my graduate students across the Gulf of Georgia into the United States where we held joint seminars (practical and theoretic) with the graduate students of Agnes Haaga and Geraldine Brain Siks at the University of Washington. Apart from the pleasure of working with these two great teachers, both groups of students were fascinated to compare the similarities and differences between practices and the philosophies upon which they were based. The quality of my own students' work increased immeasurably. I can only hope the same applied to those of Agnes and Gerry.

CANADA

We have seen that Canada is a melting-pot of many drama influences, but we should distinguish between English and French-speaking Canada. The latter, mainly the Province of Quebec with some drama work in Manitoba and New Brunswick, is still basically in the French tradition with the emphasis in schools upon 'le mime' and theatre skills. Creative drama is still virtually unknown — indeed, there is no adequate translation for the term, the nearest being 'dynamique' which has other connotations.

In English-speaking Canada there is a constant dichotomy between the objective idealism of senior educators (trained by Americans, either in the USA or Canada) and the subjective empiricism of drama teachers. Non-drama teachers have solid training in behavioural methods: teacher-training in one university, for example, permits nothing but Skinnerian approaches in all Educational Psychology courses. On the other hand, empirical approaches from Britain are paramount in the training of drama teachers — whether it be David Kemp at Queens', Ontario, Jane Benson at Windsor, Tom Crothers at Seneca College, or Margaret Faulkes at Edmonton — or Canadians with British training like John Ripley at McGill, or Helen Dunlop, the drama supervisor for Ontario

Department of Education. This dichotomy may lead to misunderstandings due to the two languages being used. Two examples will serve. Some drama teachers, when they get out into schools, may find a senior educator asking for their behavioural objectives; they then have the problem of articulating dramatic activity to a person whose classifications, and the resultant language that is used, are different from their own. In addition, post-graduate drama students in an oral examination may find themselves facing professors using different philosophic languages; idealist faculty may then consider that what the student is saying is worthless; and the empirical student may consider the questions quite pointless. Difficulties, naturally, abound but the natural Canadian good humour usually comes to the rescue.

The development of children's theatre in Canada has come in two stages. Until 1950, what little there was originated with the United States. In 1948, for example, Holiday Playhouse was founded in Vancouver by Joy Coghill who was already an eminent director in America. But in the early 1950s, the two Canadian tours of Brian Way had immediate impact. By 1969 there were 18 professional Theatre-for-Young-Audiences companies in Canada (note the use of English terminology as against the American children's theatre), while there were only 17 in the UK by 1970, and all but one of the Canadian companies were performing participational plays (including Holiday Playhouse). Universally, in English-speaking Canada, professional companies perform small-cast plays, usually in-the-round on the floor of the school gymnasium. With increasing use of actor-teachers, their influence upon the educational system is growing considerably. It is interesting to note that Brian Way's influence has been direct by the Canadian absorption of some of his past co-workers: Margaret Faulkes and David Kemp in teacher-training, and Sue Richmond and Ken Kramer who founded The Globe Theatre in Saskatchewan, which tours the icy wastes of the Prairies by jeep.

The unique contribution of Canada to drama in education is to absorb all the different influences to which she is subject, and create something uniquely her own. Let us use examples from the universities which, in most Provinces, are responsible for teacher-training. In the city of Montreal, there are two universities both with drama programmes: Montreal University, which is French-speaking, where Dr Giselle Barret runs undergraduate and graduate programmes, and The University of McGill, which is English-speaking, where Dr John Ripley has similar programmes. In true Canadian style, these two fine teachers intermingle their work, their students, and their courses — often bi-lingually. A second example is the practical approach taken by my own university, Calgary. We have a group of fine teachers, all with different back- grounds: Zina Barnieh, who was born in Italy, is the only Canadian with Canadian training; Dr Craig Elliott is a Canadian, with American train- ing; Joyce Doolittle was trained in the States, as Peter McWhir and I were trained in Britain; we have an American-trained puppet master, and a Laban-trained (in Germany) movement teacher; while those re- searching with us include a Briton with Welsh and Canadian training, a Hungarian with training in Sweden, Britain, and Canada, as well as an Australian. There is absolutely no way we can co-exist unless we recog- nize each other's differences. We try to maintain what is uniquely our own, but adapt it to the specific situation in Calgary. The same class, taught by a different teacher, can be exposed to a radically different philosophic approach — and that, considering where we are and who we are, is a factor we energetically protect.

Lastly, we should note the growing use of the Canadian term Developmental Drama in our universities. [22] Most offering under- graduate degrees, and all offering graduate degrees for drama teachers, now use the term. It is specifically all-inclusive, so that people with different backgrounds can more easily work within its framework. It is defined as the developmental study of human enactment and, in addition to teacher-training, there are courses for social workers, therapists, recreation leaders, and the like. This sets drama teacher-training in a larger intellectual framework and provides the intellectual 'bite' so necessary in a country with a mixture of philosophies and practices. This is a particularly Canadian contribution to the field, as Canada in all aspects of its life demands an 'inclusive' rather than an 'exclusive' approach. It is interesting to note that the term is already in use in Melbourne, Australia, and there are indications of similar growths in the United States. Perhaps our dichotomies are becoming less obvious.

CONCLUSION

In a comparative approach such as this, I have not intended to disparage some philosophies and practices in comparison with others. However, I have been guilty of vast generalizations in order to provide a clear picture. Inevitably there must be misrepresentations. Yet I think it is quite clear that there are two distinctive philosophies in English-speak- ing drama in education (the ideal and the empirical) with their appro- priate practices. The Canadian experience may make them mutually compatible.

Finally, it is interesting to reflect, albeit briefly, upon other inter-

national relationships. As American approaches have become more behavioural, there has been increasing interest in dramatic education
within the Soviet Union, itself behaviourally based. Some work has
begun in Yugoslavia, and experimental work may even begin shortly in
Russia. In non-English-speaking Europe, the most empirical approach
appears to be in the Netherlands. Romance-speaking countries appear
to approach drama in education from a specifically theatrical (but non-
idealist) point of view. Emergent countries are expressing great interest
in the field as a whole, and their students are training in Britain, the
States, and Canada (at least). What these countries will eventually make
of our ideal/empirical dichotomy may possibly be the most interesting
development of drama in education during the last quarter of this century.

Richard Courtney

NOTES

1   In J N Findlay (Ed) 'Studies in Philosophy' (Oxford, 1966)
2   Compare: Peter Slade 'Child Drama' (ULP, 1954); E J Burton
    'Drama in Schools' (Jenkins, 1955); Brian Way 'Development
    Through Drama' (Longmans, 1968); Dorothy Heathcote in
    'Drama in Education 1' pp 81-83 (Pitman, 1972)
3   See my 'Play, Drama and Thought' Part 1 (Cassell, 1968)
4   HMSO 'Education Survey 2: Drama' (1968)
5   Lawrence Hayes (Ed) 'Education and the Arts: The teaching of
    drama and allied subjects in the secondary school'
    (ANU, Canberra, 1971)
6   John Dewey 'Experience and Education' (NY, 1938) and other works
7   B F Skinner 'Walden II' (NY, 1962) and other works
8   Hughes Mearns 'Creative Power' (Dover, NY, rev.1958)
9   Harold Rugg 'Imagination' (NY, 1963)
10 Winifred Ward 'Creative Dramatics' (NY, 1930); 'Theatre for
    Children' (Anchorage, rev.1950) and other works
11 Charlotte Chorpenning: her many plays published by Children's
    Theatre Press (Anchorage)
12 Geraldine Brain Siks and Hazel Brain Dunnington (Eds) 'Children's
    Theatre and Creative Dramatics' (Seattle, 1961) p 26
13 Rodney Bennett 'Classroom Dramatics', 'Practical Speech Training
    for Schools' and many other books of the 1930s and 40s
14 Geraldine Brain Siks 'Creative Dramatics: An Art for Children'
    (NY, 1958)
15 Jerome S Bruner 'Towards a Theory of Instruction' (NY, 1962)
    and other works
16 Bloom et al 'A Taxonomy of Educational Objectives, The Classifica-
    tion of Educational Goals - Handbook I, The Cognitive Domain'
    (NY, 1956)
17 Ann Shaw 'A Taxonomical Study of the Nature and Behavioural
    Objectives of Creative Dramatics' (Educational Theatre Journal,
    Winter, 1970) pp 361-372
18 Graham Scott 'Structures for Creative Drama: Some Comments on
    Shaw, Langer and Kelly' (Discussions on Developmental Drama I,
    University of Calgary, 1972)
19 'Tentative Drama/Theatre Framework for California Public
    Schools: A Process-Concept Framework for a Program in

Theatre Arts for All Students, Kindergarten through Twelfth Grade' (Statewide Fine Arts and Humanities Framework Committee, California, 1970)

20   'Tentative Drama/Theatre Framework for California Public Schools: A Process-Concept Framework for a Program in Theatre Arts for All Students, Kindergarten through Twelfth Grade' (Statewide Fine Arts and Humanities Framework Committee, California, 1970)

21   Based on the Department of English, University of Oregon, Eugene, Oregon

22   See 'Drama in Education 1' pp 231-232 (Pitman, 1972)

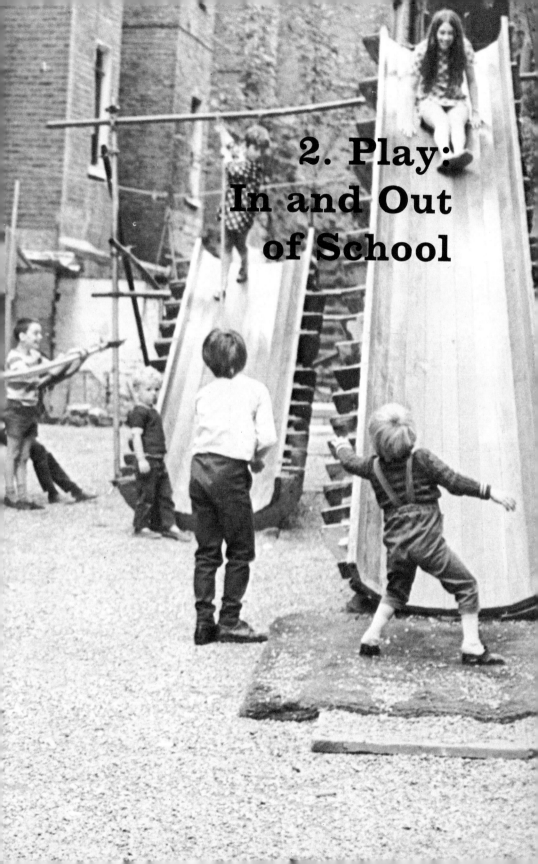

2. Play: In and Out of School

Playing and Learning

In order to balance the drama view of play we asked Michael Pokorny to set out for us the view of a professional psychiatrist

The word play is used to describe a number of phenomena. Usually, though not invariably, the context in which the word is used offers a clear idea of which variety of play is being referred to. 'Webster's New International Dictionary' (Second Edition, 1950) and the 'Shorter Oxford English Dictionary' (1964) each devote over two columns to various meanings and compounds of play. 'Webster's Dictionary of Synonyms' (1951) offers a summary of the various uses of play, categorizing play as either a verb meaning to engage in activity as pleasure or amusement, or as a noun meaning activity engaged in for the sake of pleasure or amusement, adding that play is, in general, the opposite of work.

Learning involves work, indeed is often considered to be very hard work. As such it is at odds with the notion of play as an activity undertaken only for pleasure or amusement. Perhaps there is some sense in the notion of playing the game, insofar as practising beforehand implies that it is important to win, and the game is converted into work, which defeats one of the objects of the game. Or does it? An important feature of learning is to gain not only knowledge, but mastery. By knowing one may be more able to exercise control. It would appear that this purposive part of learning, as it is incorporated in play-behaviour, has not yet reached the dictionaries. Children's play is regarded as a purely pleasurable activity. Yet there has been wide recognition for some years that children at play practise skills, and thus learn.

This phenomenon may be readily observed in infants. One example is of an infant picking up and putting down objects, when an observer can readily witness the exercise of the infant's control, or lack of it, over its hands and arms.

Gradually the infant learns the spatial relationships between various parts of its body and the way that these relationships can be controlled. Later play activity extends to the relationships between size and shape, well illustrated in the toy posting box, where shapes are pushed through the appropriate hole. Equally explorative activity can be seen as an infant manipulates objects, separating them and putting them together again.

An infant who has access to a kitchen cupboard containing saucepans, has at his disposal a large amount of experimental material in terms of size and shape and, if left in peace, will spend a lot of time fitting saucepans together, inside each other, separating them, examining them individually and fitting the lids.

At times it can be quite difficult to be sure than an infant's behaviour can really be described as play. It seems to be such hard work. Yet the happy smile which goes with achievement is evidence of pleasure gained, and the activity may then be described by using the word play.

For some time, infants play alone. Gradually they play give-and-take games with adults, but there is a fairly lengthy phase to work through before infants, when put near to each other, play together as opposed to playing alone whilst in proximity to each other.

The ability to play with others is an important step in maturation and requires the exercise of several psychic capabilities. One must be able to distinguish between self and not-self. One must be able to distinguish between an object and a symbolic representative of that object. If one plays at let's pretend, one is dealing in an informed way with symbols. A child may exhibit destructive behaviour towards a doll which is designated 'my baby'. If a real baby is treated differently, we are entitled to state that a pretend baby is subjected to specific manipulations, reserved to it. We may, for instance, infer that internal fantasies about babies are being enacted in relation to a symbolic baby. If a child is seen to treat a real baby and a pretend baby in the same destructive way, then we do not need a psychiatrist to tell us that there is something seriously wrong with the child.

One way of conceptualizing what is wrong would be to say that the child is unable to distinguish between a thing, or a person, and its symbolic representative.

Play, as I am describing it, begins as an activity indulged in to gain mastery over the motor apparatus and progresses to exploration of the relationships between objects, initially in a very concrete and direct way as in the give-and-take game, or the game of dropping things over the side of the pram and finding out whether or not they can be made to reappear. Later the relationship between symbolic representatives of objects and the fantasies about them can be explored. Pleasure is manifested when a sufficient degree of mastery is gained, and the evidence of that pleasure is appreciated by the attachment of the concept of play to the activity that appears to give rise to the pleasure.

One could consider that until mastery is gained work is being done, evidenced by the expressions of frustration that can often be observed in infants and children engaged in attempts to 'play'. Once success is achieved, one can observe the repetition of an activity over and over again. The child who has just learned to whistle does so constantly for the sheer pleasure of exercising a newly won skill. This leads to the idea that to acquire a new skill is work. Once acquired, the repetitious exercise of the skill gives pleasure. Thus there may be more than a semantic argument as to whether play is the opposite of work. Learning requires work. It leads to the acquisition of something new, or the modification of something already present. Maybe the word play should be reserved for the pleasurable activity of repeating, in which nothing new is learned.

On the other hand, learning through play is a notion that is fairly widely held amongst educationalists, and rather than attempting to insist on changing the way that the English language is used, it might be more profitable to examine the relationship between playing and learning in more detail.

There are two aspects of activity, be it playing or working, that need to be distinguished. Firstly the individual or personal relationship to the activity, and secondly the interaction in a group of people concerned with an activity. These two aspects co-exist, but the concepts that one could use in understanding individual behaviour are not necessarily helpful in understanding group behaviour. One way to describe the difference is to say that, in order to understand an individual's behaviour in relation to his world, it is necessary to know something of that individual's internal world, something of his individual view of his surroundings. Such knowledge could be gained by making inferences based on his manifest behaviour by applying to that behaviour a construct or theory of the human psyche. Alternatively one could enquire from the individual, who can not only tell you what he feels, but can demonstrate by the manner of the telling how he uses his perceptions of his environment. By contrast, when confronted by a group of individuals, one can directly observe the internal workings of the group in a way that is not possible with an individual. Whereas an individual can conceal his internal world, a group inevitably demonstrates its collective beliefs by its very existence. The group's world is amenable to examination by directly observing the behaviour of the members of the group towards each other and the effect that this behaviour has on the carrying out of the purpose for which the group got together.

The task which the group is supposed to carry out can be directly compared with the activity that the members of the group indulge in. The first step is to define the task, usually designated the primary task, and to distinguish this from subsidiary or secondary tasks which are pursued in order to facilitate the carrying out of the primary task. As an example, one could consider that the primary task of a school is to educate its pupils. Leaving aside possible arguments as to what is meant by education, several secondary tasks become essential. Some of these fall into the category of administration, another category is that of quality control, which I use here to signify activity engaged in to test whether and to what extent the primary task is being carried out. In the example of a school, this is largely a matter of testing the educational level of the pupils. Administration can be crudely described as getting the teachers and the pupils together at a particular time in a particular location so that the primary task of educating can go on. In addition apparatus to facilitate educating activity has to be provided. To carry out these various tasks, people are appointed to jobs.

Put slightly differently, roles are allotted to people. The beliefs that are held within the school can be deduced by observation of the way that roles are allotted and carried out, with particular reference to the primary task.

Furthermore, one can see whether there is any discrepancy between the declared beliefs about education and the beliefs about education which are evident from the behaviour of the members of the school. As an example, it may be stated in the prospectus that science subjects are taught in the school and that these are regarded as important. They may be given prominence in the timetable, evidence that one part of the administration is facilitating the declared belief in science. However, if the necessary scientific apparatus is inadequate, out-of-date or constantly in repair, then this would be evidence that another part of the administration does not share the belief in the educative value of science subjects. If appropriate action is not taken, then one might consider that the members of the school are in collusion to exclude science from the curriculum, in deed if not in word. Several possible conditions within the school may give rise to such a state of affairs. An incompetent science teacher has been appointed. Money is not made available, maybe on the grounds that although science is important, Latin books are also important. There are further complex chains of events that could be thought up. The point essentially is that the manifest behaviour of the group supplies evidence of the beliefs that are being acted upon and whether or not they correspond to the declared beliefs. The school governors and the headmaster may declare that science is of major importance. Observation may reveal that the dominant belief in the school is, in fact, that Latin, or football, or something else, is of major importance and science is the least important.

Two observable phenomena may give rise to this sort of conclusion. One is the physical state of the science classroom; the other is the general phenomenon, which is directly observable, of the ways in which roles are allocated: who allocates, to whom and by what criteria. After allocation has occurred, one can directly observe the manner in which the allocated role is pursued. Although the manner in which a role is pursued depends upon the person to whom it is allocated, the way in which it is allocated and the person who is chosen for it are functions of the beliefs within which the group is actually operating. A group will allocate a role to someone whom it believes will fit in with the group, and will then continuously bring pressure to bear on the person in the role to try to ensure that the way the role is pursued continues to fit in with the beliefs of the group.

In the hypothetical school situation which I have described, one could imagine there being a belief that science is a subject for cranks and that if one becomes involved in science one runs the risk of becoming some sort of crank.

Supposing that a relatively incompetent science teacher is appointed and his efforts to teach science are frustrated. What is likely to happen? In general terms, breakdown. More specifically, the type of breakdown that fits in with the beliefs held in the group about science and scientists. If scientists are cranks the teacher would justify the belief if he became impossible to work with, or had a nervous breakdown. If the belief is that scientists are unreliable and fickle, then this might be felt to be confirmed if the school had a series of science teachers in rapid succession.

This brings us back to the criteria that are in fact adopted in appointing such a teacher. Someone will be chosen who is relatively incompetent. Incompetent in relation to what? The answer is, by now, quite obvious. A teacher who is not competent to deal with the type of frustrations that the group are going to inflict upon him, except by confirming the beliefs about scientists that the group already hold. Put the other way round, a teacher will be chosen, not on the criteria of his capacity to teach science, but on the criteria of his capacity to fill the role of cranky scientist for the group. This statement carries the further implication that allowing oneself to be chosen by a group for a role means that one's own needs fit in with those necessary to comply with the group's wishes. When an individual fulfils a role within a group, there is a complex interaction happening which is only partly amenable to direct observation.

The workings of the group, the roles that it calls forth and their relation to the group task can be fairly clearly seen. The reasons why an individual fits in with those parts of the group's behaviour that he fits in with can only be deduced on the basis of applying a theory about the individual's internal world to his manifest behaviour, unless one has access to the individual's internal world. In general, one can only say that for each individual, staying in the group, or leaving the group at a particular point, must fit in with the group's needs and the individual's needs. I am using the word needs to denote a composite of conscious and unconscious wishes, fears, impulses, etc. In fact the notion of the unconscious is derived from the observation that people often do things that do not appear to fit in with their needs.

One explanation of this is to postulate that, in addition to needs that we are aware of, we have other needs that we are not aware of. These needs are, by definition, unconscious. The notion that all our behaviour is partly determined by our unconscious needs is the notion of psychic determinism and it is the essential basic notion of all psycho-analytic theories and treatments.

I am describing two interrelated, but separate phenomena. One being the individual and his relation to the group and the other being the ways in which the group uses individuals to enact or personify those beliefs that the group requires. This leads to a clear statement, that role play is a phenomenon of groups and that one way to understand a group is by the elucidation of the roles that the group evokes from individuals and the ways in which these roles are consonant or dissonant with the declared primary task of the group. The observation that the roles appear to be out of keeping with the declared primary task and yet are persisted with in the group, is taken as evidence that, whatever the declared task, the group is in fact pursuing some other task. Also the notion that the change of task is agreed between the group members is deduced from the observation that they continue to pursue their roles. The fact that the group members are not consciously aware of the change of task or of their individual contribution to the new task, is taken as evidence that unconscious determinants of behaviour predominate and that this suits the needs of the group, both individually and collectively.

Unconscious, collective agreement to continue to pursue particular roles is described by the technical term of collusion. A group may collude to pursue a task quite different from the declared task and one of the functions observable in the group will be a mechanism to keep the unspoken task hidden from the group. Thus any dissenting behaviour by a group member will be felt as an attack on the group and be punished. Dissent is in fact an attack on the collusive behaviour as it threatens to make manifest that which the group desires to keep hidden. A dissenter will thus be regarded as difficult to work with, uncooperative. There will arise pressure to achieve conformity. If this does not succeed, then a tendency to exclude the dissenter will become manifest.

The manner of the excluding behaviour will also conform to the group's unspoken needs, and often the dissenter will be pushed into a more extreme position than he would willingly adopt. Here I am describing an essential pre-requisite of the making of a scapegoat.

I should now like to use the notions I have outlined, as a basis for examining the criteria that could be used to decide whether a group is working or playing.

In the context of a group which is supposed to be learning, work covers any activity which leads to learning something new or modifying an existing skill or attitude.

Play designates any activity which is repetitive, in the sense that no learning takes place.

Roles taken up in the group are subjected to analysis with reference to whether they facilitate or hinder the primary task of the group, which is to learn.

This approach requires a clear statement of what the group are supposed to be learning.

The specific example of a group of drama students would raise the whole issue of what such students should be educated for, a debatable issue which I do not propose to tackle here. Instead I shall make an assumption, in the belief that if some other assumption is more appropriate, the principles that I am trying to elucidate will be applicable.

The only condition of applicability is that the primary task is clearly stated so that there is clarity about the point of reference.

I shall assume, or assert, that the primary task of a drama school is to teach, facilitate or enable the student to be an actor. By this I mean that the aim is for the student to portray roles in a drama in a suitably convincing manner. That is, convincing to the director and suitable in terms of the role as a part of a dramatic production. I choose the director on the grounds that it is he, or she, who will employ the actor. Unless the director is convinced of the actor's effectiveness, the theatre audience will not have any opportunity to pass judgement. I should emphasize that I am using the term drama school in a general sense, to describe a place where students of drama are taught, thus including drama departments of universities and establishments which describe themselves as 'Drama Schools'.

I assume that there are areas of technical knowledge that the student must become familiar with, and that the area of common interest is in the application of this knowledge to acting, in the sense also that through acting under supervision, the student will become aware of deficiencies in his knowledge which need to be attended to.

This supervision being carried out by the teacher and by other students in the group.

Hence one possible criterion of work emerges: whilst engaged in the work of role-playing, do the students help each other to become aware of their strengths and weaknesses, or are they engaged in making one student appear grossly deficient so that, by contrast, the others may feel good? Here the teacher's role would be to prevent the group from selecting a scapegoat and also to stop them from relying entirely on supervision from the teacher.

Of course this sort of procedure will evoke anxiety in the group, largely because, for working and learning to occur, the students must of necessity be in touch with their feelings as well as the necessary technical knowledge. This statement raises a very important issue, which applies to all learning in a group setting, namely that a group cannot learn, it is only individuals who can learn. As individuals learn at different rates, rivalries within the group are inevitably set up.

Thus we have another criterion of whether or not the group is working. A working group, in which learning is taking place, must allow the members to learn at different rates and must be able to tolerate that some will learn more than others.

Both these criteria have something to do with observing the ways in which a group deals with anxiety and some attention should be paid to the anxiety evoked in the group leader.

I am aware that drama teachers are concerned about the possibility that teaching through play may be harmful. I really do not know what the basis of this concern is. All I can say about this is that the position of leader in a group that is working with feelings is difficult. An inherent difficulty is that, as the group learns, the leader's position may be threatened. At its crudest, the group may realize that they are not as dependent on the leader as they thought, that they can manage without the leader and that, as they outnumber the leader, they can in fact take over and produce their own leader. Presumably this phenomenon is normally manifested by the student group putting on a dramatic production with little or no help from the teacher. Put like that, the taking over from the original leader is a healthy and desirable outcome of the learning experience. It is also a way of rephrasing the notion of collusion in a group.

If a group colludes to change the primary task, they are, in a sense, taking over from the leader (teacher), but in a hidden way. If this type of take-over is not allowed to occur, then there may be an opportunity for the group to reach the point of overt, acceptable and realistic taking-over of leadership and the responsibility that goes with it. I think that, in a more general sense, I am also describing a way of conceptualizing the process of personality maturation as it may occur in an individual in a group setting.

In so far as there is a concern to develop more explicit criteria of the use of 'play' in the teaching of drama, I think that the most likely approach would be for an expert in group phenomena to study a drama-group as it is working (or playing) or for a drama teacher to study group phenomena as they are manifested within institutions and apply that knowledge to the teaching situation.

Although the interaction of roles within the group is complex and often subtle, role play is amenable to systematic study which can give rise to fairly clear ideas about the ways in which the activity of a group can be interfered with in order to facilitate the pursuit of the primary task and inhibit the proliferation of collusive behaviour. This interference needs to be as informed as possible and is the specific task of the group leader.

In order to maximize the leader's ability to ensure that learning takes place, it is essential that for each specific activity a study be made of the particular application of understanding of role playing phenomena to the task in hand.

As far as drama education is concerned the area to be studied is that of the establishment of criteria of learning within a group engaged in an activity which is called playing, but may be more accurately defined as working at playing.

Michael Pokorny

SUGGESTED FURTHER READING

Grainger, A. J. 'The Bullring: a classroom experiment in moral education'. Pergamon Press, Oxford. 1970.

Hartley, R. E. et al. 'Understanding children's play'. Routledge and Kegan Paul, London. 1952.

Herron, R. E. and Sutton-Smith, B. 'Child's play'. Wiley, New York. 1971.

Klein, A. 'Role playing in leadership training and group problem solving'. Association Press, New York. 1956.

Moreno, J. L. 'Psychodrama' Vol.1 (1946); Vol.2 (1959). Beacon House, New York

Ottaway, A. K. C. 'Learning through group experience'. Routledge and Kegan Paul, London. 1966.

Shaftel, F. R. and Shaftel, G. 'Role-playing for social values: decision-making in the social studies'. Prentice-Hall, Englewood Cliffs, NJ. 1967. (Good bibliography)

Slavson, S. R. 'Creative group education'. Association Press, New York. 1948. (See chapter on Drama)

Sprott, W. J. H. 'Human groups'. Penguin Books, Harmondsworth. 1958.

Way, B. 'Development through drama'. Longman, London. 1967.

Beyond the Known

Brian Wilks, Lecturer in English and Drama in the School of Education at the University of Leeds, explores theories of play, 'the creative event'

The study of the nature, meaning and importance of children's play has long held the interest of philosophers and psychologists. Equally, there has been much exploration of the meaning and significance of the 'creative event'. It is not my purpose here to catalogue the great variety of theories, accounts and observations available,[1] but rather to examine the benefits to the teacher of drama that can accompany a serious involvement with such studies. Much that is written about 'play' has a direct bearing upon the way in which we propose to work with children, and, moreover, how we conduct our activities in school. For the experience of informal, and in many cases formal, drama in schools is in a basic and fundamental way a kind of playing. This simple fact is at once the joy and sorrow of our work; it is our freedom but also our thrall. It is also a root cause of much misunderstanding and confusion.

By here outlining some of the thinking that has gone into the presentation of theories about play I hope to demonstrate that such studies, in their relevance and perception, must occupy a central position in our analysis of the principles upon which we found our work. We may not shirk the responsibility of pondering both long and deep over precisely what we and our students are engaged upon when we work in drama.

It is a sad truth that in whatever guise we meet drama in school a large amount of the work we witness issues from the most tenuous and shallow first principles; if, indeed, it is in any way connected with penetrating and sustained analysis. But while this may be so, there is ample evidence of good work. It is as if some universal instinct for acceptable activity prevails. But upon scrutiny it becomes clear that there is wide conjecture about the aims of dramatic experience for children, which is matched by widespread confusion over the short and long-term value of drama as a worthy contribution to the curriculum of a school. While lacking in rigorous scrutiny of the first principles for drama as a discipline we do not lack accounts and models of existing practice. Practitioners diligently compose prescriptions for good habits and from time to time furnish us with glowing accounts of work accomplished. But no amount of such peripheral activity can ever substitute for the failure to study the essential nature of the subject. Examples and prophecies are in their own way enlightening, but will hardly suffice as secure foundations upon which to erect an entire edifice of educational practice.

It is my aim to indicate an approach to drama in education which is based upon a consideration of the essential nature of the experience that we try to make available to children when we 'do' drama with them. I hope to show that our apparent neglect of the psychological and philosophical approach has been doubly remiss. Such an exploration not only helps us to understand the part that drama can play in the developing life of the child, but also offers telling insights into the centrality of the dramatic experience in the life of man.

However we may choose to define those activities we call 'drama' in schools, there can be no doubt that they are some kind of playing. They are events where sheer enjoyment and willing participation are in evidence and where spontaneous and absorbing concentration occurs. Moreover, they are events where the normal restrictions of the factual world, that of discursive logic, and the limitations of time and space are seemingly suspended. It follows, therefore, that the subject of our investigation must be the nature of the experience that we recognize as 'dramatic play'. But we must also accept that drama is no ordinary activity; it is an art form rather than a mechanical physical action connected with the material world. No study of the nature of drama should be undertaken, therefore, that does not recognize from the outset that the creative enterprise which we call 'drama' can only be properly defined as an aesthetic event. Drama is essentially art and its proper scrutiny can only meaningfully occur as an investigation of the nature of what we term the creative processes of artistic making. We are involved in a philosophic study of the broadest kind when we come to investigate the value of Drama in Education.

While not attempting to provide an exhaustive and detailed account of theories of play and theories of creativity I propose to indicate the classic view of play, and after some discussion of a recent theory, to consider some ideas about the 'creative event' and their value for the teacher of drama.

PLAY

There is an abundance of literature about play. [2] Much of this literature
is excellent and most of it is humbling by reason of its precision and
clarity. Moreover it is a literature that has altered the course of education, providing much of the theory and experimental verification that is
the basis of contemporary playschool and primary education.

The study of play has interested some of the most influential thinkers
of the past, [3] and historical theories of play range from those like
Wesley's condemnation: "He who plays as a boy will play as a man" [4]
to Froebel's:

> "Play is the highest expression of human development in
> childhood, for it alone is the free expression of what is
> in the child's soul. It is the purest and most spiritual
> product of the child, and at the same time it is a type
> and copy of human life at all stages...."
>
> (5)

We shall not be surprised to find wide divergence in the definitions of
play that we shall meet. Heron and Sutton Smith (1971) in their study of
play [6] conclude that there is "no speaking with a universal and objective
voice" and suggest that any attempt to synthesize the many views is like
"trying to fit together pieces from separate jigsaw puzzles". Lowenfeld,
whose work stands as a most thorough and meaningful survey, argues
that the nature of play is so disparate that it can never be "pressed into
any single formula". [7] However, Lowenfeld does give us a definition
of categories of play that is helpful:

> "It is suggested ... that there is play that expresses
> the bodily impulses of the child; that apperceives his
> environment; that prepares the child for life; that
> enables him to mix harmoniously with his fellows."
>
> (8)

While thus categorizing recognizable kinds of play Lowenfeld supported the view that there was a duality about human nature; that there was
an 'inner life' (the egocentric or subjective life) and an 'outer life' (the
observable world of phenomenon which we all share). Play, for Lowenfeld, and for many others who share this view of the duality of experience, was an event in the 'outer life' performed on behalf of and with the
aid of the 'inner life'. We shall meet this theory later where its implications will be more fully considered. Play in such theories was seen
to have an important function in the gradual process of the egocentric
newly born infant growing to become a mature 'realistic' adult; during
the journey from solipsism to socialization.

Here are the four chief purposes of play, as indicated by Lowenfeld:
a) It serves as the child's making contact with his environment ....;

b) it makes the bridge between the child's consciousness and his emotional experience, and so fulfils the role that conversation, introspection, philosophy and religion fill for the adult ....;

c) it represents to the child the externalized experience of his emotional life, and therefore, in this aspect serves for the child the function taken by art in adult life ....;

d) it serves the child as a relaxation and amusement, as enjoyment and as rest.... [9]

If we were to go no further there would be enough here for us to ponder and set against our intention and aims in offering drama to children. It is in dramatic play that children can explore their environment and make contact with it, can essay their own emotional experience against that which they observe in the world, and no one would deny that drama affords opportunity for relaxation and enjoyment. Many of the purposes denoted by Lowenfeld are served by drama. But Lowenfeld's ideas are but one figure in the overall pattern. They are of use to us as a point of departure and an indication of the nature of play theories. They intimate the interest that such work holds for the alert teacher of drama.

Since Lowenfeld, considerable advance has been made in our understanding of the importance of play in the development of the child. The movement in the theories has been away from viewing play as an idleness proper to childhood that must fade before maturity, towards theories where play is considered essential for the mental well-being of man in society with his fellow men.

While it is difficult to define play precisely, its nature, function and stages do seem to have been discerned. In their study of play 'Children's Play' (1970), Holme and Massie present an admirable brief outline of the theories of play that are available to us:

First the nature of play. It is possible to extract criteria which are common to most theories. Giddens[10] has identified three common strands of a major kind: "play is an activity which is by and large non-instrumental in character"; "on a social level, play is a relatively self-contained activity"; and "play is essentially a non-productive activity".

Secondly, the function of play. One may look at the suggested functions of play ... and decide which ... would seem to have a universal significance. Here we suggest there are four main functions: play relieves tensions and provides an emotional outlet; play has a vital role in the socialization of children: it is part of the learning process: and play gives satisfaction of achievement and self-realization which may be otherwise frustrated. Thirdly, the stages of play. It is helpful to consider the kinds of play that are seen to occur — group, solitary, exploration, manipulative, imaginative — in relation to the various stages in children's development. [11]

Holme and Massie helpfully pinpoint Piaget's chief contribution to play theory when they quote him and comment thus:

Piaget: "Play begins, then, with the first dissociation between assimilation and accommodation. After learning to grasp, swing, throw etc, which involve both an effort of repetition, reproduction and generalization, which are the elements of assimilation, the child sooner or later (often in the learning period) grasps for the pleasure of grasping: swings for the sake of swinging, etc." (Piaget, 1951: 'Dreams and Imitation in Childhood'.)

Holme and Massie: ".... When a playing child assimilates pieces of experience through play, he adopts the experience into his own limited world; but by accommodation he meets the demands of reality and experience; in play, assimilation is predominant, so play is seen as assimilation of reality to the ego: for the child lives in an egocentric world." [12]

Again we meet the view that play is crucial for the balancing of reality with the interior life. As we age so the press of the external reality of things becomes irresistible. But drama provides the opportunity for the creation of trial situations where notions can be explored without fear of let or hindrance. It is as if drama, with its imagined places peopled by invented characters, provides an interim world, a world where the deprivations of objective experience do not automatically inhibit experiment and conjecture. In the imagined world of dramatic play there is room for the setting up of trial situations and trial responses which the bounds of normal — that is socially accepted, if not **expected** — behaviour will not permit. This is not to invoke some special licence for drama, or to put drama beyond ordered controlled behaviour, far from it. It is to suggest that the primary need for play, for the exploration of the environment, which includes the altering of that environment and shaping it anew as much as simply discerning it, comes properly within the scope of dramatic activities. As play is defined above, it clearly is what most drama teachers are presently engaged upon in their work.

At this point it would be helpful to have a definition of what precisely is meant by 'dramatic experience'. Just as the term 'play' dilates with meaning, so does this. We have the same problem of focus. What one man terms 'drama' in school is another man's 'movement', 'theatre', 'dance' or 'ritual'. For the purposes of this discussion I use the term 'dramatic experience' to mean those activities where children involve themselves, and perhaps space and objects, in externalized 'make-believe': where children act out, that is bring to being in the observable objective (shared) world, events in time that are imagined. Put another way it is that activity where children play out, by the interaction of imagined characters or things, a piece of invented history. The essence of the event is that an observer can report it in the terms of a story, ie we can say, "Once upon a time a King was seated on his throne when..." The child, in a pretend world, gives imaginary life to people and events over which he has control. It is as if in play we create little worlds, illusory worlds that come to being in the midst and despite of the mundane rules that limit our dreams and desires in the everyday 'real' world. In these invented worlds, over which the inventor has complete mastery, children can 'act out in their play what both the inner world of themselves and the outer world of people and things mean to them'.[13] This is not to say that all play is 'dramatic' and that there can be no play that is not drama, though there are those who believe this to be the case.

I would suggest that the dramatic experience is one of creating imagined events, or the recreating of them in formal and informal modes. Such dramatic play involves the skill of imitation and invention which allow the exploration of possibilities more akin to dreams than to physics. Dramatic play is the impersonation of illusory people and the experience of inventing an illusory reality big enough to contain fantasy and conjecture about the way we would like life to be, while at the same time enabling us to explore the nature of things as they are in our environment. Clearly there are many associated activities which cohere to this central identifying ideal. Essentially we engage in drama when we lay a created identity and visible 'person' upon that which we already possess and when we involve that overlaid person in equally imaginary events. We embody our egocentric ideas, dreams or fantasies, within an imagined objective form. The fun of drama comes from watching how our imagined being reacts to the events into which we deliver him. Especially is this the case when we set one 'imagined' being against another, when we put our inventions to play and to act upon each other. It will follow therefore that drama in education is not either the school play or the improvization workshop. It is something far more central to development and social growth than entertainment, pastime or relaxation. It is fundamentally concerned with the way we know our world and further, with the way in

which we are able to push forward the frontiers of what we know. If
formal productions of plays are the 'enactment of imagined history' as
Susanne Langer would, rightly I believe, have us acknowledge, then
drama itself is the art of enactment through the ability to create alternative modes of being to that of our existence in measurable flesh and
blood. It will be observed that I interpret 'drama' in a wide sense and
indeed I find myself in agreement with Joan Cass when she states:

> "Dramatic play, and in a certain sense all play is dramatic,
> acts as it were as a mirror, for as a child plays he is
> showing us (if we are able to understand) many of the
> facets of himself displayed in a variety of ways and forms
> as he externalizes his universal drama, the various aspects
> of his inner personality."
>
> (14)

Dramatic play enables us to create forms for things we feel and perhaps only dimly perceive. Often the forms are revelations which would
have remained obscure and hidden without the spontaneous configuration
that dramatic play permits.

Observation and sympathetic help can, as Cass suggests, tell us
much about the playing child or group of children.

At this point it is fitting to acknowledge the importance of Susan
Isaacs' work in this field. Her researches have been seminal and remain meaningful today:

> ".... play is not only the means whereby the child comes
> to discover the world; it is supremely the activity which
> brings psychic equilibrium in the early years. In his play
> activities the child externalizes and works out to some
> measure of harmony the different trends of his internal
> psychic life. In turn he gives external form and expres-
> sion .... and gradually he learns to relate his deepest
> and his most primitive functions to the ordered world of
> real relations."
>
> (15)

While we may imagine that Susan Isaacs' work only relates to very
young children, I believe we would be wrong to limit her ideas in such
a way. It is now believed that the process of balancing inner life with
outward reality is not solely the occupation of children but crucially a
preoccupation for all men at all times. The need to 'play out', discern,
test, refine and reshape inner tensions by projecting them into activity
does not fade with the years. To be sure, we may appear to control this
activity more but in all forms of society man is found giving high prece-
dence to some game or enactment of one form or another. In this (16)
manner, play has come to be seen as the 'business of life for the child'
and, I would suggest, for the man also.

The more we read theories of play the more resonant they become with meaning for drama teaching. They seem to be defining the very spine of the work we would seek to establish in schools and in the community.

It is possible to summarize under nine rough headings the current agreement about play's contribution to a child's growth:

1 Play permits the exploration of the 'shared' world. This leads to a closer relationship with the environment, and an acceptance of the 'real' world.

2 Play provides the opportunity for the practice of skills, both physical and mental, as they develop.

3 Play permits the exploration of fantasy in a 'safe' manner: 'play is a free unhampered activity in which the fantasy may find expression', where fears may be played out both pre- and post-experience. 'The subjective experimentation of fantasy is carried over into active expression, primarily in the form of play'. [17]

4 Play gives rise to the discovery of self and 'not self'; it enhances the defining of self and understanding of identity.

5 Play is a rehearsal for life.

6 Play can provide a harmless outlet for otherwise dangerous impulses.

7 Group play is a means of socialization. In play there is the opportunity to learn to adjust, allow, assert, and interact in a contained and safely controlled situation.

8 Play has been used as a means of therapy, as a method not only of 'letting off steam' but also as a means of acting out 'blocked' feelings and frustrations.

9 There is the theory that all play can be seen as recapitulation, that each child will live out the history of the culture within which he lives: the desire to make dens deriving from an ancestor's need for shelter etc.

A useful summary of these ideas, which seem remarkably like notes towards a definition of the purpose of drama in education, is provided by Griffiths (1934), who saw dramatic play as of great significance, and who believed that it was a process 'of continually measuring one's strength against external forces.... The child experiments and learns those directions in which he can succeed, and those circumstances to which he must yield'. [18]

It is not hard to see how relevant these researches into the nature of play can be for the drama specialist. For it is in the world of 'make-believe' that we can play in all the ways mentioned above. In drama, children will move from one mode of playing to another. They will, at times, work at the personal level and then at others as a group, now discovering a new skill, and next re-employing a familiar talent. But the realization that the case for the significance of play is also a case for the importance of provision for drama has far-reaching implications.

Professor Richard Courtney concludes his 'Play, Drama and Thought' with these challenging words:

> "Drama in Education .... is a whole new way of looking
> at the process of education. If dramatic play is such an
> important factor in a child's life as we have indicated,
> Drama in Education asks that we centre the educative
> process upon it. We must examine our whole educational
> system in this light — the curricula, the syllabus, the
> methods, and the philosophy upon which these are based."
> (19)

A VIEW OF 'PLAYING AND REALITY'

D W Winnicott's 'Playing and Reality' (1971) forms the basis of this section. The ideas in this work seem to me to be so important that I propose to examine some of them in detail.

Winnicott, like Lowenfeld, assumes acceptance of the idea that we can talk of the inner and outer realities in life. He states that we must all perform the task of 'reality acceptance' which is a task that we never complete:

> "... no human being is free from the strain of relating
> inner and outer reality"
> (20)

But Winnicott suggests that it is possible to find relief from that strain by recourse to what he defines as an 'indeterminate area of experience' which he suggests can be said to exist somewhere between the subjective view of the world (the inner reality) and the objective world (the outer reality or shared experience). I believe this to be a most significant idea for understanding the nature of the dramatic experience and the importance of the need for dramatic play. Winnicott's idea seems to suggest that play is in fact a created illusion that exists somewhere midway between subjective and objective reality.

Freud suggested that the inner life of the egocentric personality was continually adapting to accommodate what he termed the 'reality prin-ciple', and many psychologists and philosophers talk of an area, which may well be illusory, where the subjective and objective worlds meet.

It seems to me that this area is similar to the so called 'space' that is created in a painting. For the space that we appear to see, for example, in a Dutch Interior only exists as an illusion. The canvas, daubed as it is with pigment, remains flat and in no way is 'an interior'. Similarly when we enact a scene, eg the Battlements at Elsinore, we conspire to believe an illusion. The Elsinore of Shakespeare's play has never existed and can never exist in reality. It is a subjective idea which can be made to appear to exist and a large number of people can be invited to share in the illusion, that is to witness a subjective idea that has been played into being and therefore becomes visible in the objective world. Shakespeare seemed to have some understanding of this idea himself, for in 'Midsummer Night's Dream' this is precisely the joke that Snug the joiner has with us in the play within the play: that he should not realistically represent a lion for that would affright the ladies, but that he should tell them who he is first so that they believe in the lion but do not fear him. This is the essence of make-believe, not that one 'really' believes, but that one knows one entertains the illusion. The child that mounts the stone lion in the playground knows very well, and needs to know, that it does not climb the back of a flesh and blood lion. The state of the believed-in lie, the credible illusion that does not ask us to fool ourselves, offers examples of the special area where neither the wholly subjective nor the wholly objective are in being. A real ghost would not do well in Hamlet. When we 'see' the ghost in the play, we know that the ghost we see is not real: so we believe and do not believe at one and the same time. For this is the manner of dramatic play. Drama provides the opportunity for us to entertain impossibilities which by paradox illuminate our innermost being.

Children create worlds in their play that they do not believe in, but which they can pretend exist. It is the richness of this paradox that blazes like Shelley's burning coal. A real death at the end of 'Macbeth' would horrify and disgust a civilized man; because we know it is a **pretend** death we can allow ourselves to believe in it. By believing in the false death we can bear to contemplate the idea of death itself which in 'real' life challenges our competence and always runs ahead of us.

Winnicott demonstrates admirably that the subjective game must, however, be said to exist, for we can only play by doing, and doing must have duration which implies existence in time and space. Playing is doing, therefore it exists; but it must be seen to exist in some special way, for it does not seem to be subject to the 'usual' laws whereby we understand time and space. In play, for example, a chair can 'become' a castle. Now in no way has there been a physical change when a child creates a castle of a chair, and yet we can 'see' a castle. Moreover we see not a child but a king until the king falls and we have to kiss the child's knee better. Here, I believe, is Winnicott's idea in illustration. The child/king and the chair/castle exist together in a special sense and possibly in that 'special area' that Winnicott proposes. For the child plays out his subjective kingship which we objectively observe until 'reality' jars us all back into the objective world as the child hurts its knee. The child is child and king at one and the same time as the chair is chair and castle.

This may seem all very well but far from the point of this paper. The reverse is the case, for with the idea of the ambivalent special mode of existing that is brought into being through play Winnicott has brought us firmly to the central issues that define the nature of the dramatic experience.

Let us examine a further example from dramatic play, the kind that occurs daily in schools. When a group of children play a scene, be it from a text or of their own devising, the scene we witness exists in a special way. We see the real children but believe in the created characters that they portray. We do not cease to know the children while accepting the rôles they create. In the same way we remain in the classroom and yet observe something that we believe to be happening somewhere else. It is important that we acknowledge that the portrayed characters and the location presented to us do not exist other than in a special way. They are symbols having a dual existence, being at once subjective and objective. In other words, all the criteria we normally apply in identifying people and places are suspended or inhibited. At one and the same time we perceive children who are themselves and other people, a logical impossibility that is an imaginative commonplace. The children know that they are still themselves, for it is they who control the pace and form of the work they have called into being. It is the children's 'real' selves that they are engaged in exploring through the means of the invented people. In this way drama excites and fulfils a vital function in the child's personal exploration and growth. It is thus that play is enlightening. The imagined life stands for reality but is different from reality in that it allows for experiment in a docile and supportive atmosphere. Reality inhibits experiment more often than it promotes it, whereas the imagined world reverberates with possibilities and eternal second chances. Playing life into being is the true art of drama and one that carries its players beyond what they know into hitherto unknown worlds.

But this kind of play does not thrive willy-nilly, for the nature of true

play is its spontaneity and life. It will not be commanded into existence.
It is therefore essential that the teacher of drama should understand the
nature of the experience that he and his pupils venture to arouse and that
he be expert at creating the proper atmosphere of trust, sympathy and
reinforcement that pupils need.

One of the priorities that Winnicott would argue is that of allowing
'opportunity for formless experience, and for creative impulses, motor
and sensory, which are the stuff of playing.' [21]

In accepting that play is a creative experience in the terms of Winnicott's theory we are tentatively accepting a definition of the creative
nature of dramatic play. The inventive play that we call drama is a
serious undertaking, as serious as mathematics, physics or history. It
embodies the child's ideas and feelings about his life as he perceives and
lives it at this moment, at the time of the experience. The game of
'drama' is a playing into being of a 'pseudo-life' (what Susanne Langer
would term a 'virtual life') wherein are displayed, as part of its 'make-
up' the child's preoccupations and deepest concerns. Thus, the discoveries that children make in dramatic play are valuable as part of the
on-going dialogue between the child's inner personality and the objective
world. In drama children learn about themselves and about their environment in an immediate and intense manner.

In dramatic play we can enjoy a sense of omnipotence and a kind of
magical power. After all do we not 'ourselves' create the game or drama
and call it into being? It is this magical power over the world that permits experiment and exploration, the means whereby things impossible
and unheard of are summoned into the world. The delight which we have
in dramatic play arises from the sense of freedom and facility that
comes with the experimental and hypothetical world which we play into
being. We revel in the opportunity to live imaginatively in illusory
worlds which are brimming with possibilities and exist beyond the de-
forming pressures of physical laws. We do not delude ourselves in play,
but we entertain possibilities which are not permitted in the everyday
world of cause and effect and continuous consciousness in time and space.

But finally, it is in his ideas about the importance of play in our
search for a concept of 'self' that Winnicott challenges us most as
teachers of drama. He believes that playing, or the creation of subject/
objective experiences, is an essential part of the search for self:

> ".... in play, and perhaps only in playing, the child or
> adult is free to be creative, and to use the whole person-
> ality, and it is only in being creative that the individual
> discovers the self."
>
> (22)

The created 'game' (for us the dramatic play) provides a new experience for the players. It is a revelatory event embodying the developing identity of the players which is of vital concern to the people involved. We do not play to discover the nature of things, or to know something about this or that; we play to know ourselves, our feelings, fears, joys and innermost thoughts.

Believing that such enlivening play can only occur in a setting of relaxation, founded upon trust that has arisen from shared experience, Winnicott claims a central importance for the creative process of play in the healthy growth of the personality. As teachers seeking to offer the opportunity for children to 'play' we must be at pains to create such special settings and we need to consider their nature and the ways available to us of ensuring their existence in our schemes of work. We must accept our responsibility as teachers concerned with personal development and healthy mental growth and see to it that our work is conducive to continuous opportunity for creative exploration.

> "It is creative apperception more than anything else that makes the individual feel that life is worth living. Contrasted with this is the relationship to external reality which is one of compliance, the world and its details being recognized but only as something to be fitted in with or demanding adaptation. Compliance carries with it a sense of futility for the individual and is associated with the idea that nothing matters and that life is not worth living. In a tantalizing way many individuals have experienced just enough creative living to recognize that for most of the time they are living uncreatively, as if caught up in the creativity of someone else, or of a machine."
>   (23)

These ideas will serve to clarify the true nature of the dramatic experience as we offer it to children in Drama in Education. It will be observed that we are not merely concerned with what we term 'theatre', the acting of plays and its attendant skills, but rather with the creative nature of informal work of all kinds. We have seen how work in drama is work of an intensely personal kind, and we can note the level at which we must be prepared to think about the experiences we offer to children in our 'lessons'. Winnicott's explorations offer us a splendid challenge. We can accept it in the joyful spirit of the very creativity that he discerns as life's true centre. For it is in the 'drama lesson' that we meet the 'new worlds' of our pupils' dreams, the worlds that are so important in the child's growth.

> ".... on the basis of playing is built the whole of man's experiential existence. No longer are we either introvert or extrovert. We experience life in the area of transitional phenomena, in the exciting interweave of subjectivity

and objective observation, and in an area that is inter-
mediate between the inner reality of the individual and
the shared reality of the world that is external to individuals"

(24)

We have come a long way from the idea that play is mere idleness from
which children must be weaned.

THE NATURE OF THE CREATIVE EVENT

To my mind there are two writers above all others who have in the last
fifty years distilled the essence of creative play: Nicolas Berdyaev and
Johan Huizinga. [25] Each in his own way claims that there is a holiness
about the creative act. For Huizinga, 'play' transcends mere physical
phenomena and lies beyond "all the other forms of thought in which we
express the structure of mental and social life". [26] Huizinga believed
that play could bring into being "a temporary, a limited perfection".

For Berdyaev:

"Art is always a victory over the heaviness of the world
.... in art there is liberation. In Art, man lives outside
himself, outside his burdens, the burdens of life."
(27)

"In the creative artistic attitude towards this world we
catch a glimpse of another world ... we ... break
through the deformity of this world into another. In
every artistic activity a new world is created, the
cosmos, a world enlightened, free."
(28)

Drama is an art, and playing provides the opportunity for children to
postulate worlds other than that of flesh and blood. Drama is creative
in the best sense, in that it frees the child to offer his innermost ideas,
indeed to form them at the same time as forming and re-forming his
relationship with the world outside himself.

Huizinga aptly sums up this experience:

".... we might call it a free activity, standing quite consciously outside 'ordinary' life as being 'not serious',
but at the same time intensely absorbing the player intensely and
utterly. It is an activity connected with no material
interest, and no profit can be gained by it. It proceeds
within its own proper boundaries of time and space
according to fixed rules and in an orderly manner. It
promotes the formation of social groupings which tend
to surround themselves with secrecy and to stress their
difference from the common world by disguise or other
means."
(29)

Such a definition might well stand as illustrative of the contribution that
drama makes to the school curriculum. For Huizinga, play becomes a
treasure in the memories of players which not only thrills them but is

transmitted as a radiance into the community where it takes place. By nature of its sacred and magical appeal and through its essentially living forms, Huizinga believed play to be one of the most ennobling and enlivening experiences available to man.

But Berdyaev warns us of the personal, mystical and solitary nature of all creativity. Creative events are always spontaneous activity coming from within, for creative events cannot be summoned. You cannot order a child to play, for the play of children is private and precious to themselves. The event is more important than the audience and the inner exploration that the child is engaged in is more meaningful than the game which we can observe. Creativity is always the increase of life, it is the adding to the world, not by supplementing or by development of the known, but the dazzling creation of new forms and meanings in the creative event. We do not seek the development of existing powers when we explore dramatic experiences with children: we seek to liberate them into the spontaneous creation of new worlds, to the discovery of new abilities and possibilities that are not available by any other means. These new creations are visions or glimpses of possibilities, and alternatives to what Berdyaev saw as "history's hideous comedy". In enactments of a possible life, the imagined history of our dreams and searching selves, children may create intimations of freedom that discursive logic and the commonplace everyday transactions of man blur and obliterate. True creation takes place in freedom and this kind of creativity is an act of man's highest selfconsciousness:

> "A human being is required to perpetuate creation, his work is, as it were, the eighth day task ...."
>
> (30)

Man's ability to be creative is seen by Berdyaev to be the missing piece for the perfecting of the Creation. For while man lives in the finite world his spirit transcends the material world of flesh and blood – creative play implies infinity. It is with this knowledge that we can hope to enable children to rise above the 'flat insipid world of material existence' to 'participate in our creative work of conquering non-being and non-identity'.

> "Creativity is the supreme mystery of life, the mystery of the appearance of something new, hitherto unknown, derived from nothing, proceeding from nothing, born of nothing."
>
> (31)

As teachers we are deeply immersed in creativity, as teachers of drama we must seek to bring into being the 'facilitating environment' where our students will play and, if we prove worthy, invite us to share their games.

Above all we must encourage our students to embrace the saintlihood of daring rather than the dull pull of obedience. For there is "only one manner of knowing — to reach out ceaselessly beyond the known". [32]

In conclusion there can be no doubt that drama is play, as it is also a creative enterprise. It follows, therefore, that as play is essentially part of the process whereby we discover our identity and come to terms with reality, so too dramatic play is of fundamental importance for the healthy growth of personality. Clearly, study of theories of play and the most penetrating analysis of the meaning of creative processes must be given high priority in the theoretical study of Drama in Education.

Brian Wilks

NOTES

1 See Richard Courtney's 'Play, Drama & Thought' (Cassell, 1968) for an encyclopaedic view of the theories that are available. And also S. Millar's 'The Psychology of Play' (Penguin, 1968) for a survey of the field.
2 See the bibliography for details of some of the classic studies of this century. The most useful brief account of theories of play is in Anthea Holme and Peter Massie's 'Children's Play' (Michael Joseph, 1970).
3 Margaret Lowenfeld's 'Play in Childhood' (Gollancz, 1935), is perhaps the most well known single volume, but Joyce McClellan in 'The Question of Play' (Pergamon, 1970) gives a more recent survey.
4 Wesley quoted in J L Hammond and Barbara Hammond 'The Bleak Age' (Penguin, 1947) p 123.
5 F Froebel 'Chief Writings on Education'. Trs. S S F Fletcher and J Welton. London, 1912. p 50
6 R E Herron and B Sutton Smith 'Child's Play' (Wiley, USA, 1971) p 343
7 Lowenfeld 'Play in Childhood' London, 1935.
8 Ibid. p 322.
9 Ibid. p 324.
10 A Giddens 'Notes on the Concept of Play & Leisure' Sociological Review 1. 1964. Quoted in Holme and Massie (cf. 2 above)
11 Holme and Massie. p 39.
12 Ibid. p 35.
13 J Cass 'The Significance of Children's Play' (Batsford, 1971)
14 Ibid. p 42.
15 Susan Isaacs 'Social Development in Young Children' (Routledge, 1933) p 425.
16 R Griffiths 'A Study of Imagination in Early Childhood (Kegan Paul, 1935)
17 Ibid. p 320.
18 Ibid. p 120.
19 Richard Courtney. p 264.
20 D W Winnicott 'Playing and Reality' (Tavistock, 1971) p 13.
21 Ibid. p 65.
22 Ibid. p 53.
23 Ibid. p 65.
24 Ibid. p 64.
25 (1) Nicolas Berdyaev 'The Meaning of the Creative Act' (Gollancz, 1955).

(2) J Huizinga 'Homo Ludens' (1949). Ed of 1970 ed. George Steiner (Temple Smith)
26 Huizinga. p 27.
27 Donald Louric 'A Berdyaev Anthology' (Allen & Unwin, 1965) p 316.
28 Ibid. p 225.
29 Huizinga. p 32.
30 N Berdyaev 'The Meaning of the Creative Act'. p 173.
31 Louric. p 151.
32 M-M Davy 'N Berdyaev: Man of the Eighth Day' (Bles, 1967). p 3. quoting St Gregory of Nyssa.

Interrogative, Imaginative, Imperative!

Patrick Meredith, Emeritus Professor of Psychophysics and Director of the Epistemic Communication Research Unit in the University of Leeds, makes his challenge to non-missionaries

I should say at once that I am no expert on the theatre, or on the arts, or on society. But I do ask a lot of questions, I do find imagination the one experience which forever draws me on, so that I don't have to be pushed, and I do have to give a lot of orders, which means that I have to push others — for that is how I happen to earn my living, God help me, by interrogating, imagining, and empire-building.

I seem rather frequently to be asked to talk about things on which I am no expert. I never say no because even if I do talk nonsense, the initiative was not mine, so I can't be blamed, and the effort to say something about that of which one knows next to nothing forces one to find out a little more than before. Also, perhaps, the very decision to invite a non-expert is due to a healthy scepticism about experts. For as R D Laing said recently in 'New Society' in a rather sad article with the cheerful title 'Liberation by orgasm', "Professions institutionalize ignorance, and turn ignorance into a claim for status". Having lived within the protective walls of universities for over thirty years I know this to be true. The more you resolutely ignore everything outside your own subject the more you are protected. And the narrower you make your subject the higher your status. And because any meaningful question about anything inevitably takes you outside the thing itself (for meaning always depends on context) the expert develops a carapace of inhibitions through which no meaningful question can penetrate. So those who really want to ask meaningful questions have to come to ignoramuses like me, who, devoid of expert inhibitions, can at least understand the meaning of the question. The penalty of accepting these challenges is that, as a supposed expert in psychology, I am never, repeat **never**, ever nowadays asked to give a lecture on psychology. Having survived

my protective shackles through forty years I find I can bear this deprivation with fortitude, and have indeed constructed a theory of ultra-behaviourism to explain psychological behaviour to my own satisfaction, if not to the joy of psychologists.

Since ultra-behaviourism has an important bearing on the theatre it is not impertinent to say a little about it. A behaviourist is one who seeks to explain behaviour through the study of behaviour. From the literature it does not seem to matter whose behaviour you are studying or explaining, so you can spend half your time studying pigeons and the other half explaining children. For some reason you aren't allowed to do it the other way round — that would be 'anthroporphism' and that is a deadly sin. One might define it as 'dramatizing the undramatic'.

We have to be careful here. Aesop's Fables are not natural history. They are little dramas of human folly and wickedness, using imaginary animals as actors, and because the animals are unreal, and cannot physically perform on a stage, the play can be presented only as a written document. Only with the advent of the cartoon film, as in 'Animal Farm', has it been possible to portray such animal dramas visually. But even in the printed version I venture to suggest that Orwell has told us more about human behaviour through his pigs and sheep than Professor Skinner has through his pigeons and rats. And it is interesting to examine the reason for this. One does not have to agree with Aristotle that "Poetry is truer than History" — for there **are** false poets and there **are** true historians. There are false dramatists and true scientists as well as vice versa. No discipline has a monopoly of error. Orwell hits the nail on the head because he observed historical events in their historical context, which is where events inevitably happen. And when he dramatized them through animal characters he put the animals where they belong, in space, on a farm, and where they belong in **time**, namely exposed to particular contingencies. Now the experimental behaviourist does not put his animals where they belong (unless we regard the experimental animal as a new species, born and bred in and for a laboratory environment, in which case we are studying not animal behaviour but the behaviour of animal artefacts, and should say so). Nor does he expose them to the typical fortuitousness of their natural environments of events, but to a highly systematic tempo of artificial events of his own choosing. They are out of context.

But don't get me wrong here. The dramatist does the same. What could be more artificial than a theatre? And what could be more tightly controlled, more individually uncharacteristic, than the stage behaviour of actors? Yet through this artificial medium, precisely because it is a medium of art, and therefore subject to the most subtle and sensitive of controls, the dramatist who has truth in his vision can project that truth into the imagination of others. Thus we should be on very questionable ground in rejecting a scientific claim to truth because of the artificiality of its methods. Both the behaviourist and the dramatist are using one set of characters to tell us something about another set of characters. But at the same time both are telling us something about **themselves**. For what they tell us is not merely a sequence of episodes. The episodes are the vocabulary of a proposition. The syntax of the proposition, the dramatic structure of the play, the logical structure of the scientific theory, is a creative construction. Thus in bringing a scientific experiment into the context of a discussion on drama I am not dramatizing the undramatic but identifying an uncategorized species of drama. And the purpose of this identification is not mere classification for the sake of taxonomy, but an essential step in exploring the relation between the theatre, the arts and society, and in particular the society of children.

Our children are growing up in a world full of a greater variety of dangers than history has ever recorded in the past. Potentially it is therefore a more dramatic world than ever before. And the most destructive danger of all, specifically destructive in adolescence, is the exposure to what was labelled as a deadly sin in the Middle Ages, the mortal sin known as 'accidie', which I should describe as the social disease of **boredom**. And my quarrel with the behaviourists is not because they perform artificial experiments but because they have made psychology boring. There is an irony in this which will begin to appear in the very near future.

In the sixth forms of our grammar schools we are witnessing a regrettable aversion from the supposed delights of science and the university planners have been thrown off balance by an unforeseen swingover of applications to departments of arts, social studies and psychology. Psychology is not yet a school subject and so the sixth-formers don't know how boring it can be. They only know how they have been bored by mathematics, physics and chemistry. So, like the ancient Athenians thirsting for an unknown God, they aspire to an unknown subject to allay their **accidie**. If only at any time in their school career they had been allowed to discover how intensely dramatic is the scientific battle against ignorance the disease need never have hit them.

For a good many years I taught science in a grammar school. To me both science itself and the art of communicating it have always been intensely dramatic adventures. I remember with one junior form letting them put a small pellet of sodium in a dish of water, watch it dash about sizzling and spontaneously igniting and feel with their fingers the soapiness of the sodium hydroxide left in solution. Then put in litmus paper and watch it turn instantly blue. Then, drop by drop, hydrochloric acid till the litmus just turns pink. Finally evaporate the liquid over a bunsen and taste the white powdery crystals of sodium chloride left behind. "Mummy!" shouted one little girl, when she got home, "What do you think? Today we made salt in the lab!" That little girl is now a grandmother but she still remembers the dramatic day on which she made salt.

In the same school most of my efforts to dramatize science were continually frustrated by a headmaster with poison in his heart whose one joy was in spreading misery. He has since departed this vale in which he caused so many tears to be shed, and I mourn him, as I mourn Hitler, not for his death but for his life. And I pity the worms. In an impoverished mining area to which he could, through his school, have contributed so much richness, he spread fear and foreboding. He was obsessed with timetables and examinations.

But the further relevance of this slice of my educational history is the momentary impact, on the soul of this miserable little weasel, of a dramatic episode. This unlovable character, certainly not through love of drama or love of children, but through a sudden desire for publicity to improve the image of what he was pleased to regard as 'his' school, decided that the school should stage "An Evening of Masque and Ballet". He thought this could be organized by carefully dovetailing all the production and rehearsal activities into the timetable. In his bleak ignorance he had never learnt that 'the play is the thing'. As the weeks of preparation passed the timetable gradually disintegrated and the play took possession of the school. My own job was stage-managing and as my labs became workshops for the production of lighting equipment and scenery the children discovered that science could be dramatic in more than one sense. Especially when they nearly electrocuted me at the top of a ladder and then (equally absent-mindedly, I should explain) pulled away the carpet on which the ladder was standing.

But what is important about this episode is that the knot of red tape which was the heart of our bureaucratic little monster was, however temporarily, loosened by the impact of the theatre on the school society. The clockwork precision of the scholastic system had to give way to the tempo of dramatic creation. And because this is a tempo which imposes itself naturally on human beings they accepted the discipline of this tempo with joy and although the timetable disintegrated the school did not. Indeed for a while it achieved an integration it had never previously experienced, the unity of working for a collectively desired end.

Although I edit an international journal of education I can seldom bring myself nowadays to read textbooks of educational theory because they are, if possible, even more boring than textbooks of psychology. And it is important to ask why, because they are the fodder provided for teachers in training and if their training bores them they are likely to pass the boredom on to their pupils. Society is just beginning to reap the harvest of nearly a century of universal compulsory boring education. Before that only the elite pushed their sons into pedagogic penitentiaries and they could get their fun afterwards by empire-building, by shooting big game or fuzzy-wuzzies or drinking champagne out of the slippers of courtesans. When the privilege of swallowing dead culture was extended to the masses (not, incidentally, out of any love either for them or for culture but to provide commerce with clerks and accountants) the bloodless and emasculated scale of values which shaped the curriculum failed predictably to shape the desires of children. And today, with more courage because they have more money in their pockets, their thirst for drama turns them towards anything which contrasts sufficiently with the scholastic culture they detest. Is it an orderly culture? Then seek disorder. Is it a subdued culture? Then be vociferous. Is it a rational culture? Then be irrational. Is it a provident culture? Then be spendthrift. Is it a restrictive culture? Then break all bounds. Is it a sober culture? Then get drunk. Is it a calculating culture? Then be reckless. Is it a polite culture? Then be as rude as you damned well like. Is it a hypocritical culture? Then be devastatingly honest. Is it a dead culture? Then live.

But, poor kids, no one has shown them how to live, and the environment itself is being inexorably killed by a commercialism whose only vitality is profitability. So 'living' comes to mean smashing telephone kiosks, uprooting flowers in the parks, overturning cars, fighting policemen, stopping the delivery of newspapers you don't like or taking psychedelic trips.

It has become fashionable on speechdays and similar occasions for eminent gentlemen to stand up and, with a fine disregard for the contemporary scene, to declare their belief in modern youth. What they mean is that there are enough cautious ones who stay out of the orgies to provide the educational bureaucrats and pompous prelates for the next generation. Not being all that eminent I can honestly say that I don't like the way many young people spend their time today, but then I don't like the way the educational system has compelled them to spend their time for the past sixty years or more. Having worked in this bloody awful system for over forty years I have blood on my own hands:

> "Will all great Neptune's ocean wash this blood clean from my hand? No this my hand will rather the multitudinous seas incarnadine making the green one red."

But at least I have more than once nearly fallen off the ladder in trying not to freeze the blood of the innocents by draining the drama out of their young lives. Right from the start of my teaching career there was never any question in my mind that education was a system which had to be dramatically changed. "If you can't beat 'em join 'em" and I naively supposed that by working from within the system I could make a dream come true. As the vicious mechanism of the 11-plus, the O-levels, the A-levels, and the university examinations has insidiously gripped the system in its stranglehold, the dream seems more remote than ever. True, there are many exciting things happening in education but they are the peripheral, marginal, ephemeral successes of inspired individuals here and there. The system itself throws them off or swallows them as it thunders on its bureaucratic way. It is worth asking why this is and whether it need always be like this. There is time for only the sketch of an answer, but it is not without hope.

First let us distinguish drama, which is from the Greek 'to do or accomplish', from theatre which is from Latin 'to behold'. Doing and experiencing are the two sides of the coinage of learning. The theatre is the mirror in which, for thousands of years, society has compelled itself to behold itself. To its credit it has seldom allowed society to become narcissistic towards its own image, though society is always wanting to be flattered. The theatre has scolded, denounced, threatened, shocked, ridiculed, exposed, and at times uplifted society by forcing it to behold the ways of the world and visions of other worlds. In this task the theatre, because of the scale on which it works, and because of the insistent condition for its survival, namely the insatiable appetite for novelty of presentation — even when it has nothing new to present — seizes any and every art medium available, poetry, music, song, dance, ballet, tableau vivant, sculpture, painting, architecture, son et lumiere, slapstick, liturgy and can even cannibalize its own cannibals by showing film and television on stage. It thus becomes a patron of the whole community of artists and is itself the epitome of all the arts. Occasionally it even dabbles with science on stage, whilst fully exploiting its resources behind the scenes. But although itself the supreme educator of society it seldom presents education itself except as a farce.

And so there is a job to be done — an ultrabehaviourist job. Per-

haps the Institute of Contemporary Arts, whose new building is in the
Mall and so not too far from Curzon Street, may at least define the job,
though it will take a whole generation of teachers, actors and theatre
managers to accomplish it. And it is a job which the Colleges of Education and the Schools Council should be provoked into sharing. Indeed
the latter has already taken several steps in the right direction, though
without any relation to theatre in mind. But drama, as I pointed out,
originally meant doing, and the Schools Council has been sponsoring
research projects on subjects with a practical emphasis. The deliberately anti-dramatic character of the academic curriculum in schools is
nowhere more glaringly evident than in the low academic status attached
to all practical subjects — handicrafts, domestic science (now curiously
renamed 'home economics'), physical education, art and music. The
pen and paper subjects reign supreme, one principal reason being that
they are easier to examine.

Now what is the job? Michael Wood hinted at it in an article on
'Arts in Society' in the same number of 'New Society' from which I
quoted earlier. Discussing the potential role of the Institute of Contemporary Arts he says "The academic and didactic functions become
two faces of an identical job ..... For if artists need to talk to each
other less, they need to talk to their public more." Now I call this an
ultrabehaviourist job because I define 'ultrabehaviourism' as the study
of what lies outside behaviour which determines the context of behaviour,
and also of what lies inside ourselves forever making us want to change
behaviour. The theatre is the only instrument large enough both to conduct this enquiry on the imaginative scale required, which is the scale
of heaven and earth; which has the imperative of the box-office to order
the mobilization of all the arts which it needs; and the interrogative
habit, which has been its traditional function, of asking society what it
thinks it's up to. Then by all dramatic means at its disposal it should
submit our educational system to a ten-year campaign of relentless
interrogation asking it "What the hell are you doing to our children?"
And don't let the system shuffle out of its responsibility for the accidie
of modern youth by shifting the blame on to their parents. For education
is compulsory, and by thus legally obliging parents to hand over their
children to the system the state can no longer hold parents responsible
when teenagers are driven to revolt by the sheer boredom of the system.
After all teachers are supposed to be trained for their job, but parents
are not. So the Institute of Contemporary Arts should, in Michael Wood's
words "Ask questions, involve people and refuse conformities". And it
might very well start by posing a few dramatic questions to our Institutes

of Education. For it is in these megalithic empires that the whole confrontation between university culture and the teaching profession is
staged. There is more than one farce to be written under the title
"Whatever happened to the baby BEd degree?" Take any professor of
education into a pub and he'll give you your script free.

But of more direct relevance to the activities of the Children's
Theatre Association is the need for a symbiosis between the Association
and the Schools. The key to this collaboration lies in Michael Wood's
remark "The modern artist knows about the mechanics of production
and distribution in a way that his predecessors never did." Now in education the idea that there is a 'mechanics of production' (as distinct
from 'teaching method') has largely been subsumed under the still
dubious concept of 'educational technology'. If this is to rise above the
level of gadgetry and also to avoid becoming a multi-storey tyranny, it
badly needs an injection of artistic vision. For whether or not all the
world's a stage the school classroom most assuredly is, however pedes-
trian most of its daily performances may be. And, unless every teacher
can be trained to grasp the elementary fact that his profession commits
him to a life-time of stage-managing, producing and performing, our
colleges of education are not training for the real job. Schools are very
unevenly equipped in this respect. But in every neighbourhood with a
children's theatre we could have a real centre for children, teachers
and parents to be exposed to all the arts, all the machinery, and all the
visions, so that the theatre can not only educate society but start educating education.

About thirty years ago I was invited by the Devon and Exeter Film
Society to give a psychoanalytic explanation of a surrealist film "The
Seashell and the Clergyman". I pointed out that it was easier to follow
the film than the works of Freud. It followed, therefore, that instead
of asking for the psychoanalytic meaning of the film we should be asking
"What is the filmic meaning of psychoanalysis?" It was in fact the mood
behind this way of looking at things which led me to spend nine years
doing research on educational films and preaching what I then provoca-
tively called "the industrial revolution in education". Today we might
speak of the need for a "theatrical revolution in education". And although
as an amateur dramatist I would welcome this as a means of injecting a
much needed excitement into the system I also have a fundamental scientific reason for wanting to see the theatre better understood not only for
its communicative function but for its explanatory function. For what is
an explanation? It is a symbolic model purporting to portray some
aspect of reality. Now it could never do this if it was itself unreal.

This fact is succinctly expressed by Amanda K Coomaraswamy in that remarkable book 'Figures of Speech and Figures of Thought', in these words:

"Adequate symbolism may be defined as the representation of a reality on a certain level of reference by a corresponding reality on another."

Thus pictures, performances, sculptures, symphonies, formulae and words themselves are all realities in their own right as well as symbols of other realities. But their own substance, whether of ink or stone, or photographic emulsion, or flesh and blood, is presented along with the message they carry. And despite Marshal McCluhan the medium is not the message, but a parallel message which may reinforce, interfere with or bear no relation to the intended message. We have been told that:

Geography is about maps
And history is about chaps

but although the second line is true the first is not. It commits the McCluhan error. Geography is not about maps. It is about the earth. And unless the maps are at least supplemented by samples of the reality they portray they will be meaningless.

Now you may or may not regard the atom as dramatic in its own right. But man's discovery and exploitation of the atom is the high drama and tragedy of the 20th century. And only in flesh and blood performance can the message of the atom for man find a medium which can carry its full significance. It would require a Newtonian Shakespeare to write this drama and the combined resources of the ICA, the National Theatre and the Albert Hall to attempt to produce it. But with the not altogether meagre resources of some of our university theatres and drama societies, many of the scenes in this Promethean story could be portrayed. Thus in spite of the bureaucrats the epic of man's struggle with ignorance and his still more terrible struggle with knowledge could begin to be told. And this is the message from the heart of the university enterprise.

Patrick Meredith

Primary Playmaking

Paul Cornwell is a Primary School teacher who has given much thought to the function of drama work with very young children. His book, Creative Playmaking in the Primary School, *was noted in* Drama in Education I

Twice a week I take my class for half an hour in the hall for what I loosely call Movement and Drama. Altogether, with the time we spend on follow-up activities (writing, group discussions, performances of prepared scenes, painting, modelling, etc), it accounts for from three to four hours each week, and as much as double that when we are working on a playmaking project. As part of an over-brimming curriculum, with all the present-day pressures for Mathematics, Science, Languages, Environmental Studies and so on, this is a large portion of the available time. One is forced, therefore, to ask oneself if it is worthwhile. Why do we do it?

Drama contains practically all the elements that a child needs for growth: it is not an isolated study or an isolated experience. Drama is, or can be, a union of the major educational aims of a primary school. Literacy is undoubtedly the main aim, and teachers inexperienced in drama need only try a few simple experiments to see how the use of movement, mime and group improvization will provide an added stimulus for the imagination. A girl, after working on a group movement exercise 'being' the witch-like Fates, began her poem:

"A boney huddle of crooked limbs ..."

Another girl (much below average) worked with her partner on the scene where Hermes visits Hephaestus in the grotto. They used a chair for the forge. She wrote:

"Meeting of the same family"

"Eye to eye,
Face to face,
The two brothers meet;
Golden faces

And red with blush
Mix and blur together.

They speak unalike,
So unfamiliar faces:
One shy and mis-shaped,
The other proud and strong.

Collecting speed and pretty stars,
They blow up through the heavens;
Faster and faster they go,
Like clouds in a hurry."

A boy, following an individual mime activity 'being' Prometheus making man, wrote:

"A streak of terror reached his mind,
His eyes glinted with savage rage.
No confounded mortal shall have the earth,
His shaking hand fearfully reached down,
Scraping the soil, squeezing it
As if trying to squeeze it till it was no more,
Holding his hand tighter,
Trying to hold himself together,
Trying to crush and grind the soil.
The hot dies, the cold creeps in,
Running up his spine,
He is dreading the fear of that feeling,
Terror, rage and boiling fear,
Then cold as if frozen, frozen stiff."

This is clearly an emotional release for the boy, and his writing shows his complete identification with the activity performed by Prometheus.*

Oracy (the ability to communicate thoughts and feelings with spoken language) is increasingly becoming a major aim in schools, as many teachers realize the value of group discussion (as opposed to class, or teacher-centred discussion) in the social and intellectual development of the child. Group improvization (the building of scenes or happenings for the experience only or, possibly, for showing) is a twin aspect of this aim. Talking in groups will produce, in the main, a recall of the children's own experience, whereas improvization is essentially a group **creative** activity, in which they devise new ideas and invent ways of doing things. Here, as an example, is part of a scene improvized by a group and acted to the rest of the class. In the story of the Creation and the making of the first man taken from Chinese mythology, the Gods show their anger with the emperor Wu-ti, who had destroyed the people by a flood. One needs to listen to the tape-recording to appreciate the emotional intensity of the children's words.

*This drama work was centred on a reading of 'The God Beneath the Sea', the retelling of Greek myths by Leon Garfield and Edward Blishen, published by Longmans.

WU-TI: I have had enough of this flood. It is done with. I killed
              them because they were killing everything else.
GODDESS 1:   Can't say we didn't warn you.
GODDESS 4:   They are our people. They belong to us. Why shouldn't
              we destroy them?
WU-TI: They were doing complete wrong.
GODDESS 1:   They were our subjects.
GODDESS 2:   We made them to live for a long while.
GODDESS 4:   We made them to live two seconds practically. What is
              their life-span to ours?
GODDESS 1:   They ruined the earth. There is no earth left now, all
              through your people. They don't care for the gods. They
              think we're ... well, nothing to us.
GOD 1:   They do. Only the bad ones do not care. They honour us.
GODDESS 2:   What can you expect with people we put on the earth?
              They've got to eat something.
WU-TI: Silence. Look, we gave them fire as a last chance. They
              should have used the fire.
GOD 1:   Look, we should have given them gods to go down and
              teach them things.
GODDESS 2:   You can't expect to just plump people on the earth and to
              do the things themselves. They've got to learn from
              someone.
GODDESS 1:   Your people, they've ruined the earth. They've ruined
              us now ...

Social development is a major aim. Schools that are truly devoted
to the principle of non-streaming and mixed-ability are beginning to
realize that an effort must be made to **organize** this social and intellectual mix. The above scene is an example of just that. Children should
be **expected**, as they are in my class, to make groups (which change
every month) with all the other children in the class. Regular opportunities are provided for these groups to talk together: group discussions,
improvization in drama, group visits and follow-up studies in group
books etc. Drama, with its intense emotional appeal, has perhaps the
largest part in this.

One could go on justifying the major aims of a primary school, by
showing how drama can help in every respect. The control and creative
use of the body, the development of an appreciation of colour and form,
an interest in our world-wide heritage of history and literature, an
understanding of the uniqueness of mankind, and so on. All these can
emerge during explorations in drama and playmaking.

Playmaking, for me, is simply a bringing together of all these diverse aims of movement and drama. A playmaking project provides the opportunity to explore in great depth a particular story-outline; and, with the stimulus that these activities promote, the chance to integrate other areas of the curriculum. A playmaking project on the story of Rameses II and his 'conquests' against the Hittites, for example, extended into a term's project on Ancient Egypt, with individual and group studies and visits to museums. Another, on the story of the Viking journey to Vinland, promoted a parallel project on Saxon/Viking Cambridge, with a series of walks and visits to museums. And last year, our playmaking project on Chinese mythology was part of a term's project on Ancient and Modern China, integrating history and geography, as well as studies of Chinese art, music, poetry, etc. Visits were made to many museums and a botanical garden, and the children entertained four Chinese visitors in the classroom.

The actual presentation of a play that has emerged from a playmaking project will include as wide a range of these activities as is appropriate. During an intensive two or three weeks, we gather together some part of their wealth of achievement: in group invention (for example, the building of a huge funeral boat out of stage-blocks, chairs, ropes, etc), in group movement (ideas for 'being' the sea around the Viking boat during a storm), in group scenes such as the one above, in group music-making (using their own sounds for processions, dances and activities such as an Aztec sacrifice in another playmaking project), and in individual writing (poems and descriptions written during the project). Individually this means a lot of involvement in both the preparations and the performance. After the Viking project one boy wrote:

> "For costumes I made a tunic, a painted loin cloth for when I was an Indian, and my mum made me a cloak. I also made a spear, axe, sword, helmet, shield and an Indian shrunken head on a piece of cane."

And this is typical of the parts they take in the play:

> "I had several parts. My favourite parts were one of the coffin-bearers and a warrior-acrobat. The other parts I had were a soldier, a priest and a general to Ahirem."

Thus, for the children playmaking becomes the culmination of a vast range of individual and group experience, a liberation and an opening-up of their personalities; and for the teachers it is, or can be, an exciting challenge in a desire to make schools a literal 'treasure house', with the poetry that is human experience reflected in the thoughts and movements of the children.

Paul Cornwell

So the Books Shook Their Heads, and the Silence Grew

A discussion of dance and drama as an entry into the language of words by Vi Bruce, who has been engaged in research in movement education with Professor Bantock at the University of Leicester

Safely Educated

A silence curled, fleshly and cold,
unfolding in the fragrance of a still-born flower
in the chilly air

We tried to speak and cut our words in the desk —
shaped trees, but the words that we saw were new,
so the books on the shelves with their smelly breath
shook their heads
and the silence grew.*

This contribution will deal particularly with those allies of drama in education which are movement and dance, and will endeavour to speak about the value of these aspects for the stimulation of the word language for children for whom words present a problem in school.

The word 'drama' indicates doing, accomplishing. Without doubt doing is accompanied by learning, if it is also accompanied by feeling and thinking. Let us be sure that there are many children who do not readily learn by the 'anti-dramatic nature of the academic curriculum' in some of our schools.†

We will accept for the moment and make little of, the joy, the establishment and attainment of 'person', the increase in sensory awareness and bodily well-being, and the growing of relationship and understanding among people, which come about through drama and dance. This article makes a plea for a way of learning which can bring about total involvement and which may open doors, many doors, including that to the language of words. It is likely that many children who

---

* Observer supplement. January 2, 1972 — Child's poem
† Patrick Meredith. Greater London ARTS, Vol.1 No.2, reprinted in
  this volume

cannot yet define or describe in words very adequately, yet experience sharply with their senses and with their emotions, come to recognize and to link, and so to love and to use words. They become capable of the awareness of the meaningfulness of the word.

Let us look, as we must, in a non-detailed way at movement which in the hands of children may become dance or drama. Even such a glimpse must be prefaced by the name of Rudolf Laban, who more than anyone in our time, or indeed in any time, helped us to envisage the fundamental principles which underlie human movement, and to become concerned with the nature of its individuality.

Movement is universal. For a child there is a natural exploratory urge and fulfilment in movement play. We need to retain his natural enjoyment of moving, to constantly re-awaken and cultivate the movement language which in our culture is so much inclined to deteriorate through ill and limited use. We are concerned with the awareness of body, with energy and action, with the aliveness of the senses, and the increasing confidence of the body as an instrument of expression as well as skill. One needs all the time to stimulate and feed the language of words which describes it. In movement play, in dance, there is no competition, no obstacle bars the way. Movement is the first and most fundamental language, and so it is where all children can begin. Movement, the language of dance going beyond the needs of everyday life, speaks in concepts far beyond the verbal ability of the dancer. It is an important part of the language of drama, the point of decision between dance and drama being in the activities of children often very slender.

We must name for a child the parts of his body as they emerge with importance in his movement. These names are among the earliest words he knows, but the bodily sensitivity and facility needs to grow and as they do words abound. The hands he has from earliest moments seen and manipulated. His feet are to take him running, jumping, travelling and prancing as only children, young animals and dancers do. Elbows, knees, head and the middle of the body, all parts, make gesture and have particular importance in his movement vocabulary. As he grows, bodily awareness and coordination grow and become more intricate. This is the instrument which he uses for dance and drama. This is the being through which meaning becomes manifest. So, we use words which describe action; we jump, creep, punch, spin, rush, lift and twirl. We move with quality; softly, smoothly, powerfully, suddenly, heavily. A welter of words enters in, their sounds meeting naturally the movement which is so intimately the child himself.

One does not have to wait until the technique is developed for the dancing and acting to take place. As in painting the creation takes place alongside the growth of language, consolidating and embedding experience. The romantic aspects of learning can so readily be called upon, but it is not all easy fun. Effort is required, concentration is paramount, because the quality of that which happens must be the best which the body and senses can offer, and the whole person is necessary for this effort. This is what one sees when children are dancing or acting. There is often such total involvement that one looks on with wonder and some apprehension when the effort has been sustained for a period of time which would seem to be unreal.

Words and movement; these are the languages which are used. They are our means of communication — our dramatic equipment. It is likely that movement is the more ready language for most children and is where many will begin to find security and freedom. Very close is the language of sounds and of words, and if children come to hear and to use words easily, to enjoy, and to revel in their flow, as in the flow of their movement, they are well on the way to the literacy which, in our culture, they must have.

How many children need to stand as persons, to be themselves, John or Mary, people, important, respected, and recognized. Listen to Pat in 'Stepney Words'.

> Me, I'm me myself
> No one in this big
> world is like me.
>   I'm different from you
> and everyone else
> I'm just plain old
>   Me
> Me, I'm myself, No one's like me.
> And, I'm not like anyone.
> I'm just myself
>   Little old me
> I'm not quite sure what makes me different
> No one's the same especially me.

When children dance and act, given appropriate stimulus and guidance, followed by the respect which children's creative work needs and merits, they become immersed in that which they do. There is no intervening medium. What is done calls upon the resources which under such circumstances are often so much richer than a teacher ever realizes, and these 'whole' people come to relate to others in the simplest yet fullest way when they reach out, touch, or withdraw from another, when rhythm conforms or interlocks, when one questions or answers in movement, when pathways cross or coincide. Children whose language is impoverished, who find the flow of words a 'silence', who are in consequence unestablished as people, find in their movement, dance and drama the flow of their own being. So it is that when children understand and feel, they can use words if we help them to make the link.

So, words are a stimulus to dance and drama. We talk about that which we do in our language which is so rich in sounds. Afterwards there is something to describe.

> Twisting and twirling
> Romping and whirling
> Up in the air, down to the floor,
>   Legs up, hands high
>   Straddling and sprawling
>   Shooting into space
>   Light as a feather
> Up went I. Down to the earth
>   From the sky

How well the girls learnt what tortuous meant when they 'did it' movement-wise! How much better would they distinguish clearly between expanding and extending, between closing and enclosing. We use a wealth of words, ideas and concepts which come to life in this way, making the link to more words. Stories and poems are stimuli for dramatic and dance-like creation.

> "Against the broad sky, stretching and leaning
>   Winter trees"
>   Japan 20th Century

The Seagull

> The very spirit of the coast is he
> Precipitous, the high
> Cliffs shoot into the sea —
> Precipitous, the high cliffs sweep
> Into the deep
> And green reflection of the sky
>
> He moves on wings that curve
> Like sickles keen and white
> Sickles that reap
> The azure harvests of the light
>
> He moves on wings that sleep
> Quivering against the wind that drives;
> He moves on wings that suddenly
> Slant and swerve
> As his white body
>   Dives
>
> And all the while, from dawn to night,
> And through the night till dawn
> Comes his sharp, melancholy cry
> Flung to and fro in flight
> The echo of the name men call him by — 'Fuilean'

We have experience which needs discussion and argument. Often the word language must give way to dance and drama again because the word language will only go part of the way. The joy of the air, of sheer bodily energy, the smoothness of a curve, or the line which cuts cleanly through space, might be talked about, but can only really come to life through movement.

All over the country, many children are enjoying writing creatively. We are startled by the beauty and dynamic of their words, but if we look carefully they write most vividly when that which emerges concerns them greatly — Me, My Dad, My Street After Dark, My Life So Far; just as older children and students write wretched English when they are struggling to understand or are recapitulating ideas which they have not grasped, and please our sense of language when they have real comprehension. Children use words magnificently when feelings and experiences have lived.

There are many reasons why dance and drama are vitally important in education for all children. They are among the most valuable media through which learning and personal growth can take place. Here all children can succeed, those who find school difficult and those who 'learn well' and excel in their studies; all can find themselves. The need is with all, that the word — and this means ultimately the written word — becomes alive, meaningful, relating back to the self. For those whom we know to be left out somewhat in the language stakes, here one may begin, continue and achieve. The need is for teachers who believe that these things are possible, who love words and trust children, who will give security of framework, will share their talking, planning and exploring, and will appreciate and feed the results.

Vi Bruce

A Play in Ten Acts
by a Boy of Nine

A S Neill, of Summerhill School, one of the liveliest contributors to educational experiment, is now in his eighty-ninth year. His philosophy of education has always emphasised creativity, and in the following article he writes about drama at his famous school

We have always made drama a prominent feature in Summerhill. The unwritten law is that every play must be written in the school. I have often had to announce a play in ten acts by a boy of nine:

> Act I Hullo Spike. Hullo Alf (curtain)
> Act II Have you got the dough? Yep. (curtain)

The play took eight minutes to act. But older ones write quite original plays.

Our speciality has always been spontaneous acting. Here I have to give a skeleton — you are a father, you a mother, and you have been expelled from school. Carry on. The acting is never as important as the imagination: you are burgling a safe and the owner comes in. "Hullo," I say to a girl of eleven, "What are you doing to my safe?" She looks up brightly. "Are you the owner of this house? How do you do. I am from the safe company. We go round inspecting our safes."

"Oh," I say, "And why then didn't you ring the front door bell instead of coming in by the window?"

"Ah, we have to inspect entrances too in case of burglary."

Our greatest success was during the war. I said to a girl of thirteen, "You are a young lady with toothache and go out to find a dentist, but in the blackout you mistake the door and get into the office of the undertaker." (played by a boy of fourteen).

"This is awful. I can't bear it. I've had it for a month."

"Good God, haven't you done anything about it?"

"I tried stuffing it with cotton wool."

"But, madam, it must be removed."

"I'll only have it removed if you promise to give me a gold plate."

"Madam, we only make brass plates."

"But it will go all verdigris."

"That doesn't matter; no one will see it."

I was St Peter at the Celestial Gate and the children gave reasons why they should enter. A boy of fourteen went by me whistling.

"Here, you can't go in there."

He looked at me, saying: "You are a new man on the job, aren't you?"

"What do you mean?"

"Do you know who I am?"

"No," I said.

"I'm God," he said and went into heaven.

Much of our 'spont' is miming. Be a blind man crossing the street. Pick up a shilling and find it is a spittle. The younger ones prefer the unspoken. Pass a savage tied-up dog in a narrow passage. A bright girl of seven patted it on the head. "Sorry, Bruno, you haven't had your walk today."

Children won't do serious acting. For example, a love scene and they generally make a scene comic if possible. One scene they never make comic. Bill had served seven years because Spike double-crossed him. He comes to kill Spike and slowly discovers that Spike is blind — blasted by the safe blowing. No child has ever shot Spike.

Some pupils who act well in plays are no good in 'spont'. The girl with the toothache, a clever actress, acted Puck in the Dream. She made a mess of it — "I didn't understand the language". I am against Shakespeare in schools. Or for that matter any other dramatist. Imagine a child's trying to act Nora. A local cinema is showing, 'A Doll's House' and issues a bill: "Ibsen's Doll's House. Bring the kiddies".

I fancy in our free community we do better than most schools can. I saw a London school try spontaneous acting but the children were too inhibited, too conditioned by authority to be spontaneous, but I may have chosen the wrong school.

One snag about acting is the exhibitionist who would offer to play Hamlet at the age of eight. Incidentally I have often found that a stutterer never stammers when acting, possibly because he is another personality.

School drama must not be confined to acting. Our pupils make their own costumes and arrange their own scenery. We try to keep food off the stage. Once I gave them a play with a meal in it. It stopped at the table scene and ended in a gigantic guzzle.

Our lot are not too keen on watching TV plays, nor, for that matter am I. I am rooted in Ibsen, Strindberg, Chekhov, out of date I know, and I cannot appreciate or judge modern plays. To me 'Waiting for Godot' was a dull dialogue between two tramps who had nothing to say

to me. So too 'The Caretaker' the other night on TV failed to arouse
any interest. Maybe a test would be: did the play leave a memory? I
can never forget Judge Brack's "People don't do such things" when
Hedda shot herself. Little Eyolf to me is the great dramatic picture
painted by the shout from the crowd, "The crutch is floating".

Here I am wandering from school drama, partly to show that I am
not the man to judge modern drama, adult or juvenile. The lasting
feature of drama is character showing rather than the story. I find that
children seem to agree with me here; they throw themselves into the
character they are presenting. I have seen children shed tears when
acting a sad part as Duse is said to have done.

Don't ask me what value acting has educationally, for I know not
what education is — I only know what it isn't. As I have said I think the
development of the imagination is primary — the little touches, a girl
dentist using her toe to regulate the height of the victim's chair; the boy
knowing no German orders a meal in Berlin. Bacon and eggs — grunts
and cluckings; he was bright about the soup, making supping noises like
grandfather. Yes, I put my money on the imagination side.

Oddly enough we have had many a good child actor and actress, but
in fifty years only two went on the stage. May be living in a free school
allows a child to live out his exhibitionism stage early. For we can't
deny the fact that there is much exhibitionism in acting. Honest men
admit it. To Robert Morley I said, 'Robert, with your fame isn't it
awkward when people in buses or trains point to you with a 'That's
Robert Morley?' "

"Neill, I love it! " Good old Robert, and we all love it whether we
are actors or plumbers. True the desire to be recognized slowly dies
with age. It may be that our children give up acting as a means of popu-
larity and success because they feel unconsciously that it is a secondary
creation. Chopin lives but Pachmann is dead. Falstaff is immortal but
the actors who act the part are ephemeral. I was thrilled by Peggy
Ashcroft's Hedda Gabler, but Hedda will be Hedda long after Peggy is
gone. So it may be that children want more than reproducing something
created by another. In 'spont', as our kids call it, there is acting plus
creation, writing a play and acting it at the same time so to say. "Be
a couple of women quarrelling over the backyard fence." True the suggestion for the situation comes from me, but the dialogue and gestures
are creative every time.

So, I think that school drama should concentrate on 'spont' and not
on learning the lines of a play. Once a visitor suggested that our children act a play of Barrie's. Miles Malleson was there. "No" he cried,

"If I want to see 'Dear Brutus' I want to see it done by professional actors. I want to see Summerhill kids act their own plays." I heartily agree. Spontaneity is one of the treasures of living and unless school acting encourages this spontaneity I see no educational merit in acting dramas by other people. And acting and freedom must go together.

A few situations that teachers might use.

Phone your doctor and get the wrong number — the butcher. For facial expression get a telegram saying you have won £75,000 in the pools, and then another from a specialist saying you have a month to live. Try to sell a wooden leg. Advertise for an amanuensis and interview applicants — at least one child will claim to be an expert manicurist. Be a customs officer at Harwich — good fun with the language question.

For little ones: pluck flowers, load a barrow, be a native finding an alarm clock. Phone the Queen — one disrespectful girl of seven said, "That you, Liz? How's Philip?". For older ones have a host show his guests the biggest diamond in the world. The lights go out suddenly. The stone has disappeared. Some original defences given.

I have run my 'spont' class for fifty years and find it almost impossible to think of fresh situations. Children I find are not as a rule good at thinking out situations, not our children with an average school age of ten. Again I say that to have good 'spont' there must be no gulf between teacher and pupil, so that I do not advise any teacher with dignity, fear-inspiring, authoritarian to tackle spontaneous acting. His pupils will react in the way the frightened coppers react to snapping Barlow and shouting Sergeant Stone.

A S Neill

Play into Drama

Thoughts about drama in the new Secondary Schools from Caroline Benn, who is a parent, a member of the ILEA, and editor of Comprehensive Education

There comes a time in most children's activities when the word 'play' could sound patronizing — and that time is probably the mid-teens. Drama specialists in secondary schools sometimes complain that the twelves and thirteens still have that spontaneity of primary school and "so much can be done with them", but that in mid-teens, and even earlier with girls, children become self-conscious and withdrawn. There is little that can be done to interest them in drama — unless, of course, they have an interest in literature or are good at acting.

That the purpose of teachers given special drama responsibilities in a school, should be to think in terms of 'pure' drama — eg the school play — or to be exclusively concerned with drama's literary side (because they are almost always attached to an English department) is, luckily, less widely accepted than it used to be.

But how to get drama used and useful to teenagers in their own activities? That is sometimes harder to be sure about. Although just watching teenagers in some of their school activities often gives clues. Take the growing interest in self-government shown by students, and encouraged in many schools now. Anyone teaching drama would do well to sit in on the first tentative meeting of pupils getting together to run their own affairs, in a school council given (sometimes) real responsibility and real decisions to make. Boys and girls who can argue their cases on the playground, and are not retiring, find they cannot put three simple points in a meaningful order, in a voice which can be heard, using words everyone in the room can understand. Many adults have just the same trouble, which is all the more reason why helping this kind of self-expression forward should be part of the educative process and perhaps something drama teachers themselves might want to take a hand in.

Helping teenagers to say what they mean is different from saying we must teach them the rules of debate or how to have acceptable accents. What they need is help in saying what they want in the way they want, fostering natural communicative talents rather than premature coaching in artificial parliamentary manners.

Girls especially need encouragement at this age when so much research, and observation, shows that they tend to take a back seat in decision-making activities as well as achievement. They not only need help in standing up to put their point of view, but in getting used to their new physical selves. Boys on the whole are more favoured by sporting activities while girls often shy from competitive sport, and appear to dislike physical education at this time. But in fact they are very interested in what they would consider to be meaningful physical activity. One such is dancing. I have seen a group of 14-year old girls moving and dancing to music from a tape recorder around a lawn, expressing what they wanted to say without a word, for hours on end. And of course ordinary social dancing is where girls show themselves quite exhibitionist and forthcoming. Today's social dancing luckily allows girls to dance in each other's company, but all too often — especially when the activity takes place at school or youth club — some of the boys are too shy to join. Would any drama teacher think of helping? This is one excellent way to interest a wide range of pupils in drama through movement — and incidentally contribute to their own social achievements.

In schools or areas with a large minority population, the songs and dances and new movement they can bring to any social meeting are almost unlimited. In one school I know in the West of the country, all the West Indians would always get together at lunch time and dance, improvizing all kinds of steps and, eventually, building up a form of dramatic dance art of their own, expressing indirectly just what they felt about the school, the neighbourhood, the life beyond. A drama teacher in the school began working with them and eventually turned this 'natural' activity into a structured performance which was publicly performed in and around the school, and was highly successful.

The link between music and drama is well known, and so too is that between drama and art, housecraft and technical departments, since these often provide scenery, costumes and props for school productions. But how often is it only a one-way activity? A request for fifteen black capes or six swords, relayed from one staff member to a group of pupils in another department, like a mail order? The pupils are never consulted about the work, nor involved in any way so that the experience of being part of a production team is missed. But it is not just that this approach fails to involve the maximum number in drama work, but that it also risks missing out on ideas they may have. One school I know was putting on 'The Crucible' in-the-round, and the last minute scene change to the gallows presented considerable problems. These were solved by 4th year boys in the Technical Department who invented a clever hinged device to turn crucifix into gallows without a sound, a solution which never would have emerged had not the drama teacher in this case taken the trouble of getting these Technical Department boys in to see rehearsals, explaining the play and its meaning and showing them exactly what the real production problems were. In another school I know — on a large pre-war housing estate — one boy from the Technical Department got so interested in the school play's production problems that he went on to take A-level in theatre design, and after college, jointed the city's local Rep company as a resident designer. Not all 'drama education' need be for those who like the footlights side.

Another teenage passion is the film camera — both still and moving. But in schools film work is often kept quite tightly in the Art Department or even the Technical Department. As a result pupils who experiment with films are usually given full technical instructions, but sometimes less help with dramatic uses to which the film work can be put. A group of sixth formers I once knew well were taking Film work as a Minority Study. During the ten days of half term they were divided into three groups of six and each given 8 mm cine cameras and five minutes of film and told to make a film over the holidays. They were film addicts and rushed off eagerly on Day One to get started with what they assumed would be an easy task. I next met them on Day Nine, when they were all looking very dejected. It turned out they had not yet shot a single frame. They explained that they had good ideas for individual shots and perhaps a sequence or two, but building it all up into a coherent and continuing dramatic piece was very much more difficult, and they were at a loss. What they really meant was that the help of someone interested in drama was required: it wasn't enough just to know all the techniques of filming.

The examples I have quoted here are just a few illustrations of the activities and enthusiasms of secondary age pupils which any drama specialist would take into account if he or she is going to base the work on the whole life of pupils, not just their classroom life, and on the whole population of the school, not just those interested in the traditional small world of the Drama Society of the old fashioned school. The new style schools emerging merit, and respond well to, a new comprehensive style of drama work.

Caroline Benn

Games and the Actor

Clive Barker is Lecturer in the Department of Drama and Theatre Arts at Birmingham University, a professional actor, and a founder member of Joan Littlewood's Stratford East Company. In this interview he talks about his exploration of the use of games

CLIVE BARKER: I have now spent about eight years using games, some of them children's games, some of them games and exercises I've developed myself, to explore what the actor does. The games work on several levels: on one they are enjoyable within a teaching programme because many of them are 'release' games; on the second level they expose certain difficulties, certain problems that the actor faces and they explore conceptually what the actor does to tackle these problems. On the third level, in a rehearsal they let the energy out to discipline the actors towards the acting situation within a play.

DRAMA IN EDUCATION: Are these theatre games traditional games? What constitutes a game? How does it differ from a Stanislavsky-type improvisation?

CLIVE BARKER: Let me give you an example; one of the sections of games (and there are about 25 sections of these games) concerns games of meeting. These are children's games which bring people into conflict of some sort. So I start with one game which is a very old kid's game: touch your opponent in the small of the back while preventing your opponent touching you in the small of the back. You get a release of energy and flow like that, and working on you begin to get two people with mutually exclusive objectives who come into conflict. One can say that there is a dramatic situation where you have a clash of interest in that way. One can explore through this the fact that horseplay energy released is violent but very exciting. It moves actors or students or anybody into an area of movement which is way beyond their normal sort of bound movement. Then we change the game so that now you take a coin. You put it on the palm of your left hand and the game now is to distract your opponent's attention while trying to steal his coin.

We still have a conflict, but we have a situation now in which in order to get what you have and what I want I must risk what I already have, so that it becomes a much more sophisticated and subtle game. It's a test of personality in many ways: how a person can take risks.

Now from this game I can go many ways. I can make it a group game. I can make it an Elizabethan street scene in which people wander around with cutlasses, and you have to watch out for them. And I put within this a situation in which I must in some way provoke you to attack me so that I can fight you in self-defence. I can also take a boy and a girl and, say, give the girl the money and set up a Restoration comedy situation. I will then say you're an heiress, that's your dowry. That is the means by which you buy a husband. Now you want the best looking, the most elegant masculine man that you can find, but you mustn't let him steal that coin until you've got him into a position where you can trap his arm under yours and you've got him locked. Then perhaps we'll take the younger son situation. You're a man who likes to wear the best clothes, eat in the best restaurants, race at Newmarket, go to the theatre, be seen in the best clubs; your body and your style of habit requires money to keep up this appearance. You haven't got money being the younger son, she has the money. The only way you have of keeping up your situation is to get that money off her without getting trapped and whipped off to the country. Now let's explore this situation — and what you begin to see are the things which in that situation you can't do. You can't grab because the moment you grab you lose your dignity and you're out. You can't touch. So the game becomes in effect a series of elegant movements all of which are moving towards a direct point, but must always disguise themselves rather than be caught chasing the main chance. So instead of saying to the actors, we're going to do a Restoration comedy now, let's do movement like this, we can begin to work on the social pattern of motivation within that situation and let the movement itself proceed out of this. Because I must court the girl; I must, in fact, go for the money, but if I'm actually caught going for the money I must disguise my movement in an elegant way to keep my appearance.

So that here I have a game which works on all levels. It provokes conflict clash. It enables us to look at what happens when people

come into conflict. It enables us to see what happens when you provoke a conflict and to look at the simple explosion of energy. On the
other hand you are applying disciplines to this game. Obviously if
we make it a chorus girl and a North-side Chicago gangster who has
the money then it brings out a different relationship pattern.

Some years ago we did 'The Student of Salamanca' — the Cervan-
tes play where you have a wife whose husband is leaving home who
has a lover waiting round the corner. She doesn't want the husband
to be suspicious but she doesn't want the husband to stay. The husband has to go because the stagecoach is waiting. He hasn't laid a
finger on his wife for three months and this is the one chance he's
got for a quick grope and grapple! But on the other hand he can't
stay. So we simply set up a conflict game without loading the actor
with the whole situation at the start. We started in fact with a simple
game which released the energy, then we threw in rules and disciplined it.

DRAMA IN EDUCATION: Are these exclusively thought of as actors'
exercises?

CLIVE BARKER: No, I don't think they are. Many of the games explore
social relationships, and in fact within my work with actors I've
always sought, in improvisational games or anything like that, to
use the framework of social relationships, keeping it anchored in
reality instead of improvisation for indulgence. So I always bring
a game back to 'how do people interact, how do they relate, how do
they pursue their ends, how do they achieve their purpose, how do
they mask their purposes?' We do games in which it is necessary
to mask what you're doing. But always to expose to the actors what
is happening. I'm in a peculiar position now because I've pushed
these games about as far as I want to go in a teaching situation. And
I'm faced now looking one way in saying, 'the only thing I can do with
them is take them back into the professional theatre and do them
with professional actors'. Now I'm not sure whether that's looking
forward or back because, obviously, if one views education as a
process by which the individual prepares himself for the next stage
of his living then you begin with the use of simple games — energy-
releasing games to which discipline can be applied — and not with
role-playing exercises, which always seem to me to be bad directors
directing bad actors in scripts by bloody awful playwrights. This
way we are beginning to use a play situation, a pleasurable situation,

and apply quite strict social disciplines to it, working out quite clearly what the possibilities of action are within that scene; within that situation. At the same time because we can do this, we can lead a person from what he understands to what he doesn't understand or what he hasn't experienced and in this way we ought to be able to prepare the individual for the next stage of his living. Now as I say, I'm in a peculiar position because I think this work ought to be the basis of a great deal of adult education work.

DRAMA IN EDUCATION: How is this related to Ed Berman-style games?

CLIVE BARKER: There's a big difference between Ed's work and my work in that I think that no matter how much he talks about interaction a lot of their games are word-based. They are verbal games — in fact back to the old verbal literacy and verbal articulation; how can you express yourself in words? There's a hole in my work, I know. I fight shy of games which are word-based if only because it seems to me that most actors have no trouble at all in spinning words. They can do it off the top of their bloody heads and very often do this in fact to disguise the fact that they are not acting, they are not doing. So that most of my games are physically based: they're based in action.

DRAMA IN EDUCATION: What kind of professional actors would you work with, who would accept this kind of exercise?

CLIVE BARKER: Probably young actors. I do two classes a week at Drama Centre now; one with a second-year directors' course, in which we use these games but orientate the classes much more towards how the director gets his actors working.

DRAMA IN EDUCATION: I suppose to some extent you could argue that if an actor is very set in his ways this kind of game approach is for him, because it is going to attempt to get him out of the ruts and the clichés he's already got himself into.

CLIVE BARKER: I would never shove an actor into this. The other use of these games is that they allow me to set up a dialogue with the actors about what acting is. If we look at these games and keep pushing them and keep looking at them for what happens and what it tells us about acting, then I will always start with a group of qualified

actors by saying, 'The first thing we have got to do is know that we
are talking roughly about the same thing. I'm not going to tell you
how to act, that's your job; you've been trained, you're experienced.
What I'm going to do now is set up these exercises so that we can
attempt to find some communication, some dialogue between us in
which we can reach some agreement on what the actor's work is. '

DRAMA IN EDUCATION: Will it tell you about what the actor's work is?

CLIVE BARKER: Oh, yes.

DRAMA IN EDUCATION: Won't it just tell you about the way in which
the actor is using it?

CLIVE BARKER: It tells you both, I think. It very clearly exposes the
individual actor's problems and limitations in strength, but I learn
quite a lot. When I first started to do these in 1961 it was a very
rough rudimentary form. But even within the last couple of weeks
I've picked up little bits and pieces. Somebody did an exercise for
me the other day in a way in which I had never seen it done before
and pulled something new out of it. I was waiting for something to
happen and it didn't happen — something else happened. So I learnt
something else about that game.

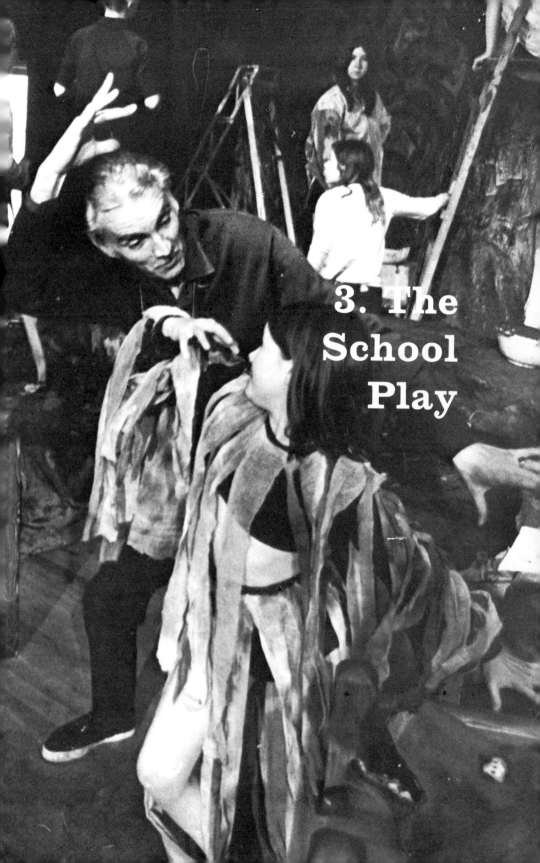

3. The
School
Play

Attitudes

Many of those who now work as drama specialists gained their first
enthusiasm for the subject from teachers with no special training, and
often acquired their first experience of the demands and challenges of
acting or working with plays via the traditional school play. How does
one define that? Probably as an annual performance of Shakespeare,
or Shaw, or Gilbert and Sullivan, and not improbably with socks stuck
down the front to enable small boys to play big girls, and all before an
audience seated uncomfortably in a hall ill-equipped for any remotely
theatrical experience. But despite the handicaps, it often worked well
enough to give a lot of boys and girls that first sense of the excitement
of drama, and that first opportunity to venture into the worlds of the
imagination revealed by 'The Play'.

Consequently, although modern thinking may propose 'better'
methods of approaching the staging and the purpose of The School Play,
it must not do so without re-examining the older methods. We must
never lose the spontaneous recreative excitement of the event by turning
drama into a classroom-bound subject. The School Play must always
be recreation, but, like all good drama, using the word positively —
REcreation. In 'Drama in Education 1' we referred to the improvisational approach to a play on racial tensions undertaken at Primrose Hill
School in Leeds. This represents one way of working, but in this issue
we look at three other approaches, two of which are apparently traditional. We do not feel that too great a sense of didacticism should
colour our attitude as practitioners towards the manner in which The
School Play should be tackled, but we do make a plea for the realization
of the educative potential of this exercise and the responsibility of all
schools and all teachers to use it purposefully. We would like to feel

happier than we do about the number of schools that, even in 1973, realize this potential.

The School Play will be more effective, more valuable, more fun, if it is part of a continuing drama experience spread throughout the school year, both inside and outside the timetable. We have to ask ourselves which is more appropriate for the situation we find ourselves in — a self-conscious rendering of a play the local Rep might do, or a piece that we can more honestly call our own. And of course 'Hamlet' can be our own just as well as 'Zigger-Zagger'. It's all in the treatment.

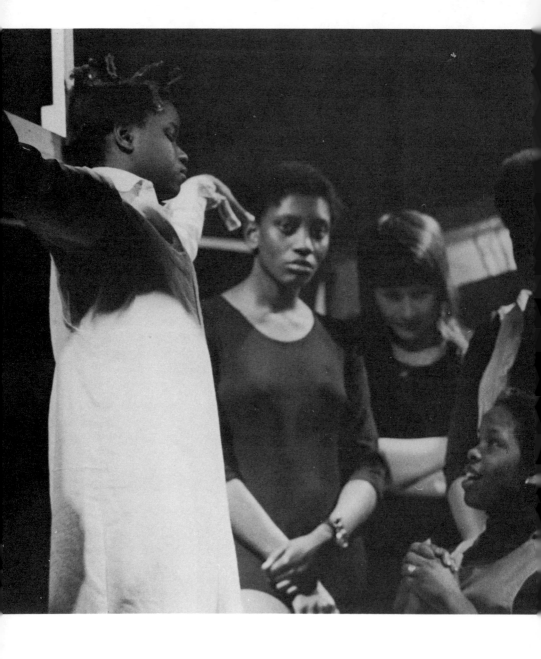

A London School Play: Ladbroke School

Christine Culbert teaches at Ladbroke School, a Comprehensive school for 800 girls (53% immigrant) in North Kensington, a densely populated area between Notting Hill Gate and Shepherd's Bush

The school occupies three buildings. The two main buildings, Upper School and Lower School, are about half a mile apart and the third building is a Technical Wing for housecraft, needlework and art. There is no drama studio but in the Upper School we have the use of the main hall which is also used for assemblies, games and examinations and at Lower School we use classrooms and the gym if it's free.

All first year classes have one drama lesson a week, second years have a double period of drama and third years have a single period. In the fourth year girls can opt for a Mode III CSE Theatre Arts course and there is general drama for the 5th and 6th forms. They have been running three drama clubs which meet weekly, a 1st year club, a 2nd and 3rd year club and an Upper School drama club.

'Mediaeval Pageant', Easter 1972

"Everyone took part and enjoyed it very much. The whole performance was a big effort. The play consisted of little scenes as well as singing and dancing. This play brought them together. Everyone was dependent on everyone. Some girls depended on others for their costume which had to be taken off somebody quickly and taken to someone else. We (the lighting crew for the second half) depended on Sara (the sound operator for the second half) with her music and in some cases she was dependent on us to start her music."

> (Quotations throughout are from 4th year girls. This was the only group which was asked to write about its work.)

"This play was performed by both Upper School and Lower School, about 100 girls took part, or more, including the Isaac Newton boys. We all had a job to do. I did part of mostly everything, I acted as well."

"Everyone did something for it. Girls from Lower School did some
acting on the first half which was excellent and most enjoyable. We were
in the second half and that was when I came into it. I was in the Crucifixion and I played the Second Torturer. It was a very nice scene."

In fact about 160 girls and 8 boys from our neighbouring school,
Isaac Newton, took part in the 'Mediaeval Pageant' which was performed
at the end of the Easter term 1972.

How It All Began

There are two drama teachers in the school, Sally Wolfenden (drama
and games) and myself (drama and English). We had decided to cover
the period of Mediaeval drama with our 4th year CSE Mode III Theatre
Arts group at some time during that term.

The idea of a grand scale pageant appealed to us and it seemed an
ideal framework to use for a school production because of the variety
of themes within it. We could think immediately of a wealth of material
that would be suitable for the whole age range and which would allow
scope for dance, movement, text work and improvisation.

Who Took Part

In fact we used ten of our teaching groups: three 1st year groups, three
2nd year groups, 1st year drama club, 2nd and 3rd year drama club,
4th year CSE Theatre Arts group and the Upper School drama club (this
is where the boys came in). We aimed to use every girl in the group
and to have a short, well-organized scene from each. We knew that it
was important not to give any group more than it could cope with.

Rehearsal

All the work was done at the times when we normally see these groups,
except for the two afternoons when the whole thing was put together and
one Saturday afternoon when the Upper School groups came in.

It was essential that this final putting together was absolutely clear
in our minds and that the performers knew their 'base' positions and
acting area quite clearly by having worked in simulated conditions in
their rehearsal space.

Space

We have a large hall 60 ft x 50 ft, covered by a lighting grid and with a
small, low stage at one end where we built Hell Mouth. There were
four acting areas, three mansions and the centre of the hall.

A London School Play: Ladbroke School

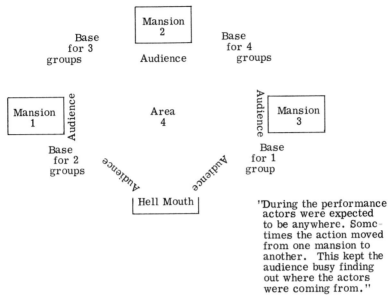

"During the performance actors were expected to be anywhere. Sometimes the action moved from one mansion to another. This kept the audience busy finding out where the actors were coming from."

Technical

The CSE Theatre Arts group (two double periods a week) and the Upper School drama club (one two-hour session a week) were made responsible for the technical side of the production, as well as performing the last two scenes. All the technical work, especially lighting and sound, provided a considerable challenge, but it was obviously enjoyed. It seems from this that the 4th year is a good time to introduce technical work to girls.

Work Period

We started work on February 14th and production date was March 22nd and 23rd. Half term came during this period, so we had four weeks and two days before the first full rehearsal.

Integration

During this period the whole of the 2nd year was involved in a team teaching project which included English, drama, music, dance and art, and they were working on the theme of 'Entertainment through the Ages'. Two of these groups had chosen entertainment in the Middle Ages. They were using the Canterbury Tales and their contribution to the pageant was a dramatization of the Pardoner's tale and the Wife of Bath's tale. A project concerned with the Middle Ages is ideal for integrated studies and could include English, humanities, drama, dance, music and art.

What Form Would the Pageant Take?

For the first half we decided on an historical survey which would be done through improvisation and dance and for the second half a series of plays from the Mediaeval Cycles which would enable us to use text work with the 4th and 5th years. In fact 1st year drama club and four of the 3rd year drama club girls also did text work in Part 2 of the Pageant.

Choosing the Material

I asked for suggestions from the 2nd and 3rd year drama club. We talked about the historical events of the period and after discussion they decided they would like to work on the Murder of Becket and the Black Death. (A weekend visit to Canterbury was organized later; there was no time for this during the rehearsal period, though that would have been a better time for it.) Reference books were taken into working sessions to read the stories again and check on details. It is important that lots of resource material is readily available for the use of the children in preparing their contribution.

Programme

PART ONE

An historical background including events that took place between the 12th and the 14th century.

'The Murder of Thomas à Becket' — 2nd and 3rd year drama club

      Scene I   A banquet at the court of Henry II
      Scene II   A quarrel between Henry and Thomas
      Scene III Murder in the Cathedral

'The Canterbury Tales' — 2F, 2M, 1F

      Scene I   The pilgrims meeting at the Tabard Inn
                      to go to Canterbury
      Scene II   The Wife of Bath's Tale
      Scene III The Pardoner's Tale

'The Black Death' — 2nd and 3rd year drama club and 2B

      The year 1349 was the year when the Black Death
      swept through England. The villagers believed that
      this was God's punishment for the wickedness of
      the people.

PART TWO

A series of mystery plays from the Mediaeval Cycles.

      'Man's Disobedience and the Fall of Man' — 3rd year drama club
      'Noah's Flood' — 1st year drama club
      'The Nativity' — 1Z
      'The Crucifixion' — 4th year CSE Theatre Arts group
      'The Resurrection'   — Ladbroke and Isaac Newton
      'The Harrowing of Hell' — Upper Schools' drama club

The Plays

The first play of Thomas à Becket used the central area and one of the mansions. The banquet scene showed Henry and Thomas, servants and visitors, feasting, joking and dealing with a beggar and ended with a formal line dance. Scene II showed Henry ordaining bishops and being discovered by Thomas who reprimanded him, ending with, "Who will rid me of this turbulent priest?" to lead us back to the Cathedral scene in the central area. This is a marvellously dramatic scene with a strong ritualistic feeling which cannot fail to capture the imagination. Music set the scene. A Gregorian chant immediately gave the feeling of church ritual and the children loved filing silently into the Cathedral, kneeling to pray, and fleeing silently as they saw the terrifying aspect of the four murderers.

Next came the arrival of the Canterbury pilgrims at the Tabard Inn. A 1st year group did a line dance into a 'snail' and a jolly circle dance to entertain the pilgrims and then we had the Wife of Bath's tale and the Pardoner's tale. (The Mediaeval dance tunes are beautiful to dance to and appealed enormously to our girls.)

'The Black Death' was based on a passage written by the Leicester Cloisterer Knighton:

> "In those days (1348) there arose a huge rumour and outcry among the people, because when tournaments were held, almost in every place, a band of women would come as if to share the sport, dressed in divers and marvellous dresses of men — sometimes to the number of forty or fifty ladies, of the fairest and comeliest (though I say not the best) among the whole kingdom. Thither they came in parti-coloured tunics, one colour or pattern on the right side and another on the left, with short hoods that had pendants like ropes wound round their necks and belts thickly studded with gold or silver — nay, they even wore, in pouches slung across their bodies, those knives which are called daggers in the vulgar tongue; and thus they rode on choice warhorses or other splendid steeds to the place of the tournament. There and thus they spent and lavished their possessions and wearied their bodies with fooleries and wanton buffoonery, if popular report lie not .... but God in this matter .... brought marvellous remedy .... rain and thunder and lightning .... that same year and the next came the general mortality throughout the land."

The play began with an authentic Mediaeval children's game, 'Hot Cockles', which was found in one of our reference books. After this we moved to a presentation of the diamond, ruby and sapphire to the winners of a jousting competition which was the cue for the 'Flashy Women' as we called them. The idea of being a flashy woman was amusing and gave an opportunity for the 3rd years to let themselves go on a wild dance. The dance was abruptly halted by a warning from a wise old woman that God would be sure to punish such wickedness.

Part 1 ended with the annihilation of a village by the Black Death. This was a dance sequence which first showed people at work, then being stricken by the plague and dying.

The most important factor in Part 2 was how to use the text work and where to find suitable rendering of the Mediaeval texts. A search in school libraries and public libraries produced versions which were much too long and indigestible. Cutting, adapting and varying with movement, dance and vocal sound effects were essential to make these plays enjoyable and interesting for the performers and the audience.

'Man's Disobedience and the Fall of Man' began with the Dance of Creation using a modern piece of music (we thought it was too restricting to stick entirely to music of the period — much better to use something that worked for a particular part). Also in this play was the Dance of Good and Evil when the serpent and God vied for the souls of Adam and Eve; here we used music from 'Godspell' — this dance had been done independently of this play but fitted so we used it.

Four of the 3rd year drama club girls did this play using a short excerpt of text, just two pages. They enjoyed using text for the first time and appreciated the 'ring' of such lines as:

Satan: "For woe my wits are in a whirl here.
               This moves me greatly in my mind."

and

God: "My curse I give thee here
              With all the might I say
              And on they belly shalt thou glide
              And be ever full of enmity
              To all mankind on every side
              And earth shall all thy substance be
              To eat and drink."

'Noah's Flood' ran to four pages of text and included the dance of the animals going into the ark. A track from the LP 'Swingin' Safari' was used for this: it was perfect. In fact this was one of the highlights of the pageant. Simple, full of life and obvious enjoyment, Noah's Flood was a very humorous play in lively rhyming couplets:

Noah: "Now wife come in! Why stand you there?
              You are too stubborn. That I swear!
              Come in silly old woman ere
              It raineth and we drown."

'The Nativity' was done in tableau with another group singing the Coventry Carol. Then we had the problem of getting from the Nativity to the Crucifixion which seemed rather a sudden step to take. Here was a chance to use everybody at once and this linking passage was not tried until the first full rehearsal. We used the words 'Teach us', 'Feed us', 'Save us', 'Praise Him', 'Crucify Him' as being symbolic of the life of Christ. Each phrase started as a murmur round the hall as Jesus walked through the central area, then built up to one cry in unison as Jesus stood on one of the mansions.

'The Crucifixion' scene was two-and-a-half pages of text much adapted and arranged chorally:

1st torturer:	Here I have a band
All torturers:	A band, a band
1st torturer:	Here I have a band to bind his hand
2nd torturer:	Hammer and nails
All torturers:	Hammer and nails, hammer and nails
2nd torturer:	Hammer and nails to fasten our foe to this tree

With the cross on the floor of the mansion the torturers managed to tie Jesus to it by the wrists, then they raised Jesus to a standing position, now apparently crucified. A good opportunity for lighting and sound effects came as the blind knight was made to pierce Jesus with a sword:

> "Strike up fast
> Strike up fast, strike up fast"
>
> (Darkening sky — thunder clap)

Passion music from Handel's 'Messiah', 'Behold the Lamb of God', was used to link to the removal of the body by Joseph and Nicodemus and to the Quem Quaeritis at the sepulchre.

The last scene, 'The Harrowing of Hell', was where Hell Mouth came into its own, a pink, glowing monster-mouth belching smoke (dry ice). The scene began with the Devils' Dance which led into just over two pages of text work. This play was where the boys were used as Jesus, Satan and the Saints in Hell. Unfortunately their parts were rather static and so, I felt, not really suitable. The Devils, played by 4th and 5th year girls, had lots of movement; perhaps it would have been better to have used the girls as the saints and the boys as the devils, though both girls and boys like plenty of movement in their plays. This is part of the whole question of choosing suitable excerpts for text work and deciding on the best way of interpreting that material. This last play was the least successful, I thought, as the boys were not really happy with what they were doing. They were, in fact, much happier with the technical work, which was their main contribution to the production (see next section).

Technical Work

All the technical work, except costumes, was done by 4th and 5th years, the 4th year CSE Theatre Arts group and the Upper School drama club. There were no facilities for costumes to be made during our working sessions.

"Some people did design while some helped to make props, others helped to build the mansions and some did lighting and sound."

"Technical work involved a great deal of concentration as well as acting — in fact more."

We had two sessions a week with the CSE group and one session with the Upper School drama club. It was very important to have each session planned in detail as every minute counted and both groups had a scene to rehearse as well as all their other jobs. In fact the technical work alone would have been enough for these groups, which were the only ones to be pushed for time.

Before each session we made a list of the jobs that everyone had to do, eg paint base cloth, paint and decorate masks, hang lamps and so on.

"We decorated the boxes which were very smart indeed. We painted and decorated the masks and props and they were all very effective."

Set

Hell Mouth was made under the direction of one of our art teachers who worked with us in three drama club sessions.

"We made Hell Mouth which looked fantastic with the dry ice and the red lights haunting it."

We built three mansions 8 ft x 3 ft using every available rostrum block. The superstructure was made from 2" x 1" timber nailed to the blocks at each corner. The mansions were decorated with calico base cloths and pelmets. Mediaeval resource books and the Bayeux tapestry gave ideas for designs which were painted on to the calico.

"The four stages were in the form of a square. As they were cycle plays we tried to capture the atmosphere of the mediaeval times by making the acting areas take the form of carts which they used to perform on."

"I think what made this play so good was that the stage wasn't on one place. The acting was done on three mansions and on the centre of the hall."

Use of Set and Placing of Audience

We planned very carefully how we would use the acting areas, the first consideration being which plays needed the large central area 4 (see diagram). All the way through the Pageant we used the acting areas as interestingly as possible, so that the action would move from one area to another each time a new play came along, and often during the action of a play. This was good for the audience who might find themselves 25 ft away from one scene and 2 ft away from the next. We used science laboratory stools for audience in front of the mansions and chairs on each side of Hell Mouth. The audience was made up mostly of performers and we had room for about 80 parents and friends.

With 240 people, mostly children, we did not have a completely quiet audience and at times incidental chatter made it difficult for the performers to concentrate. This problem should be considered when planning a large-scale production.

Lighting

"We had five areas to light. The LX plot was the most difficult we are likely ever to do. "

"In our plot (Part 2) we had 33 cues. There were four of us doing the lighting, three working the dimmers and me reading the plot. "

In our hall there are 30 lighting circuits, most of them on bars suspended about 25 ft from the floor. Our LX box consists of 3 junior 8 dimmers attached to the back wall of the hall which means the lighting operators have their backs to the action:

"Your neck is half screwed off during a performance. "

We have 6 Floods, 14 Pat. 23s, 8 Pat. 123s (Fresnels) and 2 follow spot stands. We also hired 4 Pat. 23s and extension cable. All this equipment would have been useless without our Bantam Tower.

"We also angled and hanged up the lights on our dear tower. "

There were 2 LX crews, one for each half of the Pageant, five girls and three boys in all. None of them had done any stage lighting before, so we began with safety.

"I did lighting with three boys. First we had to learn to fix plugs and know the different kinds of lamps, also how to hang them and make sure they were safe. The first time I went up the tower I was absolutely terrified but after some time I got quite used to it. "

Together both crews allocated the lamps, arranged a hanging plot and arranged the circuits in the dimmers. Then they split up to work out a Dry Cue Plot for each half. They were very enthusiastic about this as they were entirely on their own.

"We had to decide approximately how much light each play would need to have without seeing them and we even went in one Saturday to angle the lamps — we didn't mind though. "

There were obvious disadvantages letting the crews do their own working out — it took longer that way — but come the big night we realized it had paid off. Here are two different accounts:

"It was the first time I had done the lighting and what a job. You really have to concentrate on the dimmer board and what was coming next — all I can say is that lighting is one big responsibility."

"On the big night — the first night as Crew One we had to put on the houselights but disaster! We didn't! We quickly but carefully checked that the plugs were in their right places and the switches correct, then we put up the houselights. We made one mistake. On the second night though things went well."

The girls and boys were very ambitious and creative in their use of lighting and looking back on the way we left them to do all the planning work, in spite of apparently wasting time, we felt we were right to put them into such a demanding situation.

"I thought acting was a nerve-wracking job but I've certainly changed my mind, lighting is worse but just as rewarding."

Music

We used music extensively throughout the Pageant to create atmosphere, to dance to, to link two plays and to cover action. I have mentioned already that we did not stick rigidly to the music of the period; however much of the music we used was from 'The Mediaeval Sound' (Oryx EXP46, Cost 79p). We were lucky in having our Media Resources Officer to prepare the sound tape for us.

Costumes and Props

It was obviously impossible to try to costume everybody. We decided to costume main characters very simply and asked the rest to wear jeans or tights and a man's shirt to serve as a mediaeval tunic. PE Department leotards were used for the dance groups and later for Adam and Eve, the torturers and the devils. We needed to make twelve long tunics, some of which we dyed to suit the character, eg purple for Herod, scarlet for Satan. The only other costumes we made were for the Flashy Women. For them we made parti-coloured hooded tunics, a lot of work. They made eye-masks for themselves and we dyed tights red or blue.

Props such as the swords for Becket's murderers and the crown of thorns were easy to make. Masks, which some of the girls had made in art class, were adapted by them as devil's masks.

148

Organization

It would have been better for Sally and me not to have relied on our own resources for a production of this size. We should rather have enlisted the help of other members of the staff through the Head. If there is not an adequate and well-organized production team, drama teachers can easily be put in the position of being made to feel they are asking personal favours. This is not a good way of working.

All the areas where help is needed should be covered before work begins, taking time to involve other teachers from the beginning rather than going to them for help when it's too late for them to be really part of the project.

It is being able to leave someone responsible for one area that is important. If a teacher says she will be responsible for the making of twelve tunics, then you need to know that she will buy the material, dye the material, measure the actors and have the costumes ready on time. Of course it is better if one of her teaching groups does the work rather than the teacher herself.

Similarly the responsibility for the organization of Front of House, the whole area of invitations, programmes, refreshments, supervision of cast and duty on the door has to be covered completely, delegating work as necessary and trying to involve as many children as possible.

In order to ensure that this machinery works well, there should be a production meeting before the work starts and several more during the work period.

Disruption of the timetable is to be avoided as far as possible. If some time is necessary to bring everything together, this should be arranged with the Head or Deputy Head well in advance.

Comments from Staff and Audience

"It interested me because it was an overall picture of the Middle Ages and didn't confine itself to one area. It was something different from just an academic approach."

"A marvellous patchwork pageant of the Middle Ages. It could have been visually enhanced by the addition of costumes throughout."

"There were several solemn moments during the Pageant. I think they worked best in the unscripted plays, eg the murder of Becket and the Black Death."

"A fascinating production, so much variety and scope for so many enthusiastic children to participate — I left wanting to use the outline plot and script in my own school" (drama teacher).

Questions, Thoughts and Ideas

During and since the production period I have considered several points relating to a school production and have also questioned and examined the value of production approach in school drama.

The School Play

The size of the audience is important.
Are there some occasions when a small invited audience would be more suitable?
How should the audience be placed in relation to the action?
How long should the rehearsal period be?
Should you aim at perfection in all departments? Is this a practical aim?
Should school allow extra time and money for a production?
Should the same drama teacher always be the leader of the team or would it be better to share the load?
A teacher's enthusiasm must be able to carry the production cast through the inevitable low phase during the rehearsal period.
How far should you involve a 'difficult' group in a school production?
How do you approach the problem of audibility when performing for an audience?
What place should text work take in school drama and when should it be introduced?

If text is written in suitable language, preferably with a lively rhythm, is of an appropriate length and is used imaginatively, it can be a rewarding experience for the children.

"It was a very exciting experience because it was the first time we had ever learnt our lines from script."

There comes a time when a group needs to meet the challenge of a writer's language, concepts and attitudes — something to wrestle with intellectually — the extra dimension of being involved with and thus interpreting a character created by a writer.

Should a production date be fixed before work starts, or should you wait until something is developing before you decide on a production?

Should you first choose a production team and let the theme arise from common interests or first choose the theme of the production and select the team later?

Production approach

In an improvised production does the end experience justify time spent on organizing and polishing a scene which reached its peak at an earlier stage?

A school production gives any number of children:

a)   the opportunity to share common experiences by working with others towards a common end;

b)   the satisfaction of seeing something they have made as near perfect as possible;

c)   the inspiration and impetus to use every ounce of their energy, mind and body working together in a period of concentrated effort.

If children are motivated and involved then they will be enjoying their work. The process is at least as important as the product.

Conclusion

Nevertheless it seems that, although there are conflicting viewpoints, for the children to be able to create together this Mediaeval Pageant invoking a collective memory of the Age which could never be realized in any other way, and to have the final satisfaction of sharing their work in production, is for them a very valuable experience. At best this gives them a heightened awareness of the universal, timeless themes such as anger, fear, superstition, revenge, the politics of human society, ritual and celebration, the forces of good and evil, catastrophe and death.

Christine Culbert

A Leeds School Play: Intake

Intake School, Leeds, is a Comprehensive Senior School, and was previously a Mixed Secondary School. The headmaster is Charles Gardiner. His enthusiasm for the theatre has been the inspiration for a quantity and quality of dramatic activity that has earned the school a national reputation

In an annual 'Summer Festival' Intake School presents a major play, and supports this with activity throughout the school that complements the production and allows a wide range of activities to flourish with an equal sense of independent purpose. The nature of the production is unashamedly 'theatrical', and whilst a performance before an audience would not be regarded by any means as the only purpose of the exercise, it remains a central point of the activity. Some attitudes towards the use of drama in schools would conflict with Charles Gardiner's performance-orientated approach — but, then, few would envisage a school so given over to creativity, experiment and exploration in the wake of the theatre stimulus. It is sometimes commented that Charles Gardiner does the wrong things with the right results! DRAMA IN EDUCATION, in this discussion with Charles Gardiner, records the main points of his philosophy and practice, and also offers comments from pupils and visitors in response to the drama work. Here is one supremely successful, but nevertheless controversial, approach to The School Play.

Plays presented at Intake School over the last few years have included 'Julius Caesar', 'Macbeth', 'A Midsummer Night's Dream', 'King Lear', 'The Tempest', 'Romeo and Juliet', 'Hamlet', 'The Lady's Not for Burning', 'The Firstborn', 'Under Milk Wood', 'The Boy with a Cart' and 'A Sleep of Prisoners'.

DRAMA IN EDUCATION: Can you describe how you started drama at Intake, and why?

CHARLES GARDINER: In the war years during time off I talked with all sorts of people and with one man in particular who was a painter.

We talked a lot about the unity of the arts. I had always been greatly
moved by music and also by the visual arts, having been trained as a
teacher of art, but the greatest appeal of all to me was the spoken
word. I had always had an interest in theatre, but not been able to do
much about it, as I went to a country school and was brought up in a
village.

When I came out of the forces I taught in Middleton boys school
in Leeds, and it was art, really, which was the first thing. There was
already some drama going on in the school, in that they performed a
play annually. I, as the Art Master, was asked to do the sets, and
ultimately the costumes, and gradually, I suppose, I did a take-over,
because it eventually finished with me choosing the play and producing
it, and with my art people making the sets and the costumes, and
gradually getting a team of the staff to work with me.

Then after a couple of terms in a junior school, during which
time I did produce a play with them, I became Headmaster of Bramley
and as Headmaster I was then able to try out the ideas I'd had about
drama. By this time I'd moved over from the field of art, particularly
having worked with Cross to establish a sort of ladder for the non-
academics, and I became really more interested in drama as a motivation for education, because I'd seen at Middleton the sort of things
that were possible, the sort of enthusiasms that could be engendered.
I realized that with drama there was an enormous educative tool and
at that point I knew no more than that.

DRAMA IN EDUCATION: Were you thinking here of an educative tool for
the less able child or in general?

CHARLES GARDINER: Oh, in general. I don't think I knew then that the
use of drama can be every bit as academic in education as history or
the study of a literary text in a literary way. I didn't know that, but
I suspected it. Then when I became Head of Bramley County Secondary I was responsible entirely for directing the education of 250 boys.
I started movement training, movement into dance, and movement
into drama, which I had originally begun at Middleton, where I had
been encouraged by an Inspector of the Authority to experiment in
this way. It was regarded as a very weird activity, and indeed in the
city I was known as 'that 'weirdy' who is larking about up at Middleton'.

DRAMA IN EDUCATION: Was there any resistance from the boys towards movement. Did they think it a cissy activity?

CHARLES GARDINER: Oh yes, definitely, at the beginning. It was a very tough school this. It was a rugby league school and even in those days knives would appear. I found this when I went: you see as the Art Master I had this very fact to deal with. One example of it is that I decided that the school looked like a prison. It was absolutely bare. It was immediately post-war and there was just nothing. It wasn't their fault, but it didn't look very beautiful, and I encouraged them to bring flowers. Well, there was enormous resistance to this to start with, but they did eventually bring them, but they brought them wrapped in newspaper. We then arranged them and put them round. But that had to stop when the local cemetery keeper arrived and complained that the graves were being stripped! And although I thought it admirable that we should decorate the school with flowers, I really couldn't condone this, and so that had to stop. We then moved over to wild flowers! When we started this movement lark, as it was known, I demanded that they wore bathing trunks and I wore bathing trunks with them. But they were not really with me until we were able to black out the doors leading into the hall, so that nosey folk couldn't look in. It was entirely with my own Form, with whom obviously I had developed a relationship, and with me on my own in the hall these forty boys would work, and eventually we got to the point where they didn't mind other members of staff coming in and eventually they didn't mind Dr Hooper, the local Inspector coming in. This is the point when he started to encourage me. I didn't really know what I was doing at that time.

DRAMA IN EDUCATION: Dr Hooper was an Inspector of Schools in Leeds?

CHARLES GARDINER: Yes. He was actually the music adviser, but he was a general inspector as well. He was responsible for Middleton. It was Dr Hooper who put me in touch with Rudolph Laban.

DRAMA IN EDUCATION: Where was Laban then?

CHARLES GARDINER: Laban was starting his Art of Movement Studio in London, along with Lisa Ullmann. I had not read 'Modern Educational Dance' and I had not met Laban or Lisa Ullmann and I didn't know anything. I was merely on my own feeling after something. Eventually Laban and Lisa Ullmann came up and ran a course in Ilkley which I attended, by which time I'd read 'Modern Educational

Dance'. It didn't mean a thing to me. I couldn't understand it. It
was his attempt at notation which I now can see, but didn't then, and
I heard him lecture, and at the end of the lecture I thought, "I can't
understand this. It must be my lack of ability. I just cannot understand it." There then followed a practical session with Laban. At
the end of the hour-and-a-half working practically with Laban and
then with Lisa Ullmann I knew and I saw that one of the great basics
about this business of drama is that it is not really a thing you can
write about — the things that happen you can't really write about —
the things that happen you can't really **know** about as a spectator.
The really important things you only know if you **be**, if you **are** (my
grammar is going all to pot), but this is the thing. This was a great
burst of light on that particular course.

By the time I got to Bramley I had progressed quite a way, I'd
begun to see that there was a system. Because the one thing that
was worrying me about this business of movement into drama, movement into dance, the whole activity of using drama as a teaching
instrument, was that I accept the fact that you cannot teach anything
unless it's systematic — that order is the first essential.

The whole act of teaching involves movement. This is why I was
so keenly interested in movement. It seemed to me that the whole act
of teaching is progression: is movement from A to B. And what is
movement? This is where I was interested and this burst of light
illumined the area of system in teaching and I was then able to map
out for myself a progressive programme of work with the children.
It was then that Dr Newell, HMI said could he come and see my work.
I said of course. So he came and got very excited about it, and brought
up Frank Tandy from London, who was HMI for Drama and it was at
Bramley that the first Ministry film loop of movement into dance or
drama with secondary age boys was made.

I carried this on and at the same time I produced two one act
plays with the boys. This was the beginning of the Theatre Workshop
idea; this was really the inception, because we were a small school
and a small staff (there were only five of us) and we all mucked in.
Every member of staff did something towards these productions. It
was then that I got my first experience of one thing, 'project', 'idea',
whatever you like to call it: motivation, sparking off a whole school
thing. This was possible in Bramley where there were only 250 and
five staff (or perhaps eight staff at that time). I was there for two
years and a term and then I went to Intake which I opened as a brand
new school. I put movement on the timetable and there was no one

else to teach it so I taught it myself. I taught it myself for about four years.

DRAMA IN EDUCATION: Again was there any resistance to Movement on the timetable in the new secondary school? Did this raise the eyebrows of your colleagues on the staff?

CHARLES GARDINER: Yes. They didn't raise their eyebrows to start with, because they didn't know what the hell it was. But once we'd started and they'd experienced it, indeed yes. And also the fact that on occasions it made a lot of noise. But later on my Senior Mistress became interested and she watched what I did and learned, and went on a course or two, and eventually she came to help me. It's only later, as the staff grew, that I was able to appoint an actual teacher of movement.

DRAMA IN EDUCATION: How late in fact? When was that appointment made?

CHARLES GARDINER: She came in 1961.

DRAMA IN EDUCATION: It must have been a pioneer appointment in a secondary school?

CHARLES GARDINER: It was indeed. There was no other school in Leeds in which movement training was being given to boys of secondary age. It was a pioneer appointment, I suppose, because who ever saw advertisements in those days for either teachers of drama or teachers of movement? There weren't any! The School opened in September 1955, and we put on our first play at Christmas because I was determined that I was going to start as I meant to go on. And if there was anything in this drama lark as an educative instrument, here was my opportunity to find out.

Now I've always had to be two people. I've had to be the teacher of drama, the Director of theatre workshop, but also the Headmaster. And as Headmaster I must always be able to sit in my study and look at this bloke Gardiner who is teaching drama and directing theatre workshop and say, "Now look what he's doing — is it really worthwhile or is it an utter waste of time, and ought I, as Headmaster, to say to him it is a waste of time and it's not having beneficial effects, cut it mate". And I've always had to do this, and I still do it because

otherwise I would not fulfil my function as a Head, and I admit that
there have been times when I have had very grave doubts. But then
I've realized that this is the bottom of the wave, I'm in the trough,
and I'm only in the trough because there is a crest to the wave.
Simple child-like philosophy, but this is mine. And so one has gone
on. We started drama in two ways. First as a school production
which we did and then we decided to do it again the next year. I was
working then with members of staff who were interested: we were
working out of school most of the time — lunchtimes and 4 till 5. I
asked for the cooperation of my needlecraft department, my art
department, woodwork department.

So, I began to get a little nucleus of enthusiastic folks working
on this annual production. At the same time I began to find that one
or two members of staff were in fact using dramatic techniques in
their teaching and would ask if the Hall was free, could they come out
and use it, and this we have always done: we still do.

Drama began gradually to assume an importance in the school's
existence because of the standards we were achieving, and we were
achieving these standards, in my view, because we set our sights
high. There was only one standard as far as I was concerned, and
that was what I understood as the standard of performance of the professional theatre.

Eventually I said that we would take a week of school time for
rehearsal. I realized that we would have to pull people out of lessons
and that in doing so I would give rise to the usual belly-aches in that
when the actors went back to their lessons they would say, "Please
Sir, I wasn't here then", and then the member of staff would say,
"Why?" and if the reply was "Well, I was away ill" nothing would
happen, but if the reply was "I was at rehearsal" there you have
immediately a sparking point for the disintegration of staff relationships, and for an enormous build-up of anti-drama, anti-theatre. So
I, as Head, laid down that in that week's rehearsal there would be no
new work done. The rest of the school would use it for revision, and
the duty was laid on the actors to do their revision at home. If they
wanted to play in the Play then they would have to do the extra work.

We went on like this for two, three, four years possibly, because
we sited the Play prior to the May exams — internal only at that time.
We still were doing this when we had taken on the external exam —
the RSA. There then came a crisis when people who were taking external exams also wanted to act, and I thought they couldn't do both.
But Harry Pashley, who was District Inspector HMI at the time, said

to me on one occasion, "Well, you know Mr Gardiner, a good school
should be able to cope with both." The crunch came when we did
'The Lady's Not for Burning'. In that case there were six who were
taking RSA that year and there were murmurings among the staff,
"Well, he can't possibly pass because he spent all this time rehearsing" and so on and so forth. So I waited with bated breath for the
results. When they came they had all done well, and three of them
had done better than anybody else taking the examination at all. So
there was a quiet sort of victory for the attitude I had by then adopted.

Then came the moment when Mr Metcalfe, who is now Headmaster
of Manygates High School in Wakefield (he was then Head of my English
Department) and Alan Gummerson (who was Head of my Art Department) came to me and said, "Look, we think this theatre business is
a good idea, but it seems that the system at the minute is a bit negative educationally, and we've got an idea we would like to put to you,
which we think is a bit more positive."

Their idea was that the rest of the school who were not engaged
in theatre workshop production, should divide into sets, where we
would break down the 'streaming' and indeed break down the age
grouping and arrange them vertically or really not have any set
arrangement, and that the staff should be asked, over the period of
the actual school time rehearsal of the Play, to offer courses which
would be entirely related to their own enthusiasms, again working on
the thing that the most effective teaching aid is enthusiasm. I thought
this was an excellent idea and it was put to the staff and they 'caught
on'. So eventually we moved into our present system, which is
exactly this. So that from a week, it became a fortnight, Festival
Fortnight. It is a wholly exhausting business and it's now three
weeks. Looking at it, it really embodies the idea that I had when I
opened Intake, and I really would have liked to have opened this new
school with this new idea, but I didn't because I was a coward. The
idea being that I never ever wanted the pill-box timetable aped from
the grammar school or any school, whereby at the end of 40 minutes
a bell rings and everybody changes. I really wanted to be able to
allow work to come to its natural conclusion, whether that was a good
conclusion or a bad one, because all the things one does in education
obviously are not all good. But here we have developed exactly this
sort of thing in that in our summer Festival there are no bells and
sets, courses last sometimes half a day, sometimes a day, sometimes as long as three days, depending upon the sort of time we think
is necessary.

Drama in Education

What I would like to enlarge on finally, is what I feel are the
values of drama in education, of theatre in education, because I now
make a distinction.

I set out to find out whether drama, the activity called drama
and/or theatre could be an educative instrument, and by now I am
entirely and utterly convinced that it not only can be, but is. Because
it has been demonstrated to me that it deals most pertinently with
this business of relations. It also involves the business of intellectual understanding; it also involves the business of finding out whether
you've got a heart or not; it also involves the technical skills of the
body. You discover whether, for instance, you can hear an inflection
or whether you can't. You discover the sensitivity, the literal, physical sensitivity of your own hearing apparatus. It has been demonstrated to me that it is a great aid in social education with a small
's' and that it develops sensitivity to other people's demands, other
people's offerings of relationships; it develops tolerance as well as
intolerance, but the development of intolerance is really the development of tolerance because where intolerance appears, one deals with
it, and it's really talking about tolerance. It has developed, as far
as I'm personally concerned, a very very large number of personal
friendships between me and the pupils with whom I have worked over
the years, who are now, many of them, adult.

I put at the very end the fact that it has helped them, I think, in
their lives after school, in that many of them have gone on into youth
drama, into amateur theatre and find it a rewarding and absorbing
hobby, if nothing else. One or two, or more than that, have gone
into the professional theatre or into television, and still perform on
television, but this comes right at the end, because we are not setting
out to train professional actors at the moment. We are setting out to
do two things: to assist the real object of our school, which is to
teach people or to help people to learn how to think honestly. To help
them to solve problems. To help them to see that there are such
things as standards which they can either accept or reject, and values.
And to give them as much help as we can in solving the basic trio of
questions about their own existence as people — who am I, why am I
here, and what the hell is it all about? This, to me, is the bedrock
of education. This is what we ought to be trying to do. Because we
all ask ourselves these questions sometime or other, and they are
the fundamental things to me. They are the things, at least as far
as I see it, at the heart of our being. We can't answer them as
adults. I can't satisfactorily myself: I have a shot, but it is the

having of this shot which is to me my life and all I'm really trying to do as a teacher is to say to my pupils, "Look, this is what makes me tick, what I've just been talking about I think makes **you** tick, not in my way, but in your way, because you are unique as I am. That if you can see what makes **me** tick I hope it will help you to understand what helps to make **you** tick". And I have no bigger hope for the work I'm doing than that.

I use the word 'drama' to cover the sort of activities which we do when we do movement into dance, movement into drama, each week of the timetable. The work we do when we use the techniques of drama to illustrate a situation or to ram home some facts. By training in improvisation, theatre games, which we do all the time. **That** I would put as drama in education. **Theatre** in education I'd define as the working in and putting on, eventually, for public performance, a play with all the attendant things that happen, all the bits and pieces and all the various branches of its organization. But throughout the whole thing we are concerned with the setting of standards and the solving of problems.

The setting of standards is fairly obvious. I can give an illustration. When we were doing 'The Dream' I was screaming at one point for a bench which was eventually to be a marble bench — therefore it was blocked in with ply. I kept sending messages over to the shops and it wasn't ready, and it wasn't ready, and it wasn't ready. Eventually I marched over to the shop to see what the hell was going on with this bench, whether they were making it out of solid gold or whatnot. When I arrived, there were these two boys patiently filling the holes in which they'd put the panel pins to put the plywood on, filling the little holes, tiny little holes they'd made, with putty. Then the putty had to dry, then it was to be glass-papered before it was painted, and I hit the ceiling! And my handicraft master, quite rightly, said, "Mr Gardiner, we are concerned here with the setting of standards" (after I'd said who the hell's going to see this from the front row of the stalls). "We are concerned here with the setting of standards, that is what I hope these boys have been taught." And I shut up.

The solving of problems. We realize we can do this in two ways. We can allow a problem to appear and then the pupils solve it as part of the team or give up — in which case we would help. Or we can come across a problem and so arrange it that the two or three adults of us are seen and heard to be solving the problem in an adult way. Or not being able to solve it, and having to find some other solution. And sometimes we deliberately set up this sort of situation —

they don't know we deliberately set it up — but we do in fact.

When we did 'Lear' I knew the boy playing Kent had lost his father about six months before and he was having enormous difficulty, not only with the scene in the stocks, but also particularly with the scene at the end and with the line "Vex not his ghost". Now I knew, or at least I thought I knew, why he was having this difficulty. Eventually when we were rehearsing the stocks scene I said, "Let's sit down and sort this out" and I sat down on the set and he sat down and moved very close to me. I sensed that he was at that time seeing me as a sort of father figure and realized that what I'd suspected before about the "Vex not his ghost" line was in fact the trouble. So gradually I stopped talking about the stocks scene and moved into talking about him and his father and his relationship to his father, and life after death, and so on and so on. Eventually he grew over this in the most wonderful way, and the end of 'Lear' as far as I was concerned, and the audience, was extremely moving in performance. But it was at its most moving, and this to me was an absolutely marvellous demonstration, on the morning after the first night. I had not been entirely satisfied with the way in which I'd arranged a salute as Lear was picked up and carried out through the audience. I wasn't happy about the timing and the fall of the soldiers' swords. So I called them for rehearsal at ten, and they were there in their jeans and their ordinary 'get-up', in the cold theatre and no lighting apart from the house lighting, and as far as I was concerned, it was a purely mechanical thing. And we took it before the death of Lear and ran it through. There was only me there and we all knew, and this was the marvellous thing, that this was when we really did it — there was no music, no lights, no costumes. Nothing. There was the bare bones of us and the text and the situation, and we all knew that this was one of the great experiences of our work together. And it really sprang from Kent's inspiration, revelation — I don't know. But I have never forgotten it.

Just to return a minute to the business of academics. I have never yet had, apart from one boy who played Horatio, any boy in the cast of any of our plays who has ever been selected by the 11 + Selection Examination. They've all been the people who have not been selected. And I would now, having seen what they have done, say that in a number of cases these pupils have a far deeper intellectual understanding of what the text is about, than many 'A' level students and even university students with whom I've talked. And this has come about simply because they have worked with the text, where we have not said this is Shakespeare, hands together, eyes closed, bow

down. We have said that in our opinion here is a good text. What is
it all about? And have worked on it and where we have not known we
have not been ashamed to ask for help. We've never hesitated to go
anywhere for help. Brian Mosley, a professional actor, a fight
arranger, has always come and helped with our fights. Again, because we are setting standards, we want the best we can possibly do.

My one fear used to be that all I was going to do was to produce
little Charles Gardiners; that I was merely giving to them, and they
were reproducing. In the beginning this was true. It is not true now.
I've been going long enough for some of my people to have left me,
and to have gone on into the amateur theatre and to work on television
and so on, where they are working with other directors, with other
actors, amateur and professional, and when I see the results of their
work I know they are not copiers of me. They have grown their own
wings and are in fact flying in their own way. This is just marvellous.

* * * * * * *

Charles Gardiner makes it clear that he has always been fortunate in
enjoying the support of the local education authority for his work in
drama. Miss M O Woodward is Chief Inspector of Schools for the City
of Leeds Department of Education and Arts. In the light of her support
of Charles Gardiner's work 'Drama in Education' asked Miss Woodward
for a comment on the Intake approach. Whilst what she has written is
inspired by one school, the case is presented in terms that allow a
wider application.

* * * * * * *

In some schools the production of a play provides for adolescents an
educational experience so intense that traces of it remain in their personalities, attitudes and interests long after they have left school. After
a memorable performance in such a school, members of the audience
often ask "How do they do it?" and the question is cogent when the pupils
are drawn from homes lacking a literary tradition and have not previously
appeared particularly gifted.

In order to achieve the creative vitality that wholly engages the enthusiasm of the participants, the Head and teachers have abandoned preju-
dices that die hard. They no longer assume that a school production
must crave the indulgence of fond parents or that mediocre plays or
home-made improvisations are the best medium for young actors. All
who participate, and such commitment must be voluntary, accept that
they are undertaking an inter-disciplinary exercise to which each will
contribute in a thoroughly professional manner, so that the pupils, also

volunteers, will acquire new insights and skills, not only into play production, but into living.

A distinction is made between the routine practice of movement and similar activities and theatre, an experience which older pupils demand as they become more self-conscious and critical. They welcome the masks provided by scripted plays and need the support given by the characterization, plot management and language supplied by the best dramatists. They do not always understand the meaning of every passage initially, but they have a phenomenal capacity for memorizing; once the inhibiting script has been dropped and they speak on the stage, every move and action illuminates the lines and as rehearsals continue, comprehension grows. The actors are not only preparing for a successful performance of a great play but are gaining a deeper insight into human behaviour, into the nature of comedy and tragedy, into the significance of language.

Those who design sets and costumes, lighting and effects teams, the stage crew, those who make and sell programmes are expected to observe high standards of craftmanship and because their contribution is recognized as integral to the success of the production, involve themselves fully in the total effort. The text dictates the strategy of production and poses problems that must be solved. An actor cannot make an impressive entry if the steps he descends are rickety, nor can an inexperienced boy walk like a king in a dyed sheet slipping off his shoulders. Pupils raising funds to purchase the best materials lend their support to the actors, as do those who raid the library for illustrated books so that properties, costumes and furniture are precisely in period, or write to the British Museum to enquire exactly how ancient Egyptians raised their hands in greeting. This is the scholarly approach in action.

In performance, the players and audience together create a magical experience of theatre, through which no-one passes quite untouched, because they have been involved in an enterprise of excellence.

M O Woodward

An Ethiopian School Play: Wingate School

Derek Bullock is Headmaster of Abusi Odumare Academy in Ijebu-Igbo, Nigeria. He has been Principal of two other schools in Nigeria and of the Wingate School, Addis Ababa, Ethiopia. Problems of language and culture clearly arise when producing Sweeney Todd *in Nigeria or* Twelfth Night *in Addis Ababa, but Derek Bullock maintains that these productions are far from irrelevant*

In the past eleven years I have, I find, directed twenty full scale productions in three African Secondary schools. Fifteen of them were at Government College, Ibadan, in Western Nigeria, between 1960 and 1967; three at the Comprehensive High School, Aiyetoro, also in Western Nigeria, in 1968 and 1969, and the last two at the General Wingate School, Addis Ababa, in 1971. Certain names occur more than once — two 'Julius Caesars' at Government College, for example, 'Sweeney Todd' at all three schools, and 'Twelfth Night' in Ibadan and Addis. Certain memories are stronger than others, particularly of 1964 when, at Government College, we did 'A Man for All Seasons' and 'Galileo', with the same Lower Sixth boy playing both main parts. Some are memorable for the technical difficulties involved: I remember particularly a double bill of 'Androcles and the Lion' and Soyinka's 'The Strong Breed' which required much ingenuity to accommodate it on the extremely cramped stage of the Government College Assembly hall. Two plays, 'A Man for All Seasons' and 'Andorra' made a real impression because they carried a strong and relevant message for the Nigeria of their times. 'A Man for All Seasons' came about eighteen months before the military coup which overthrew governments in whose members personal integrity was scarcely a prominent virtue. 'Andorra' was relevant to what was already felt to be the danger of tribalism, though no one in April, 1966, could have realized how great the danger was or could have foreseen the near catastrophe it was to lead to.

But the production of which I have chosen to write for this article, is the 'Twelfth Night' we did in Addis in May, 1971. Government College, and the Comprehensive High School were after all only two of many schools producing the school play in Nigeria. The convention is

165

well established, and though standards are often indifferent or downright bad, the school play has made its contribution to the healthy state of amateur and professional theatre in Nigeria today, especially in Ibadan and the West as a whole. Things are otherwise in Ethiopia, which seems to be missing out in the surge of literary activity which is going on all over Africa in the French and English speaking countries. Far more is written in Amharic than in English, and there seems to be little dramatic activity of quality in either language. It is, of course, difficult to judge accurately productions in an unfamiliar language; but my impression is that the few television plays I watched were far below their Yoruba counterparts. The only group that brought an Amharic play to the Wingate — admittedly an ad hoc, amateur group — was very bad indeed.

For many years there seems to have been no serious drama in Ethiopian schools, and there is virtually nothing in the University. Excellent work is done in some of the private foreign schools, which cater mainly for the children of the large expatriate community. I saw a most moving 'Amahl and the Night Visitors', for example, at the American community School, which defeated the terrible odds of its setting in a vast echoing gymnasium. The Good Shepherd School, an American Mission School, again catering mainly for expatriate children, also do some very enterprising things — a good 'Noye's Fludde' towards the end of 1971 among them.

But most, if not all, Ethiopian schools are going through a barren patch as far as any cultural or sporting activity is concerned. The sheer size of the schools is one reason for this. Many of the schools in Addis Ababa are all Grade Schools (Grade I - XII) and have several thousand students, who can only be accommodated in a double shift system. Directors and teachers are far too busy struggling with the all but intractable problems of administration, and shortage of space, teachers, books, etc. to have time or energy to devote to any of the frills of schooling. Add to this the endemic student unrest which makes it impossible for any school director to predict with any certainty whether his school will be in session next week, and it is not altogether surprising that sport, school plays and so on have fallen into the background, if not out of the picture altogether. The Wingate is unique amongst the Ministry's schools, in being of moderate size (400), boarding, all boys, and highly selective in its intake. It is a Senior Secondary School with only Grades IX to XII, and admits boys from all over the Empire. There is strong competition to get in, especially to get one of the quarter or more of the places for which free scholarships are awarded.

Drama in Education

Even the Wingate has not been immune from strikes and violence, and the boarding and extracurricular sides of school life were not exactly flourishing. I went, not knowing whether it would be possible to do any sort of work in Drama, and met with several dampeners before I had even opened my mouth on the subject. It was known before my arrival that I was interested in Drama, and the first member of staff to speak to me about it made pretty plain his opinion that that wouldn't do here. Ethiopian boys could not act; they were much too individualistic and withdrawn; they were only interested in their studies; in any case they would never accept the discipline of a sustained enterprise like putting on a play. The other major dampener was my first sight of the School Assembly Hall. I had spent my retirement leave from HMOCS treating myself to a year at Central School taking the Advanced Teachers' Course in Speech and Drama. At Central 'play' and 'theatre' are almost dirty words as far as teachers' courses are concerned, and I was intending to try to start with something other than formal productions. But the Hall turned out to have a permanently tiered floor and balcony, with fixed seating. There was a brazen and unalterable proscenium arch with a magnificent span of fully fifteen feet. There was no lighting.

These first impressions were fairly quickly modified. Other members of staff had different views about the potential and attitude of the boys — views which happily turned out to be correct. I unearthed some photographs which showed that the Wingate had had an active Drama Club up to only just over a decade earlier. One or two boys individually came to ask that we should have a drama club, and the School Council made a formal request to the same effect. The Assembly Hall too was not all bad. There was a six feet deep fore-stage which also extended a couple of feet on each side of the proscenium arch; there was quite reasonable wing space and back-stage space; and at the back of the balcony was a projection room which would clearly make an excellent control room. Acoustics were very good, and though the width of the auditorium relative to the width of the proscenium arch made sight lines from some seats difficult for the main stage, sight lines were on the whole good.

Even so, it is unlikely that we would have been rash enough to launch into a formal production, had it not been for the Silver Jubilee Celebrations, and the strong suggestion from the Old Boys' Committee that the school should put on a play for the occasion. The play somehow chose itself. I was still toying with the idea of a programme of miscellaneous items, when I woke up one morning with the idea of 'Twelfth Night', quite my favourite play, and the play which had been my first essay in

168

direction at Government College, eleven years earlier. Even the most enthusiastic colleagues were a bit doubtful at that one, but I decided to go ahead for a month, and then decide whether or not I had bitten off too much. About 50 boys turned up for auditions, which occupied three long sessions during a whole Sunday and showed that we could cast the play convincingly, and after warning sermons about the effort involved, we started work.

I rehearsed the play according to what has become my established pattern for the second language situation:

1 A couple of weeks taking individual actors through their parts, working for basic comprehension and basic diction (two of us shared this);

2 Three weeks on reading rehearsals in my office;

3 Three weeks on movement rehearsals;

4 Two to three weeks for beginning and endings of scenes, technical rehearsals, runs and dress rehearsals.

A boarding school usually gives the benefit of two or three rehearsal times a day, and really long sessions at weekends. At the Wingate we were able to have one 30-40 minute session during the lunch break, two between afternoon school and supper, and two between prep and bed-time. Saturday and Sunday mornings and evenings usually accommodated three sessions each. The play was divided into just over 40 rehearsal units, averaging 50-60 lines each. In each of Phases 2 and 3 of the rehearsal schedule, we first worked through the play at the rate of one unit per session, and then through the play again doing rather more per session. Units were not, of course, rehearsed in sequence. A weekly timetable was drawn up which allowed for the fact that three members of the cast were in the school basket ball team, and several were active members of the Wingate Scheme and were away for at least one week-end each on expeditions. We were to give the play during the Jubilee week in May — three weeks after our vacation. All the cast came back to school for the last week of the holiday; some didn't go away at all. From beginning to end, there were about 150 hours of rehearsal, though no individual actor was called upon for anything like this time.

By the middle of Phase 2 it had become apparent that we were in business with a viable production. Most members of the cast were showing real understanding of their characters, and morale was sky high. We were well on in Phase 3 when morale even survived a school strike. I was able to tell the actors that even if we were delayed, we had gone so far that we should be able to resume when things got back to normal without any difficulty. However, they had obtained a dispensation from the organizers of the strike to carry on with rehearsals, and for a whole week this was the only department of the school (apart of course from the dining hall) that functioned.

Even before embarking on the production I had ordered some lighting. Six Pat. 23s, 6 Pat. 123s, 2 8 compartment battens, and 9 Junior floods, and 2 Junior 8 boards. This arrived and was installed during the vacation preceding the production, and proved reasonably adequate. The two boys, young 12th Graders, who were to lead the lighting crew of five, were both Eritreans and so did not travel home during the Easter Vacation. They were the school electrician's mates throughout the installation and so understood very thoroughly the connection between the switchboard and the rather distant lanterns.

The set was simple. There were black wing flats and a cyclorama. In front of the cyclorama, a black curtain could either be completely off (for the garden), or arranged in four columns for the street (Malvolio and Viola's ring scene, and the duel), or completely closed for interiors. Orsino's had the addition of a looped purple half-curtain. The various parts of the garden were made of arrangements of some or all of two free standing rectangular trellises, and two square topped garden arches. These were made of eucalyptus (the imported tree which made possible the existence of Addis Ababa) of about two inches diameter. The same wood was used to build the one side and two half sides of a hexagonal summer house used for "What a plague means my niece" and for the carouse. The summer house was on a trolley, and the trellises and arches were light enough to be carried easily by two small boys. They were all painted with black gloss paint with random patches of gold spray paint over. Real branches of a kind of fir were attached, sprayed gold and silver. The box tree was a frame of eucalyptus, similarly painted, with real branches tied inside, again sprayed gold and silver. The table and chairs for the summer house were of woven bamboo, bought in the market. Orsino's chair was my office chair, a low backed arm chair with a leather upholstered seat. Olivia's chair was from Jimma where there is a craft of carving chairs and stools from a single block of wood. They are by no means cheap, and this chair was the most expensive single item of the production, costing the equivalent of £7. Had our Malvolio not been a native of Jimma with the right connections, it would have cost even more.

Feste carried a small Jimma stool with him wherever he went. The original idea was to use the summerhouse reversed for Malvolio's prison. This did not work out in practice, and we cut a trap in the forestage. It was just possible to get under the forestage from the cellar under the main stage, and crouch there among the timber props. Scene changes were carried out by Olivia's pages (dressed as miniature Malvalios), two sailors from Scene 2 and Orsino's two 'officers'. None occupied more than a few seconds. Except for a few of the more obscure jokes, we played a full text in two Acts of ninety and fifty-five minutes each.

Costumes were 'Jacobethan', made from materials bought in the market. They were designed by the Assistant Bursar and the wife of the Maths master, and most lady members of staff and teachers' wives had a hand in the sewing. There was no existing wardrobe to be mined and cannibalized, so the work was fairly extensive. The final bill for costumes, props and set materials came to just over Eth $1,000 — about £170.

The music was quite a problem. We used the traditional tunes, for which one of the teachers, herself an accomplished guitarist and folk singer, composed simple guitar accompaniments. The tunes were slightly modified in the process of arranging and adapting for the talents of our Feste, and the final result was most attractive. Singing is not much of a problem in Nigeria, where the majority of pupils and many of their parents have been strongly influenced by Church primary schools and where church going is still popular. Hymn tunes and harmonies at least, therefore, are widely known, and it is not difficult for boys and girls to 'hear' and learn simple Western tunes. Ethiopian music, however, has its own scale, and it is not easy for boys who have known no other to learn Western tunes. Feste learned his songs all right with much practice, and he learned the guitar accompaniments. But putting the two together proved rather too much for him. He did manage a single chord accompaniment for 'O Mistress Mine', but rather than sacrifice the lovely rippling accompaniment for 'Come Away Death' we had it played from the wings by the composer, with a miming accompanist at the back of the stage, releasing Feste for his acting and his attractive, dusky singing. He remained apprehensive right up to and including the final dress rehearsal, and it was only when he experienced the pleased reaction of his first audience that he was able to enjoy his songs as much as the rest of his part. For link music between scenes we used the Capriol Suite. It was a great pity that the style of production was not suited to the talents of our brilliant blind pianist, Abduke Keffene, who was to make such a contribution to the 'Sweeney Todd' of December.

So far as the boys who took part in it were concerned, there is no doubt that the enterprise was a great success. Their enjoyment was apparent throughout rehearsals, and shone through their performances. They experienced the play in a very real and meaningful way; all the more important an experience as there is no literature of any kind in the Ethiopian School Leaving Certificate Examination. They all learned something that they would not have learnt without the production. To a lesser extent this was true also of other boys in the school, most of whom managed to see it at least twice. Their experience of the play could not be as profound as that of those who actually took part, but they certainly enjoyed it. And everyone, actors, technicians, audience, had at least a real experience of **theatre**, which I trust no one, however dog-matically anti the school play, would begrudge to schoolboys, many of whom had probably never even had the experience of a fleapit cinema before coming to Addis Ababa to go to school at the Wingate.

All the performances were competent and one or two were excellent. At Ibadan, we had worked in close collaboration with a girls' school. But unless, as was the case in Ibadan, there is a like-minded and enthu-siastic Headmistress, the administrative problems of such a shared enterprise can be daunting. For a first effort in Addis, I shirked the difficulties, and we had an all-boy cast. The Viola was, therefore, in-evitably more boy than girl, but turned in a spirited and witty perform-ance that was greatly appreciated. Olivia was taken by a boy of slight physique and demure good looks, quite out of keeping with his skill as a football player and prowess as an athlete. Feste, slight, gravel-voiced, wistful, gave just the sort of interpretation I had envisaged for him. Andrew thoroughly enjoyed himself. But the two major performances were undoubtedly those of the Malvolio and Toby. The boy playing Toby had to overcome a diffidence of speech, which in conversation amounted to a speech defect. But he produced a good rich voice, and if his arti-culation sometimes left those who did not know the play guessing, no one was left in any doubt as to who and what this Toby was.

As for Malvolio, he was quite simply one of the two best schoolboy actors I have ever seen. He was one of those boys almost destined to be Head boy of any school he finds himself in. An outstanding athlete, a competent student, a strong personality (incidentally he did very well when we were able to send him to Kenya to join a Duke of Edinburgh's Award Commonwealth Gold Scheme expedition), and now discovering a totally unexpected talent for acting of a really inspired order.

We gave a total of six performances. The first a private, Saturday morning performance for the censors. Woizero Mary Tadesse, the charming Vice Minister in charge of Culture in the Ministry of Educa-tion, tried to get us exemption from this, the play being what it was, but without success. The censors are not prepared to work on the script, but insist on seeing the whole play exactly as it is to be shown to audi-

172

An Ethiopian School Play: Wingate School

ences, before they will give authority for a licence. They sat through
the whole two-and-a-half hours, stolid and unamused, and left with
what seemed the rather ominous promise to let me know their decision
on Monday morning. 'Twelfth Night' was judged to be harmless, however, and we got our licence. (We were less lucky with the special
Jubilee edition of the School Magazine, from which one English and three
Amharic pieces were entirely cut.) We gave a performance to our own
boys, and Saturday afternoon and Sunday afternoon performances for
other schools. We were lucky having a hall that blacked out, and a climate which makes it possible for an audience to sit in a closed auditorium. (This is impossible in Nigeria.) There were two public evening
performances. Both were well attended and the second was something
of a gala in the presence of His Imperial Highness the Crown Prince
and with the Diplomatic Corps well represented in the audience. The
performance was extremely well received, and there was a good deal of
surprise that we had been able to achieve such a standard. The only
serious criticism was of the diction. People who were unfamiliar with
the text had some difficulty in hearing some of the actors properly,
particularly Sir Toby.

I am in retrospect extremely glad that the Jubilee pushed me into the
production. In the event I stayed at the Wingate only a year and a half.
I like to think that the two play productions that I did in my time there
helped towards an unfreezing of student attitudes, and helped other members of staff to make progress in their own efforts to establish closer
relationships between teachers and boys, and a greater degree of trust
among the boys. I found the Wingate a school without a soul (I know that
not all the teachers agreed with me in this, but I think it is not an unfair
assessment of the situation). It had, I gather, not always been so, but
the troubles of the last few years had done the Wingate, as other schools,
much harm. The very solid work of the Drama Club gave a considerable number of boys an engrossing and positive interest in at least one
aspect of school life and a very rich personal experience, and also gave
all the boys in the school something to feel proud of.

I hope that by so doing it helped the school on its way to finding its
soul again.

Derek Bullock

4. The Players
In Conference

Drama Education for What?

This conference, organised by the Drama Department of the University of Hull in March 1972, attracted a large number of teachers of drama at all levels, members of theatre in education teams and representatives from various fields of the professional theatre. Vivien Bridson has compiled this report of the study of conference

THE CONFERENCE BRIEF

Ostensibly three distinct attitudes now prevail in higher education where drama is concerned: 1) At theatre schools students are trained to become actors; 2) In colleges of education students are trained to become teachers; 3) In universities students are trained to appreciate drama as an art form and historical phenomenon.

But the real situation is that many actors and university graduates teach and that most young men and women who enter the three modes of training harbour a desire to act professionally.

The end result seems to be: a few gifted actors, a few gifted teachers and many people who are only adequate in both fields.

THE QUESTIONS

1   In what circumstances could the strength of each form of education be fully realized? What could these forms contribute to each other?

2   Should the emphasis on all avenues of training lie on the personal development of the student in relation to his understanding of the subject and its role in society?

3   Should the acting schools neglect teacher training? Should the universities neglect teacher training and what attention should they pay to practical work? What does the college of education achieve through its conception of drama as an educational force?

4   If students are educated as creative people able to take responsibility will this answer the problem?

5   What does the last question mean?

On trying to draw together the findings of the Conference I have found it difficult to know where to start, where to place one contribution in relation to another. Drama, because of its nature, because it involves the human being, demands such profound questions that perhaps all of us are guilty of myth-making in relation to the solutions which we accept.

Perhaps Ronald Knox, in his reply to Berkeley, hit on something of our problem, when he wrote his famous limerick:

> "There was a young man who said "God
> Must think it exceedingly odd
> If he finds that this tree
> Continues to be
> When there's no one about in the Quad"

> Dear Sir:
> Your astonishment's odd:
> I am always about in the Quad.
> And that's why the tree
> Will continue to be
> Since observed by
>   Yours faithfully,
>   God"

The doubt which Berkeley raises is 'What can we possibly **know** beyond sensation', with the further corollary that we construe our sensations relative to our own experience and attitudes. We therefore tend to perpetuate our own mythical view of life unless we are jolted into new ways of sensing and perceiving, unless we are able to look at another person, their situation, their experience, and relate to this with freedom of attitude.

Why then do we adopt, at times, an attitude which is primarily mythical, and what is the role of myth-making in society?

Michael Pokorny: Myths

What is a myth? I looked in the Chambers's Twentieth Century Dictionary which gives, I quote: "An ancient traditional story of gods or heroes, especially one offering an explanation of some fact or phenomenon: a story with a veiled meaning: a figment".

The dictionary goes on: "Mythical — relating to myths: fabulous: **untrue**". Even more interesting: "Mythologist, a **maker** of myths".

Now these statements taken together, are really very strange. We are told that one can make an ancient traditional story, which offers an explanation of some fact or phenomenon and which is fabulous or, to put it bluntly, untrue.

What sense can there be in such a paradox?

One starting point that may help in understanding the phenomenology of myths is contained in part of the definition of a myth, namely " ... especially one offering an explanation of some fact or phenomenon".

Amongst the most painful and terrifying situations that any human being can encounter, is the situation of not knowing. Of being uncertain. When we do know, we can, and do, fill the gap with ideas. In some circumstances we may have the means available to test our ideas, but if we have not, then the only way to change the situation from one of uncertainty is to convert ideas into beliefs.

The drive toward certainty is a universal phenomenon which we can all observe, both individually and collectively. Individually it is not too difficult to recall the discomfort of uncertainty — is it going to be all right? Collectively one can point to the saying "Better the devil you know, than the devil you don't". We are all familiar with the notion of primitive man, faced with the inexplicable phenomena of sunrise and sunset, rain and drought, etc, making myths to explain them. I wonder whether there is equal familiarity with, and recognition of, exactly the same process occurring today?

Where would we look for parallel situations?

Well, we could think of initiation rites of primitive tribes and then take a look at the ritual ceremonies at which universities present degrees to their graduates. Is the system of examinations in education really any different from systems in previous civilizations in which parental figures explore the extent to which the new generation have absorbed the cultural beliefs that are held to be essential for the continuation of the tribe in its present form? I put the question of examinations in this form, because, in my experience, one important question that the examiner is asking is "Do you think in substantially the same way that we think?" You will have noticed that I passed from individual and collective uncertainty, via some concept of primitive man, straight to some hidden aspects of examinations and degree ceremonies. The link by which I connect these, is the concept of omnipotence. This concept is used by psycho-analysts to describe a normal stage of infantile development. However, this notion of omnipotence is widely held.

Many years ago a cartoon appeared in a widely read magazine depicting a child being wheeled in a perambulator across a street, whilst a policeman held up the traffic. The caption reads "His Majesty, the baby". I don't know how many of you are familiar with the writings of Truby King on infant care.

The major thesis put forward was of regulating the baby. Feeding by the clock. This may sound odd when compared with modern notions of feeding on demand. The pendulum swings between control and permissiveness. But the struggle underlying the swinging is ubiquitous, and is at its crudest in any situation which is felt to be one of control, or be controlled. Either/or. Parents and children struggle with this over the years of growing up.

The picture of primitive man creating explanatory fables can be seen as a situation where man feels himself to be at the mercy of the elements. If he can make a story about wind and sun and rain and so on, he provides himself with a guide to activity that he can undertake to propitiate those aspects of his surroundings which he feels are hostile to him. It matters not in the slightest whether his activities **really** have any effect on the seasons, provided that he can feel more in charge of his destiny and less at the mercy of arbitrary, external, change.

So, before going hunting, he indulges in activity designed to let him feel that it is going to be all right. Uncertainty is replaced, to some extent, by assuredness.

An important aspect of the formal giving, in a strictly prescribed manner, of university degrees, is that it solemnizes the notion that if you obtain a university degree, your future is assured. It matters not in the slightest whether this activity **really** has any effect. The university degree has become a totem of our civilization. The fact is that for a number of years university graduates have had increasing difficulty in finding suitable employment. Nevertheless, the universities expand

and ever more aspirants flock to the seats of learning. The myth is exploded, long live the university degree!

Notice that I use the word 'exploded'. That is the word we commonly use to describe the abolition of a myth. Why?

Because a widely held myth is usually only given up in the face of a catastrophic event. A myth enables us to feel that we have taken control over hostile and arbitrary external events. To relinquish that feeling and return to a state of being at the mercy of, to return to a state of unrelieved uncertainty, is, in itself, a catastrophic event.

Now, I want to go back to the dictionary. I quote "An ancient traditional story". Let us leave aside the word 'ancient' and concentrate our attention on the word 'traditional'.

'Tradition', according to the Chambers's Dictionary, and I quote, "Handing over: oral transmission from generation to generation: a tale, belief or practice thus handed down: anything bound up with or continuing in the life of a family, community, etc". In addition, may I quote "Traditor (obsolete) — a traitor, betrayer: one who under persecution gave up sacred books or objects or the names of his fellows".

I think that we can discard the word 'ancient' as giving superfluous dignity to the notion of tradition.

There are two aspects of the definition of tradition which I want to look at. The first are the references to family, community, etc, which underline the fact that myths are phenomena of groups of people. The second appears in a slightly hidden manner in the definition of tradition, I quote, "Anything bound up with or continuing in the life of a family, community, etc". The notion of being 'bound-up-with' is an interesting one. Part of the definition of the obsolete word 'Traditor' throws some light on it. I quote, "One who under persecution gave up".

We are dealing with a phenomenon of group life that is bound up with notions of ensuring the continuity of life in its present form, of which an ingredient is the holding of beliefs in the face of persecution.

The interplay of belief, continuity and persecution in the life of any group, is complex.

A situation that points up some of the complexity in a way that makes it sharp enough to be looked at is the situation of the minority group.

Even a fairly superficial examination of a minority group will reveal the fact that the actual degree of persecution that the group is subjected to, bears little relation to the beliefs held in the group about the nature and extent of its persecution.

If a minority group is going to stick together and continue in its present form, if it is going to adhere to its traditional beliefs, then a minimum degree of persecution of its members is essential.

If the actual persecution is not enough, means are sought of increasing it. Much has been written about that aspect of what has been called ghetto mentality, in which a belief in the discriminatory behaviour of outsiders increases distrust and bolsters the conviction that 'They' are against us. This system is operative only on the condition that the minority group feel a pressure to stick together and not become absorbed into the community around them, pressure to stay the same.

Which of us in this room do **not** belong to one, or more, minority groups? And, as we are all aware: "Better the devil you know, than the devil you don't".

So much for the traditional aspects of myths. What about the aspect of the word mythical? I quote, "fabulous: untrue". The holding of a belief which will only be given up under persecution leads us to the observation that myths are myths and are not to be questioned.

To believe in an explanation of some fact or phenomenon inhibits the ability to examine that phenomenon for further evidence, unless any evidence which is available confirms the belief. What I am describing is a situation in which evidence is perceived in such a way as to confirm existing beliefs. Of course, none of us would behave in such a way — after all, we are gathered together to examine some of the myths which are held about drama and about education.

After what I have said about the intensity with which a group holds on to its beliefs, who would be so bold, so foolhardy as to question current cultural myths about the purposes and functions of the holding of a conference? After all, the working conference is a very popular institution these days. It is widely held to be a good thing.

There are a number of ways in which one could describe a conference, and I would like just to draw your attention to some features of conferences in a way that allows comparison with other situations, such as universities, schools, clubs and commercial undertakings. A fairly wide net.

The essential concept is that of the institution, which is a collection of a number of people, a group, who get together to carry out a task or tasks. It has a boundary in time and in space. There is a declared task, not always very clearly defined, but nevertheless held to be the primary task. There are, inevitably, a number of subsidiary tasks, many of which may be very difficult to identify.

Within the boundaries of the institution there are sub-groups, either structured or arising spontaneously in response to internal pressures. One of the major tasks of management is to so regulate the inter-group

relationships as to minimize the generation of group rivalry within the
institution. If groups start fighting each other, their energies will not
be available for the primary task. Groups will start fighting each other
if they feel a need to control what is perceived to be a hostile environment.

The quickest way to produce this state of inter-group warfare is to
generate uncertainty within the institution. One sure way of doing that is
to have as wide a gulf as possible between the declared task of the institution and the actual task or tasks, the actual tasks being kept hidden or
unofficial.

Example The primary task of a university is to promote learning.
One subsidiary task is to give degrees. One hidden task is to produce
middle-class citizens. If the hidden task becomes more important than
the declared task the result, sooner or later, is upheaval. Sub-groups
form, whose object is to take control of the institution.

Well, what has all of this to do with the focus of this conference,
which I understand is to explore the interrelationship between drama
and education, maybe even to examine some myths.

I should like to offer you the suggestion that drama is one way, and
a very important way, in which myths are re-presented to a group of
people who are called the audience. The impact of the drama on the
audience depending upon that area of myth which is mutual to the audience
and the actors. Some dramas are concerned with widely held myths and,
though easily acceptable, make little impact. Some dramas deal with
myths not generally held and, although they may make a great impact,
they will, on the whole, be largely unacceptable.

There is an area between these two extremes in which much serious
drama operates. The area of the statement of widely held beliefs in
such a way that some aspect or aspects are amenable to scrutiny, but
not to the extent that the audience feel too affronted or threatened. If
you seek to say something which will be widely acclaimed, then it must
be neither a repetition of what many people say, nor something entirely
new. Before a really original idea is appreciated sufficient time has to
elapse for it to become felt as familiar enough.

Rapid widespread recognition is reserved for he who states plainly
something that many have been tending to think for some time.

Groups make and hold traditional beliefs which are only given up
under persecution and which are felt to be an essential part of maintaining the status quo.

Uncertainty generates anxiety. There are many variants of anxiety,
but in groups that feel under attack and in danger of disruption, the most
appropriate description of the anxiety is to call it persecutory.

All groups are subject to the experience of persecutory anxiety and all groups resort to generating myths to deal with this anxiety.

Although the myths that are generated take a number of forms, the similarities of the basic ingredients are quite remarkable.

Mythologies of previous civilizations are still meaningful today. Nursery rhymes are recognizably similar, whatever the language of origin.

There are, according to Wilfred Bion,* three basic myths that a group has available to it to deal with persecutory anxiety. According to which of the three basic myths the group assumes, it will behave in one of three ways.

These behaviour patterns are, dependency; pairing; or fight-flight. Bion arrived at his conclusions by observing the behaviour patterns of psychotherapy groups and concluding that, when the group becomes anxious enough, it seeks to act on one of the three models for dealing with anxiety: dependency; pairing; or fight-flight. His conclusion was that a group manifesting one of these behaviour patterns is acting upon a basic assumption. Because the basic assumption is acted upon, and not tested, it has all the hallmarks of a myth. So we have arrived at a bit of psychiatrists' jargon — the label, 'A basic assumption group'. This label designates a group which is showing basic assumption behaviour patterns, such as worshipping a sun-god, and this behaviour arises in the face of sufficient anxiety within the group to divert it from its primary task. What is a sufficient degree? Any degree of society which is felt by the group to threaten its existence and which must, so the group feels, be dealt with in order that the group survive. Survival has become the primary task in the face of a threat of disruption and the survival behaviour engaged in is the manufacture and implementation of a myth.

My suggestion is that serious drama is largely concerned with examining the basis of persecutory anxiety using techniques of re-pre-senting some facet of a myth.

I will go further and suggest that good drama rouses an optimal degree of persecutory anxiety in the audience.

Neither too little, nor too much.

You will have gathered that I know something about myths and about groups and about anxiety.

I know little about drama and what I know is unsystematic.

I am, however, much concerned with education. Particularly the

WR Bion 'Experiences in Groups', Tavistock Publications, London, 1961 areas of education which can be described as the seeking for techniques to enhance the capacity to learn.

In terms of learning, a lecture is of very limited usefulness. Partly because of the inherent tendency for the situation to become one in which the lecturer displays skills to an audience. The notion that erudtion can rub off onto those who come into contact with it, is a myth. A magical belief. Learning requires active participation and is hard work.

Of course, active participation is not in itself a guarantee that learning will take place.

* * * * * * *

Michael Pokorny's statement that "the only way to change a situation from one of uncertainty to one of certainty is to convert ideas into beliefs" may help us to rationalize certain preconceived ideas which we may have formed relative to the nature of the acting school, the college of education and the university.

One of the general problems apparent during the weekend seemed to arise from a lack of understanding of the aims and directions of each of these specific avenues of drama education. It should be helpful, therefore, to consider the views of those people who are responsible for these courses of training.

What follows can be regarded as three statements of 'identity' arising out of a considerable degree of 'persecution' as each speaker was asked to consider their educational programme in terms of 'failure and success'. Now each statement, if one compares one with the other, may seem to be mythical in intent, but each indicates a common area of concern, education through drama. The differences arise because the theatre school is attempting to prepare its students for a specific career, that of performing in the theatre; the college of education, although concerned specifically with training teachers, has to educate its students to enter a profession where no one school or situation could be remotely said to resemble another; the university has both a wider and a narrower brief. The aims of a university in our present society do not encompass preparation for a professional career. However the question which needs to be asked is whether these three year initiation rituals are serving any purpose in modern society, whether in fact the present overall situation requires a totally new mode of outlook?

Nat Brenner: The School
of Drama

The job of the theatre school is to feed the profession. This means that
we must provide selected, talented young men and women with a basic
training which should be sufficient to enable them to function, at least
competently, in an industry in which no one has time to waste on ignor-
ant beginners. We select about thirty of the four hundred or so applicants
which we get each year through a series of weekend visits to the Old Vic
Theatre School. It is a pretty exhaustive process now, but I look forward
to the day when we can be even more careful in the preliminary selections. When we've got them, we try to train them accordingly and can
only measure our success relative to the degree of their success when
they attempt to make a start in our catastrophically over-crowded profession.

The first theatre school of any significance was the Royal Academy
of Dramatic Art, started in 1904 by a few of the most prominent men in
the theatre of the time, notably Herbert Tree, the actor/manager and
the playwrights Pinero, Barrie and Shaw. They called their school the
Academy of Dramatic Art, the 'Royal' came later. Today there are
over thirty-eight drama schools offering full time courses. A few of
these were founded before the war, but the bulk erupted between 1946
and 1962. University drama departments were also setting themselves
up during these times. All these developments were indicative of a
flush of euphoria in the face of the theatre. The theatre had begun to
experience something of a renaissance after the war. Classical drama
was booming, the Old Vic was absolutely marvellous. We were enjoying
a wave of verse drama from Christopher Fry and T S Eliot; distinguished
novelists such as Graham Greene were writing plays. The educationalists
could no longer cavil and chant at the triviality of the theatre. In the
mid-fifties there were Osborne, Arden, Wesker and Pinter, and Joan
Littlewood was in full cry at the Theatre Workshop. Samuel Beckett's
'Waiting for Godot' came to London. A change of climate occurred in
the fifties which encouraged the building of new theatres for repertory
companies in spite of television, and of course at that time television
seemed to be expanding the need for actors. So we saw the beginnings

of many more drama schools.

At present the purely professional schools are non grant-aided apart from the fact that students accepted usually qualify for discretionary awards which provide maintenance and the payment of their fees. We have, however, failed in obtaining direct financial aid from the Department of Education and Science. I think they would, in principle, like to give some help, but there are too many schools requiring help now, and also the time is out of joint for such a venture, because of unemployment.

Now, what about the training which we offer in order to enable our students to 'function competently in the industry'. We have to prepare people for such a wide range of requirements, the Royal Shakespeare Company, subsidized repertory theatres, children's theatre companies, experimental groups, television and film. Well, let's ask the users of actors what they think about training. Tyrone Guthrie, who published a book shortly before he died, implied that we were failing. He dismissed out of hand the study of drama as literature and dealt with acting. He felt, despite the problems of the industry, that it remained absolutely necessary to have well trained actors. He dealt with the balance of training. He said that classes for stimulating the imagination were pretentious, and largely a waste of time. Those who acted professionally should not need to have their inspiration stimulated, they should have their aspirations examined. He did not subscribe to the emphasis now put on improvization, seeing this as a cheap, easy way to fill up time and to entertain large classes. I don't quite go along with Guthrie on improvization. I have found it extremely useful in some contexts.

For example, when one is working on classical plays with a young actor who finds that his concentration is going, and that he cannot make sense of the lines and so is unable to develop his relationship with the people on stage. It is much better here that he forgets the text for a moment and just talks to people, in the situation. Returning to the text he suddenly recognizes his father, his mother on stage and so can go on from there. Guthrie goes too far on this. Above all Guthrie emphasized the need for more voice and speech training. He considered that sixty per cent of a first year student's time should be devoted to this, allied to more musical training. But of course, this related to his experience and he was mainly concerned with the masterpieces of renaissance drama with occasional excursions into opera and Gilbert and Sullivan. His assignments in recent years were to direct 'The Alchemist' at the Old Vic in 1963, and 'Volpone' for the National about four years ago. Well he would need virtuosity of speech for Ben Jonson, and such

186

a commodity is now in short supply. Drama schools certainly give the matter a great deal of attention, but not as much as sixty per cent in the first year. Now I find that the standard of voice and speech, particularly for male applicants, has been getting worse and worse, so we have to budget more time than we did eight years ago. The reasons for the decline in voice and speech technique lie in our own social, democratic development since the war. It is a subject that could be fascinating, but I haven't time to go into it now.

On the matter of style Guthrie cuts through the mystique by quoting John Gilbert, "Style is knowing what kind of play you are in." But of course to know this requires a knowledge of plays, a knowledge of various roles and practice in performance. So, a drama school should inform the students of a sense of style giving them a range of practical exercises from Greek drama, Mediaeval, Elizabethan, Jacobean, Restoration Comedy, Molière, Ibsen, Chekov, Shaw, Wilde, Coward, Brecht, the lot. I am not unduly worried if we find we have neglected the contemporary scene: the students live in our time, they get it extramurally. I do think it is our job to give them a fairly catholic background, to train the actor for all seasons.

At a conference between representatives of drama schools and repertory companies a few months ago, the view was expressed that actors, on leaving drama school, should be able to do everything — act, sing, dance, even ride a one-wheeled bicycle. I thought that was taking the ideal of the well trained actor too far, although I sympathize with the basic concept. Another view expressed by some television producers who visited the school was that our preoccupation with the masterpieces of the theatre was unrealistic in the light of the time that our students would spend, after leaving school, devoting themselves to comparatively trite, naturalistic pieces, on television. They felt that we should give them some practice in the trite. Our point is that masterpieces inform our standard, and that these can be brought to bear on lesser material, enriching this material in the process. Good actors have in their time made third-rate plays look quite second-rate.

Perhaps the greatest influence on the training of actors in this country has been Michel St Denis, who founded the London Old Vic Theatre School in 1946. It lasted for only six years and its breaking up was a dire tragedy. Apart from Michel St Denis there were Glen Byam Shaw and George Devine as co-directors. Laurence Olivier, in the introduction to St Denis' book, writes that the decision in 1952, that the work of the school was dispensible, was unimaginatively misguided. It closed because the Old Vic could no longer use its grant of £12,000 from the Arts Council for the school. The money had to be used for the company. For the want of £12,000, the school actually closed and I cannot see that it can be recreated on the same level, in our present time. But then perhaps it was not just the money. It may very well have been because people in the theatre were embarrassed by an ideal and a standard which admonished them.

However, more drama schools now exist, and we have succeeded in helping to maintain professional standards in spite of the erosion of the industry. For the future, a regulated entry into the theatre seems necessary to reduce unemployment. For this reason, the new restrictions which Equity have imposed on entry into the theatre, no matter how painful, are an attempt to treat the problem. The National Union of Students may argue against the evils of restricted entry, but it is felt that the evil of unemployment is greater. For this reason, drama schools should be able to restrict their entry to applicants of the highest standards, and their graduates should be reasonably assured of career opportunities and work.

For the past few years I have had a few post-graduate students in the school; students who have their degree and come on to a drama school for a year's practice, before they pit their talents against others in the professional world. Most of them, after a term, feel the need to stay longer than a year, and if they have talent I arrange for them to do so. You see they become aware of their technical inability, all the critical faculties which their university education has developed become directed to themselves. But I think this whole business of going to a university first then going on to some other milieu is wasteful and ridiculous. There are people who at eighteen have enough academic qualifications to get into a University, but they may also have a muse. These people, with a kind of 'Renaissance' ability, do exist. We should have an institution in this country, in which these young people, who deserve a place in a professional drama school and who are also bright enough to be offered a place in a university drama department can do both things, through coming to one institution for four years. They should get the degree by association with the drama department, but under the control, discipline and cultural influence of the professional drama school. Through this process the best spirits in the land might emerge.

This I feel is the necessary step forward and breakthrough in the training of the most informed actors in the country, and I am going to get this instituted, certainly put into the climate of our times, within my lifetime.

John Hodgson: The College of Education

The words **failure** and **success** are so final, so inhuman, that I am going to avoid them and substitute two other words which you may find easier to grapple with — they are **problems** and **aspirations**. So, I am going to talk about the problems which we, in colleges of education, are facing in our attempt to train teachers of drama, and to look at some of the attempts which we have made in order to try and solve them.

John Allen says that there are one hundred and sixty colleges of education with main courses in drama, and I think, that if you have read that report, you will very quickly see that the **first of our problems is one of aims and directions**. Drama is such a young subject and has been in the school curriculum for such a short time that I feel we are still fumbling, which is why I feel it is necessary to draw attention to writers like Aristotle, who did a lot of good thinking a long time ago. If we could stop feeling that we are doing it all for the first time, and opened our eyes and looked around and saw that some of these ideas have already been contemplated, we would be on a firmer foundation and so be able to see a little more clearly, where we ought to be going.

I think it is necessary to do a lot of hard thinking in order to examine and evaluate what we are doing. At Bretton we have done this several times and at present, this is where we think we are trying to go. We have said that we have five main aims:

1 We are trying to develop the personal qualities of the individual
2 We are attempting to provide opportunities for increasing the knowledge of aspects of drama, past and present.

This is perhaps one of the differences between where Nat and I stand. I think that the present is very important, that we need to look at it rigorously and can see it best in relation to the past, in that the value of the past is that it throws light upon the present. Our training tends to start with an attempt to look at the present time, to see what drama is now, before we turn our attention towards the things that happened in the past.

3 We are trying to develop an appreciation and understanding

of the actor, and of acting, as an educational force.

There needs to be a great deal more thinking and examination of this means of investigation that we have, built into ourselves. You only need to look at the way any child uses this in his or her investigations, to discover that we have this fantastic force. We should know how to look for it, and try to understand how it works, with greater clarity and certainty.

4   We are concerned to foster an understanding of child
     development with special reference to the way in which
     a child forms relationships.

In what ways does a child respond to other people and what opportunities for response do we give him within the classroom? It always worries me that in our schools we herd together hundreds, now thousands of children, and the one thing we deny them is the opportunity to talk with each other, to meet each other, to relate with each other. We present them with an ever narrowing series of boxes, classrooms, desks and so on, which make for separation.

5   We hope to give experience of a range of methods of
     approach in teaching drama.

So you see we have these two-fold aims, but they are not so two-fold, not so separated as they may appear to be on the surface. We are trying to keep these ideas firmly in our minds and to make sure that the course works out as a survey of these aims.

Secondly, there is the problem of teaching drama and this is another area in which I feel we have a long way to go. At the present time, we have as our external examiner Professor Bantock of the University of Leicester School of Education. Last year, he suggested that Colleges of Education should narrow their sights and stop trying to teach such a wide range of skills. He formulated three areas of teaching: on the one hand that of mere instruction and to the other extreme that of the full involvement of the person. He said that Colleges of Education should confine themselves to teaching people how to instruct. Now this would immediately cut drama teaching out of the syllabus entirely, but it does at least pinpoint the problems. Teaching drama is **the** most difficult job and to expect anyone, on leaving college, to be immediately able to cope with a job which entails involving a class of children creatively through the use of voice, mind, body, imagination, feeling, the whole lot altogether, is asking a great deal. I think we have to think about the problems of teaching drama but that also we have got to stop imagining that at the end of three years a student is trained, and that's it.   The more we can emphasize that this is **initial** teacher training, that is just the beginning, the more positive our attitude can be. Perhaps this is one of the ways in which the James report is beginning to help, in its suggestion that the first teaching year in school should be very closely related to training, with opportunity for discussion, advice and further help.

The third problem is that of the schools themselves. I am continually being faced with the fact that I am failing and that we are failing in what we are doing, because the students are not all that keen to go into the schools. I find myself in a very tricky position here, because I have no wish to perpetuate the present school system. I have felt for a long time that it is time that we got rid of schools as they are constituted at present and thought again, in terms of something more organic — like an education centre — from which and to which you could go, sharing ideas, pooling experiences, leaving the centre to accrue experience and then returning in order to develop skills in certain areas, then going out again. We should be more more transport orientated in our schools. If things remain as they are at present, I am very worried as to how we can go on getting people who are resilient enough to withstand all the pressures that they find in the schools, who are able to go on working within that framework without accepting it as the necessary thing. I look forward to the Theatre in Education team as being one of the more useful ways of breaking through this barrier and perhaps, of bringing life into both those conservative institutions, education and the theatre.

Fourthly there is the problem of student motivation. This is something which has very much concerned me in recent years, the problem of how to sustain interest. It is all very well, and fairly easy, to make exciting courses for one year, but everybody eating rich diets may well tire of them. I will tell you later on how we have attempted to deal with this one.

The fifth problem is that of time, the time allocated to the area. When you are dealing with human growth and human individuals working with each other, you cannot do it quickly. It is quite foolish to attempt anything in the nature of a rich experience in a short period of time and it seems that more and more, over the last few years, extraneous matters have been taking up time, and that courses instead of becoming more integrated seem to become more fragmented.

The sixth problem is one which I think all of us as teachers share, and I think that perhaps this is one of the values of conferences like the present one. It is the problem of **sharing and knowing what other people**

are doing. We need to meet other people, to appreciate that the problems which we have are not isolated ones and that there is no need to be overwhelmed by them. Even if people have not got the same problems it is often very reassuring and helpful just to discuss them. This is often a first step towards some kind of solution.

So, these are the problems. Now, how have we attempted to meet them?

At the present time we have a three year course which involves twenty to thirty students. I will confine myself mainly to that course in that perhaps you can see best the opportunities which are there.

We attempt to divide the course into a number of phases, not years. Usually a phase lasts about two terms. The first three phases are patterned. Each phase has a theme, and the first theme is 'Drama in the Present Time'. The second takes a look at 'The Origins of Drama' and the third at 'Theatre and its Relationship to Education'. From this term onwards we are attempting to meet the problems of student motivation by handing over to them, after these three phases. They will then have had examples of the way in which we pattern these courses and so we shall ask them what sort of pattern, what sort of framework they would like to work with, over the next few terms. We are going to have what will be about a fortnight's discussion and through sifting and sorting the ideas put forward we hope to pattern the second half of the course relative to the experience and suggestions of the students. This is in fact how we have stated the matter to them:

> "The first half of the course is planned in order to give you grounding and insight into the subject, the last half will be patterned as a result of student ideas and experiences, and needs. Make notes about your reaction to the course as you go through it so that you can build the last half in the light of your **considered** experience."

So, we are going to try and prevent, through the second half, student feeling about whatever is happening and we hope that by that stage they will take an even greater part in the organization of the day-to-day practical interchange of teaching experiences. During the first half of the course there should be a lot of feedback, and we should encourage this, so that there will not be any sudden change when some of the responsibility is taken over by the students.

What we have tried to do is to present four kinds of opportunity:

Opportunity through class work and workshop sessions;
Opportunity through individual assessment;
Opportunity through teaching practice and teaching experience;
Opportunity through project work.

Each phase has its own project at student level and at teacher level; each phase has at least one personal assignment and perhaps here it might be interesting to hear about the kind of things which we are asking the students to do. We feel that perhaps we don't need our students to ride one-wheeled bicycles, but that we can nevertheless require them to be aware of the wide range of skills which the drama teacher needs. And so we ask them to do the following six things:

1   To have a file which is concerned with teaching material which is collected throughout the years, relating this to a long essay, that is, a piece of their considered thinking. By the end of the course this will have formulated the beginnings of a philosophy of drama in education.

2   A piece of creative writing arising out of work done on their project, concerned with the building of a documentary, a very useful and important means of structuring some of the drama work in schools.

3   A long essay, which takes well over a year in its preparation.

4   A movement and speech assignment concerned with story telling, aspects of communication.

5   An individual production.

6   A lecture demonstration concerned with some aspect of their knowledge of the history of drama.

Up to the present time we have been very careful to structure the weighting of this, but from now on, we are going to ask the student to talk this over with us so that not everybody will offer the same amount of weighting for each assignment. If a person feels his strengths lie in a particular field he can choose a greater part of the weighting in that area.

With regard to the other problems, we hope that this kind of feed-back, this kind of organic course can help us to meet them and to go on meeting them. We hope eventually to see this through into the schools themselves, now that there is a growth of fresh thinking and of wider understanding and of a much happier, more imaginative approach to the general education pattern as a whole.

*See 'Uses of Drama' by John Hodgson, published by Eyre Methuen

Donald Roy: The University

Academic interest in drama as a degree subject must, it seems to me, be based on the assumption that drama is a field of human activity that is worthy of attention in its own right: not primarily as a means of earning one's living, or as an educational force or tool, but like music, an object of study. The theatre has a long, by turns respectable and disreputable history, and is still very much with us; it is at once an art form, a social phenomenon, an ideological form and a business venture; it involves the exercise of skills and crafts which render it aesthetically distinctive and require special training; and its cultural ramifications are such that its study calls into play faculties otherwise associated with literary criticism, history, sociology, psychology, archaeology, the visual arts, music and various forms of physical address. All of these considerations entitle it to autonomy as a separate academic discipline and, by the same token, all must find their place in any university degree course in drama. At the same time, when I call drama an academic discipline I am conscious that I am using the term in rather a different sense from that which is normally implied. As places of learning, universities are traditionally expected to provide an intellectual discipline, a training for the mind. Drama certainly does this, and integrates it with training of the body, so that the response it calls for is not entirely conceptual, which is why I regard it as the most humanizing of the humanities.

There seems to be some misunderstanding about what drama departments actually try to do and I feel I must attempt to put the record straight. It might help first of all if I give some account of our teaching at Hull and then try to evaluate it. We offer two kinds of degree course, a Special or single Honours course, to which we admit eight applicants per session, and a Joint course, to which twenty are admitted. Joint students combine drama with one other degree course and they may select this from a wide range: English (the most popular), Latin, Greek, French, Italian, German, Spanish, Swedish, Russian, Music, American Studies and Theology. We have deliberately kept the choice as wide as possible so as to produce a wide spectrum of interests amongst the members of our Joint classes. In these circumstances, given the nature of the dramatic impulse, real cross fertilization between cultures becomes possible and the atmosphere is congenial for the comparative approach which we take to the study of European theatre.

Both the Special and Joint syllabuses cover much the same ground. There is a three year survey of dramatic literature examining the work of more than two score playwrights from Aeschylus to Peter Nichols, and a course of the same length in theatre history, which looks at physical conditions of performance, theatrical organization and the place of the theatre in the community at large throughout its evolution. In these courses we follow a chronological pattern. There are, of course, other ways of teaching the subject, but we have stuck to chronology because we like to regard the theatre as a continuously evolving phenomenon. This outlook naturally commits us to studying not only accepted masterpieces and the work of dramatists with a literary reputation, but plays whose only claim to fame is that they sustained the repertoire and were popular and relevant at the time. To counterbalance these survey courses in dramatic literature and theatre history, we offer, in the third year, a number of special options. Some of these are predominantly critical, others, like those on 'Masks' or 'Management in the Theatre' and on 'The Play in Production', have a more practical bias, but all allow the students to pursue, in depth, a topic which interests them. After dramatic literature and theatre history, the third area of work is a rather more speculative course entitled Art of Theatre which attempts to explore and define the distinctive characteristic of theatre as a performing and communicative art and which ranges freely over primitive drama, types of popular entertainment, theories of the drama and dramatic criticism, and the peculiar implications, both social and artistic, of the mass media today. Finally I come to our programme of practical work. Here our aim is to give students tuition in and experiences of as many areas of expertise involved in dramatic action and in performance of a play before an audience as possible. To this end we have devised an interlocking system of practical classes and studio productions. Weekly classes are backed up by two vacation courses in the first year and a further course of three weeks at the end of the second year, which is given over to the preparation of a production. In the third year timetabled practical classes are concerned exclusively with the techniques of radio and television and are taken by the Director of our Audio Visual Centre and his staff. The ratio of practical classes to formal teaching over the entire degree course is in fact 3 : 4. Obviously I do not suggest that this constitutes a professional training; that is not, and should not be our objective, but it does provide a solid introduction to the performing skills without which drama cannot properly be studied or fully understood, and it affords a basis from which to take off into individual specialization in production work outside the time-table.

This part of our work is quite extensive and in an average session we expect to stage between fifteen and twenty public productions. Some are directed by staff, but most are directed by students, and all are acted, lit, designed, crewed and managed entirely by students, with varying degrees of staff supervision. The range of plays presented is nothing but eclectic. For example this session we began with our version of the English Miracle Cycles, a conflation of eighteen plays, newly translated and performed with an emblematic setting and costumes. Since then we have had John Bowen's 'After the Rain', Ibsen's 'Ghosts', Synge's 'The Well of the Saints', 'The Oz Obscenity Trial' and Brecht's 'The Tutor'. In these productions students may either diversify their experience or concentrate on one particular area which interests them. Here, the Gulbenkian Centre is a tremendous asset: not only is the studio theatre maximally flexible and capable of reproducing almost all conceivable stage forms, but the technical installation of the building is superb. The whole emphasis in its design was in fact the provision of adequate working space for students and staff rather than audience accommodation — in short, it is a teaching theatre. It may be an ideal situation compared with the playhouses students are likely to encounter outside the university, but no more ideal than having the time and opportunity to discover and perform Sophocles, Molière, Strindberg, over a period of three years. All our students share the opportunity for learning empirically, though naturally enough the Special class are in the best position to benefit from it, since they are our students exclusively, and thus can be given more practical coaching as well as more time for seminar and discussion, more options including one on film making and another on theatre in education, and an entirely separate course on 'Popular Entertainment' which is conducted through individual research and group project work.

I hope this brief summary of what we do at Hull will have given you some idea of our objectives as a University Drama Department. The extent to which we reach these objectives is another matter and one which will require of me acrobatic feats of objectivity if I am to assess it at all accurately. The task is complicated by the fact that drama, as a degree subject, is still in the process of discovering its identity. The result is that I think it is still viewed with fairly general suspicion, from one side as a renegade and from the other as a parvenu, and in my moments of bleakest self-questioning, I wonder whether it has yet found its own distinctive academic feet. That the feet are there and that they are capable of breaking new ground, I have no doubt.

Perhaps my confidence will seem less airy if I single out a few of our achievements at Hull. For one thing, I am fairly happy about the balance we have been able to strike between formal and practical teaching. It is a balance which most students seem to like and which the better have no difficulty in sustaining, and has been accomplished and nourished in a number of ways. First, by the choice of teaching staff. I am fortunate in having a team of colleagues who not only have interests and qualifications covering a wide range of European studies, but colleagues who manage to combine the scholarly with the practical to a quite remarkable degree. I believe this to be vitally important; if the staff of a drama department are compartmentalized, its syllabus will rapidly go the same way and there will be a disjunction between the two main aspects of its teaching, which might soon cease to inform each other. In the same spirit we have now begun to admit post graduate students whose research projects cannot satisfactorily be completed in libraries and archives alone and need the dimension of performance. They are able to stage productions in our studio theatre in connection with their research. A similar balance characterizes our methods of assessing undergraduate students and these have undergone considerable modification in the light of experience. We still retain a two-part final examination with some written papers, but to these we have added assessment of course essays, an optional dissertation, progressive assessment of practical work throughout the three years and for Special students a final practical assessment in the form of a viva voce with the external examiner. But the ultimate safeguard is the emphasis we place on the play in performance, rather than the printed text, as the fundamental criterion and the centre of academic interest.

Lastly, you will want me to come to the proof which with drama courses, as with all academic puddings, must I suppose lie in the eating. Here I have been very heartened by the extent to which the integrated dual nature of our course work is reflected in degree results and the careers which our graduates take up. Not only have we registered three first and about thirty upper seconds in the past three years, but according to the latest report of the university Appointments Officer, eighty per cent of the department's brood have found drama — I quote his measured words — "A useful background." In actual bodies this means that of eighty-four graduates, twenty-four are actively employed in the theatre, two in journalism, two in television, one in advertising,

197

ten in teaching, while twenty-eight are engaged in postgraduate research or further training.

It seems to me that this catholicity of careers is a good thing, not a sign of ambiguity or indecision in the course. If a student develops a consuming desire to enter the theatre and we think he has some of the necessary qualities, we give him the opportunity to gain as much experience as possible and do our best for him. Similarly if a student knows he wants to teach, after further training they may make it. But we certainly do not set out with the express purpose of training people for the professional theatre, and we do not, as Peter Plouviez alleges, believe that we can do so better than the acting schools. We aim to give students a good grounding in the academic discipline of drama and within the distinctive forms of that discipline to create a congenial atmosphere which allows or nudges students to develop their minds, talents and imagination, and thereby grow as people. It is a discipline which might allow them to learn about humanity and about themselves. Compared with that, the job of grooming people for the theatre seems, at least, to be on an entirely different wavelength. It is not the minutiae of training for the theatre as it exists now in the provinces of a small island, off the west coast of Europe that should interest us, but an apprehension of the theatre as it has been, the theatre as it might be and the theatre as it is.

* * * * * *

These statements should help us to consider the first two questions posed under the heading 'The Conference Brief'. They agree on the point that all speakers are concerned with the personal development of the student, although this is apparently of prime importance to the tutors in colleges of education and an adjunct of the work in drama schools and universities. There are several complementary viewpoints and some parallels in the concern for a need for change. Both John Hodgson and Nat Brenner call for a change in the form of the educational institution, the former relative to the school environment and the latter within higher education. One can see the dilemma of the drama school which sees its best potential applicants accepting university places and it is also possible to see the dilemma of the university in that it has to fight the rituals of academic tradition.

The dilemma of the college of education, the problem of communicating through drama **and** educating as a conscious rather than an accidental occurrence, makes perhaps for a more acute awareness of the value of learning through first hand experience and also of the need to provide an environment which will encourage discovery and investigation.

George Brandt sees some of these problems as crises or moments of persecution which promote change.

George Brandt: A Slight Ache and Other Matters

The present situation of crisis which exists generally in society today may also be applied to the fields of drama and education. Let us use the situation in order to reconsider fundamentals rather than to panic and remember that the theatre has always been stimulated by crisis. As an example of this we may look at Moliere and the scandal of 'Tartuffe' knowing that the Comedie Française is still alive and well in 1972. Similarly Ben Jonson saw the early seventeenth century as a time where through 'Volpone' he tried "to raise the despised head of poetry again". In retrospect we look back on Shakespeare, Beaumont, Fletcher, Heywood, Dekker, Middleton and Webster — it surely was **not** a barren time in the theatre.

Today, however, what are the criteria of success? On the one hand we have 'A Girl in My Soup', 'The Mousetrap', the pornographic attitude and the crusades of Mrs Whitehouse and Lord Longford, and on the other hand, original work by authors like Tom Stoppard, David Mercer and John Arden. It is difficult to tot up a simple comment. Perhaps what is at the heart of it is the question of the function of the theatre today.

There is the 'happening' and its emphasis on the nature of chance interaction, which I had experience of at Schloss Leopoldskron, Max Reinhardt's former château. At the end of three weeks working with a group of people of mixed nationalities, under the leadership of Ken Dewey, 'it' happened, but it would be hard to state the values of 'it' or its impact as a performance. The element of discovery, however, may be of some value when it is considered relative to theatre, also the element of communal interaction between participants, and between participants and 'audience'.

Drama has always been a communal art. If it did not expressly articulate commonly held myths, as in Greek or mediaeval drama, it has always rested on the unspoken assumptions of a given society. This is what has given it its enormous impact, at the peak points in theatre history. The community saw its beliefs, values, patterns of thought and feeling given visible shape, and these beliefs made flesh gained enormous force from the audience responses that amplified them.

It is this rootedness in community concerns that has made theatre
a largely conservative art form. It has not, in the past, represented
the thought of the lonely thinker decades ahead of his time. When it
reflected controversy as it did in the polemical drama of the Reforma-
tion like 'King Johan' or 'Res Publica', or the social critique of Ibsen,
Shaw or Hauptmann, the notions put forward had already gained wide
currency before drama articulated them.

This is self-evidently true of the serious drama. But it can plaus-
ibly be argued that the comic drama, including perhaps especially farce,
represents social value judgements as well. In fact, since laughter as
the response to comedy is spontaneous and bypasses the filtering of discursive thought, it may be an even surer guide to deeply held social
beliefs and attitudes.

Thus, many of Touchstone's lines still draw an instant laugh in the
theatre. But what is our response when he says, as he plans to marry
Audrey:

"A man may, if he were of a fearful heart, stagger in the
attempt; for here we have no temple but the woods, no
assembly but horn-beasts. But what though? Courage! As
horns are odious, they are necessary. It is said, 'Many a
man knows no end of his goods:' right; many a man has good
horns, and knows no end of them."

(As You Like It, III, 3)

Horn humour is relevant here, but perhaps not relevant to our culture, although it may still ring true in Northern industrial countries
and in parts of the Mediterranean, because of the inferior status of
women.

The fragmentation of society may, however, make these 'gut' reactions no longer dependable. Fragmentation of audiences is certainly a
fact, but the theatre as a unifying force comparable to that of the
Elizabethan theatre — that is something else again.

Attempts have been made to broaden the theatre population during
this century, and theatre as a community building enterprise is not a
new idea, for example Max Reinhardt's work. But perhaps we have
learnt to mistrust the mass spectacle which conjures up the unhappy
associations of party rallies and crowd manipulation. However, the
desire of the individual to merge with the mass is still apparent, as
is seen in the pop festival. These, of course, show too limited a form
to permit any interesting development.

The essentially middle class nature of the bulk of drama seems to
cause a narrowing of vision. This is shown in different ways in the
drawing room drama of T S Eliot and the tougher world of Pinter.

Pinter himself has rejected non-communication as a clue to his characters, they understand each other all right. But neither Eliot or Pinter paint a panoramic view of society.

Another symptom of the fundamental uncertainty as to the role of theatre in the life of today is the volatility of audience taste, which makes it increasingly difficult to predict whether a play will be a box office success. Here we are back with 'The Mousetrap' and Mrs Whitehouse again.

Thinkers in the theatre in this century have tried to come to grips with the problem. There is Stanislavsky's commitment to individual idealism in the actor; Brecht's concern with social function; Artaud's desire to stimulate on a sensory level and to probe into the unconscious, into the mythical substratum. Grotowsky has borrowed from both Stanislavsky and Artaud with his concern for the ultimate importance of the actor in his 'Poor Theatre', stripped of the trappings of realism. But even this does not dissolve the traditional barrier between performer and spectator. This was left to the Americans, who through the 'Happening' have made the most drastic attack on what have hitherto been considered the irreducible essentials of theatre. The 'Happening' does away with the idea of a plot; events are deliberately alogical, devoid of causality; even the character of the actor disappears in the person. As an event it represents a contemporary attack on the literary element in drama. In the 'Happening' randomness does not allow for duplication. Drama, however, has usually been embodied in fixed repeatable theatrical performances and as a basic principle, through the ages there has been the division between actors and audiences. 'Happenings' blur or abolish this division altogether, the audience are swallowed up by the event, participate in it and help to shape it. It follows that 'happenings' are not, in contrast to much though not all of drama, committed to being performed in a special playhouse. They can take place anywhere. The particular scene of the action governs it and in fact becomes part of it.

"Theatre," according to John Cage, "takes place all the time, wherever one is, and art simply facilitates persuading one this is the case". [1]

To turn to the other side of our concern — education. Here we know as familiar, crises within the student world. Because this is an age of social disorientation the aims of education at all levels come under question.

Are people being trained for their allotted social functions in a grossly unequal and divided society? Is this training effective? Should people be trained for this, or for the greater development of their own potential?

At school level, the use of drama in education can represent an attempt to engage the child's personality in the act of learning instead of just his intellect, although there are obvious pockets of resistance to such a concept. The development of the personality is not at the top of every educator's list. But let me confine my last remarks to my own field, the place of drama studies at university level.

In the university field, drama is a growth subject and connects naturally with the study of history, sociology, architecture, music and the visual arts. It has obvious links with various technologies, and attempts to get away from the older concept of a one-sided literary education. But we have been anxious to preserve academic respectability, and what does this mean? As often as not, a mistrust of any form of education other than the conceptual one, leading to verbal expression. That, of course, is not really the point of drama studies. We must face the problem of the dislike of theatre practice among academics, and also consider the question of the learning method.

How much latitude should a student be given in setting the syllabus, in selecting their own areas for investigation?

What of relevance? There are enough pressures in modern life making the past inaccessible and closing off valuable historical perspectives.

How much weight should be given to the creative component in university drama work? Should post-graduates be allowed to submit creative work as in the American universities? Should a playwright get a higher degree, rather than the publication of a text, not to mention professional production?

Should a director or scenic designer get a higher degree, instead of a diploma from a professional school, or better still, employment in the theatre?

These questions and allied matters will require a good deal of thought in the future, and they call for answers. Educational drama presupposes a living theatre, and one's view of theatre inevitably involves one's view of society. To ask the question 'Drama, Education, For What?" involves our view of society. It involves our view of where we are going, and how we can live, and how we are to survive.

NOTES

1   'Ahead of the Game' by Calvin Tomkins

* * * * * *

Drama in Education

It seems then that this element of 'persecution' may promote change, and it is interesting that Grotowsky, perhaps the epitome of twentieth century theatre persecution, is now also in a state of change. He appeared in Paris during May of this year, having been on an Indian pilgrimage. An interview in The Times gave the following picture.

He (Grotowsky) asked for questions and then talked for three hours. The substance of his remarks was that he had outgrown the idea of a "poor theatre" and of playing to a "circle of hermits". Nor was it much fun to be treated as caviar for the elite: human brotherhood was a noble ideal but "not everybody is your brother" and the great problem was to find the right audience to play to. He was at pains to deny his reputation for imposing a monastic discipline of harsh, rigorous work, and the words he used most often in describing his present method were "delicacy and gentleness".

Of course it is easier for one man to break out of the restrictions he has placed upon himself than it is for a conservative institution to be similarly influenced by experience. But some of the problems which Mr Brandt cites are being tackled in other areas of higher education. Perhaps the next conference should focus itself around the problem of student motivation — or should it be an investigation into why we value qualifications? For instance should it matter that a playwright be awarded a degree, do qualifications really matter at all? Do they bear any comparison with the experiences which have contributed towards a student's work in general?

Can we break some of these rituals of academic puberty which are adhered to in such a rigorous fashion?

I think Clare Venables would like to, if she had the opportunity.

Clare Venables: University Training and the Provincial Theatre

I wish to limit myself particularly to the topic 'University Training in relation to the Provincial Theatre', to forget London completely and to talk about the area which I know.

Can universities change the theatre and if so, is it possible through what is going on in University Drama Departments at the moment? From my experience there seems to be more confusion in the universities than in the Colleges of Education or Drama Schools, in that in the latter there is some expectation of training for a specific field.

What I am concerned with is what goes on in the three years of university training and whether this does equip a student for what he eventually decides to do. There seems to be a hesitancy about a university admitting that they may be going to train an actor, perhaps less about a potential director, but nobody, in my time at Manchester, would dare to say that they were setting out to train a technician, or a designer. That would really have been pushing it. We used to worry for hours about applicants who did show acting potential, as to whether to advise them to go to Drama School rather than university. Should this worry be necessary?

In my experience quite a few actors and actresses do come from universities and there is absolutely no reason why Drama Schools should not "Stand up and be counted". The university world certainly has some assets in relation to training people for the theatre. They have money, they have facilities, they have time, they have books and all that entails, they have no need to be competitive. The problem is that these assets are directly contrary to practically any condition that may be met in the provincial theatre, and that ninety per cent of the actor's career will involve competitive contact with other people. This is something which the Drama Schools have over the universities, in a rather sick way, but through this competitive aspect, they can also turn out very nasty, single-minded star maniacs. This is obviously not what one wants a university to do, but it is important that we are aware that the university's assets are not necessarily assets at all, in relation to the theatre profession.

First might I suggest that the universities think of changing their names from Drama Departments to Theatre Departments. This sounds a petty, but I think very important, thing and arises out of the problem that many University Drama Departments grew out of English Departments. They, therefore, tend to think in a literary rather than a theatrical way.

I think Drama Departments desperately need contact with the professional theatre and that a whole system of exchange could be set up there. Take Hull for instance. How much contact is there with the Hull Arts Centre? Do you discuss together the work they are doing, the work you are doing? Is it possible to avoid the university's cocooned atmosphere through contact of this sort?

I think also, that at some stage, the Drama Departments should say "Yes, we are going to train actors, technicians, directors, and some who are unsure of what they want to be", that there should be some element of vocation within the student's training. Lastly, in this context, I think we must think in terms of making the degree largely practical. One of the great problems I have as a director when I meet an actor or actress in audition, who has been to a university, is that it is not relevant at the moment for me to ask what kind of a degree he or she has got. Well, what kind of a qualification is that? It's not relevant at all.

Now let us look at what is going on in the provincial theatre at the moment. There are obviously the much publicized growth areas such as Birmingham, Sheffield, Leeds, where they have every facility in the book. They create a sort of 'After Eight' chocolates sort of atmosphere but at the same time they do some good work in their community. They are just beginning to find their feet as sort of sub-West End theatres. Then, you have a whole series of Reps, such as Lincoln; usually working in old buildings; spending as little as possible on actor's salaries and as much as they can on costumes and sets. Sometimes they have a very frustrated Theatre in Education team, who are expected to inspire fifty thousand schools, with very little money. There are some which are doing very much more than that, where a director discards the money to spend the rest of his life in the provinces — Peter Cheeseman at Stoke being an obvious example. These people commit themselves to that place at that time and try to make that theatre work for their area. There is also the area which virtually all theatres are trying to go into — the idea that there is more to be done than the 7.30 pm performance, that there are lunchtime shows, work in schools etc. It's all very piecemeal, but the actor's day is beginning to crack, so that he can go out and start to work inside the community. It's all very idealized in that we hope it will mean that people will begin to come together, it is leading towards a communal activity.

I think that this community awareness has led to a rethink of actual working relationships between actors, technicians and above all, directors, who are beginning to realize that there are people who have a genuine creative ability of their own, and that their relationship to the actor is a coordinating one, an inspiring one, not a dictatorial one. And it's also now okay to talk about Stanislavsky again. If you talked about him ten years ago people looked embarrassed and thought "University Intellectual". Now it's au fait, it's okay, the actor is beginning to turn into a person, instead of being a sort of celluloid identity.

The University is obviously brilliantly equipped to sort out the right kind of people for this world, if that is the way theatre is going. But, at present, the student emerging from the university, because he has done a lot more talking than doing, has a tendency to believe in the idea as being sufficient, to believe that the working out is a secondary, slightly irritating factor. There is also an over-emphasis on the experimental side of theatre which can make a university student impatient when he goes into a rep theatre which is putting on 'Hamlet' one week and 'Hot and Cold in All Rooms' the next. There is this terrible danger that the graduate will think that it is only the set plays in the syllabus which are right. There is also a lack of humility. One generally finds that an actor, who has experienced personal criticism, because every time he acts and receives comments it is he himself who is criticized, has humility.

There is also the factor that a university course can create more interest in discussing the point of a play rather than the telling of a story through the play and that it builds within the student, creative naivety.

We have tended in the past to divide intelligence, separating IQ from creative ability; that instinctive awareness of what is going on around you, the ability to gel all sorts of things together. Now, to my mind, the creative actor is the intelligent actor, and I think this is terribly important, which is one of the reasons why I am saying let's make the practical work an enormous part of the degree. I think that this is the crux of the matter as far as the training of theatre people is concerned. The great thing that the University Drama Departments can be proud of is that their work is grounded in history, not dead history, but all the sociological factors and developments which created the theatre. The university student is in the perfect position to relate to his own theatre and to himself.

The university, therefore, with its facilities, offering a good technical and a good creative training, a course in history, could train the sort of person who is going to lead the theatre out of what is undoubtedly a muddle at the moment. It's bits and pieces and nobody is quite sure what is going to happen. I think they could really pull the theatre streets ahead of its time.

* * * * * * *

The universities are under attack, I expect both rightly and wrongly. However, the emphasis which Clare Venables places on the development of a student's creative confidence is vital and gives some food for thought relative to question five on the 'Conference Brief'. I suspect that this criticism of the general education of a university drama student could also be levelled at the drama schools and at some colleges of education. Responding to a director, responding to a teacher, does not stimulate a student to be able to use his creative resources so that he can respond with originality and purpose to the problems which he may have to face in professional life, whatever the job may be. There is a vast difference between the ability to present factual information which someone else has put forward, either verbally or literally, and the ability to discern meaning, either logical or in the realms of fantasy, from information which has been discerned by the student's own investigations, both of himself and of the sources of stimulus available to him.

What matters here is that the reactions of assailant and defenders are not those of fight/flight, but as Dr Pokorny suggests, involve listening and consideration, so that the criticism is not assigned to the level of "the tree in the Quad".

John Fernald, in this context, has his own 'tree' in that he attempts to explain how a director works and can be stimulated by the creative response of a well-trained actor.

John Fernald: Problems of being a Director

In terms of the attempts made to popularize the theatre it is important to remember that goodwill, enthusiasm and vitality are not enough by themselves; skill is required. The image of the theatre should be something more than insipid, the theatrical muse being, in the words of Oscar Wilde "A lady of repellent aspect remotely connected with education". It seems to me that at present the theatre is very remotely connected with education, although given the attitude that those who promote it require skill, there could perhaps be a more direct connection.

I feel, as a director, that it is possible to equate the role of the director with that of the orchestral conductor, although there are differences between the ways in which players respond to their director and musicians to their conductor. The musicians work together as a team doing exactly as the conductor wishes, whereas actors are all egoists, and the better they are the more egotistical they are. This is what makes the director's job truly exciting. However, the health of the theatre is not really dependent upon the director, but on those who create for it in a permanent way. However good a director is, when he's dead he's dead, but Chekov and Shakespeare are alive today. Their plays remain for us to recreate, and re-evoke for all time through the creative response of the actor, and the primary concern of the actor is the creation of his own character. Everything else pales in the actor's estimation.

The dictatorial director, however brilliant, stamps on these complex and mysterious creative forces that exist in the individual actor. The good director's skill lies in his ability to manipulate these forces within the actor. Here I think it is a good idea to remind ourselves of Stanislavsky, to read him again, to put him through a sieve, to see how much is really pretentious and inimical and how much is of value. There are two things which I think are of importance: the first is that Stanislavsky expected the actor to explore his part from every conceivable point of view, and the second is that he was also concerned with the skill with which an actor was able to express the result of his explorations. I would like here to quote a passage which is not often referred to:

"There exists a natural, musical, resonant form of speech which we note in great actors in moments of genuine artistic inspiration. An actor must acquire this musical speech for himself by exercising his voice under the control of the sense of truth almost to the same degree as a singer does. An actor interpreting a part, in terms of his own understanding of it will not forget that each sound which forms a word, each vowel, as well as each consonant, is a separate note which takes its place as the tonal chord of a word. It expresses this or that small part of the soul of the character that filters through the word."

We have come to think of Stanislavsky as the exponent of what happens between the words, but we forget that Stanislavsky made this strong point for the development of the actor's vocal skills. The training of the actor's skills, both in movement and voice, take a long time and require a good teacher: it is the actor's equivalent of the learning of musical scales and of the work which a dancer puts in at the barre.

A director assumes that his actors will have these skills and will know how to use them. He also, through knowing his actors, is able to spark them off and to react accordingly himself. He is aware of the delicacy of their interplay where everybody is playing for and with everybody. This means that the element of chance, the unexpected sparking off of one member of the group by another, the interplay of the actors with the audience, is always there when you are directing. These factors explain why live theatre is one of the most exciting things in the theatre arts and completely apart from television and cinema in these respects.

Audiences go to the theatre for various reasons and their attention is held through a complex pattern of tension and relaxation, built up through their response to the play. All the way through a play the actor exercises power over the audience by building up these responses. There is, of course, a certain danger in this, as some forms of theatre can wield an enormous power over an audience, to no purpose at all.

Writers like Brecht have reacted against this idea of magic in the theatre, although some of his plays, because he was an artist rather than a politician or polemicist, were enchantingly magical. However, from my experience of meeting Brecht later in life, I felt that he no longer took the theories of his youth very seriously. The same is true of Bernard Shaw, who thought that he was teaching people through the theatre, but in fact was stimulating, amusing and asking people to use their imagination.

It is therefore the responsibility of the director to wield the actor's power over the audience, not as a vulgar power but as a power of truth. This power is dependent upon skill and it is here, in the attempt to bring theatre to the masses, that failure often occurs, because the executants lack the skill which is going to enable them to maintain their audience's attention.

Another job of the director is to control movement on the stage, to control spatial happenings, for movement is a very powerful thing. In this field the director's power is very great, because actors have not got eyes in the back of their heads and cannot be aware of what is going on behind them. Awareness of this power of the director can also make them suspicious. I remember Donald Wolfit for instance. He had to take over the role of Pastor Manders in a production of Ibsen's 'Ghosts', and to join a group of people who had already staged the play. At first he rehearsed alone, and although I told him very carefully where other people were, and what they were doing, he didn't have them there, so he didn't take it in. When he finally joined the other actors I watched him getting increasingly agitated, until he said "John, John, this won't do." At the end of the act we stopped to sort it out and in the course of the argument it turned out that he was very worried about Flora Robson. She was at the back of the stage, with a pair of knitting needles and this troubled him. He said "John, you haven't been an actor for thirty years, you don't know what that woman will get up to with those knitting needles." This is an illustration of the importance of movement, you see. One pause, and a bit of knitting — fine — the eye goes immediately to her and she becomes emphatic. It's the kind of thing a director does, but it must happen in a pause. What Donald Wolfit feared was that it wouldn't happen in a pause.

Movement is very fascinating, because it is one of the areas more under the director's care than anything else. And here, if the actor or actress has skill due to controlled movement, just as there can be skill due to controlled verbal expression, he can give the director the moments of inspiration which can cause the audience to react with excitement.

* * * * * * *

The activity of a director is a personal one, but I think that some directors in the theatre may build up a relationship with their actors which is symbiotic unless they are very careful. Of course the director should be enriched through the reactions of his actors but equally well, the actor should be enriched by the director. Provided the actor is well educated as a person who thinks, feels and responds with a certain amount of skill, there may be the possibility that they might outdo Donald Wolfit and manage to have, if not eyes in the back of their heads, enough sensitivity to be aware of the dynamics of the group situation which they work within. But perhaps this is just a necessary qualification for any-one who enters the teaching profession?

What then is this thing called drama and how can we best use its potential educationally?

Can we try to look at the present situation and try to bring forward some positive suggestions for future development?

As drama is essentially something which **necessitates** participation, I am concluding this report with the consideration of 'A Case for a Practical Approach to Drama' presented by John Hodgson with the help of students from Bretton Hall College of Education and Hull University Drama Department.

John Hodgson: A Case for a Practical Approach to Drama

The present state of affairs in our drama departments and colleges and even to some extent in our training schools, leaves a great deal to be desired. It seems fairly clear to me that for the most part what we have in universities is a dramatic literature course or some kind of approach to historical theatre, and that this makes most of the inroads through lectures, seminars and papers plus practical sessions. In colleges there is a very much more mixed practice, but generally I think the direction is ill-defined and uncertain. In theatre schools the stress is to the practical side and the plus there is a kind of broad literary background which gives a few glimpses of history. The practical and the academic are for the most part kept very separate in training.

When travelling in the United States last year, I managed to look at some fourteen programmes and I was again struck by a variety of approaches. Usually I can say that the quality of the work was in inverse proportion to the size of the plant. Somehow the vast buildings did not stretch the imagination anything like as much as in those places where people needed to stretch their imaginations in order to make their buildings work at all. It may just be that the teaching staff in the latter places were better, it may be merely coincidence, but this was the general feeling which I derived. I saw directors training, working with actors, on very feeble themes and very uncertain material. In Moscow, where I also saw some training programmes, there seemed to be two poles: at the one extreme those who worked on very traditional, very formal lines, and at the other those who worked more on an educational line, where they were less concerned with keeping up appearances and more concerned with the development of the individual. So, I have come to think that we really need to return to first principles and ask ourselves what the whole business is about.

Let me take you back to very, very elementary, basic thinking relative not only to drama but to education as a whole.

I am here, and presumably because I am here, I am meant to be alive, so may first premise is that life has to be lived and if I am going to live it at all I want to live it pretty extensively. Secondly, I would suggest that I want to extend my life, to develop it fully so my third premise is a question: how am I going to do this? It seems to me that the way to extend your life is to be concerned with the **resources** you have for living and that it is through using these **resources** that you will be led out to appreciate your environment, to appreciate the people and the ideas you are likely to meet. If as educationalists we can recognize these things, then we have a fairly strong yardstick with which to judge what is happening. If we look around our universities, colleges, schools, training establishments, I wonder if any of our training keeps really close to these basics.

It is also important, in order that we understand ourselves as people, that we appreciate that **growth** is part of our **change** and **development**. We must be aware of these factors so that we can adjust to these changes, adjust to growth, adjust to all those things that are going on around us and which make up the factor of going on living as a human being rather than as a piece of machinery. We have to make full use of our resources.

Education then should take some part in trying to further this growth. There are two things which we all need, physically we speak of food but educationally we are concerned with the other side of the coin, with nourishment and exercise and it must not only be nourishment of the body but nourishment for the mind, imagination and feeling. Up to now in our educational establishments we have focused our sight almost entirely on the mind. Our educational pattern has not involved that richness of nourishment which will ensure that every aspect of the person is involved, that we are nourishing the whole man, and this has led us into the problems which we are now having to face.

How do we get this nourishment? There are two factors here which are so basic and simple that we often overlook them. The first is that we have to have **intake**, we have to have something which will go into our body, into our mind, into our feelings, and this can only come from the senses. Education, therefore, must be concerned to make these senses, which are the only means of intake, sharper. The second is that we cannot just put experience, and thus information, into the person. This is where we have been mistaken in education, until very recently. We thought it was just enough to give information without giving adequate attention to the fact that time is needed for circulation and that we must learn to find some means of outlet, some means of expression.

All this may seem irrelevant, but it is basic to what I wish to go on to, to ask what drama has to do with this whole process. First of all we need to remember that the first thing which any child does is to respond to immediate stimuli; therefore education at the beginning must be concerned with the immediate environment of the child. As he becomes more aware, more mobile, imitation and play begin. The child begins to observe, and one of the ways in which he copes with his environment is by watching others — he sees things happening and begins to adapt to life and living through observing others and taking on something of their characteristics. There seems to be an inborn capacity which enables the child to cope with all kinds of problems and situations. As an illustration of this, I remember taking the small daughter of a friend of mine out — she was eighteen months old at the time. Now I got lost in thought and left her behind. When I turned round I found that she was doing the most incredible imitation of my movement pattern. Now, had she been older I might have thought that she was sending me up, but it seemed to me that she was much too young to be able to appreciate what she was doing. The more I thought about it, the more I realized that she was coping with this enormous creature in front of her, bringing it down to size and that this was a basic use of dramatic skill. Impersonation had begun to creep in. As this ability develops it begins to help us to understand, to have a sense of character, and through the developing capacity to associate ideas, the imagination grows.

In addition to this, the young child also delights in both destruction and building, and we can use this delight and attitude of enquiry through a wide range of involvement in dramatic situations; similarly we can develop the sense of pattern and order and the desire to classify things as we acquire more dramatic skill. As the child grows older the imagination, provided it is nourished, becomes stronger, thinking develops and so we begin to be able both to analyze and synthesize. In our universities and colleges we tend to place too much stress on analysis, giving inadequate stress to the development of the capacity to synthesize and here again drama is one of the ways which we have of exercising and developing this capacity, of bringing together those faculties which make for the whole man.

Within these considerations then what is the whole business of drama? What do I mean by drama?

Drama is a means of making us more aware of others, an awareness which education tends to block. We may be critically aware of others but this does not mean that we are more aware of ourselves, in fact it can be just the opposite. I have discovered that often, people with university training have become so critical that their creative forces have been completely blocked, and I have found students who having followed a three year degree course were completely unable to tell a simple story.

Others were quite unable to look at a newspaper and discern what was dramatic within its contents. These people have completed their three year training, which would suggest to me that their course has been concentrated upon the development of the critical faculty to the exclusion of some very important aspects of education: not enough attention has been paid to the development of the capacity for creative expression.

Drama then is not simply texts, it is not simply theatre form, not simply dramatic criticism, nor should it be simply physical and vocal agility. It has to do with one central thing: the human being, the actor, and I suggest that if we are going to place drama in a practical form, we have to put, at the centre of it all, the actor. We cannot, therefore, afford to neglect the practical side, which should really be concerned with the human being, or give it separate sessions unrelated to the other work that we are doing. Surely the actor is the central person, the central part of drama, and all other things should grow from this consideration. If we are going to study theatre form it must be in relation to the actor; if we are going to study the text it must be in relation to the actor; if we are going to study criticism it must be in relation to acting and actors past and present.

So, I am taking a broad view of acting: I want you to think of it as involving the human being imaginatively and creatively, where the actor employs himself as the instrument in both investigating and expressing something of his nature and conditions. Surely this is worthy of a university course. If we can use ourselves and this fantastic built-in instrument which we have got, in order to discover something about our own potential as human beings, then we will be making some useful contribution, not only to the education of the individual, but to other people who are going to be concerned with education after us.

Drama is both a method and a subject. We can use the dramatic method to investigate dramatic subject matter; we can set up laboratory situations in which we can make discoveries about ourselves as communicating human beings, about other people and about the way we live with them.

So these are a few of the basic things which I think are so important for us to understand and grasp and I suggest that there are three areas which we should not neglect when we come to planning our syllabuses and our way of approach. We should be concerned with the development of the **central acting capacity**. We should have a genuine knowledge about drama which grows from **the inside,** and is not just derived through mental activity. We need to concern ourselves with the skills, but **they**

do not need to be taken in isolation. There is no need to be working on the voice to the exclusion of other aspects of ourselves; things can and should be interrelated. The most important thing is that we need to know **where** we are going. It is very easy, in such a complex subject, to lose direction or to be uncertain about what that direction is. Drama is a very old subject in many ways, but it is also an incredible baby in the educational pattern of today. For this reason we must be much more certain of our techniques and approaches so that we can attempt to clarify our thoughts each time we take a drama session.

* * * * * * *

The following diagram of the points which John Hodgson has presented may help to show their relationship. It should also help us to see the progression shown in the illustrations which were presented practically, where the source material was the play 'Macbeth' by William Shakespeare.

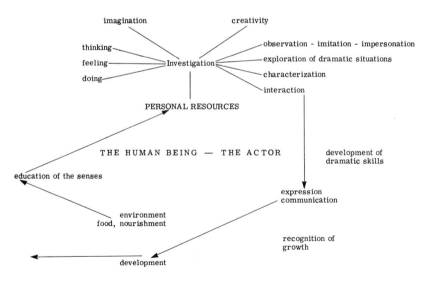

THE DEMONSTRATION

The first point which emerged from observing the students at work was that they must already have had a certain amount of 'nourishment' because not only were they responding to the text of Macbeth, they were already able to investigate. Those who have attempted to work with students will realize that this indicates a certain amount of understanding and skill. The creative and technical resources soon run dry and require feeding when areas of knowledge are limited; then, of course, as someone commented in the discussion, one is only aware of the student and his experience rather than the student's ability to make a personal investigation of a text or other topic.

The illustrations arose from the students' guided investigation of a scene, a situation, a speech, a style and a theme.

The first investigation concerned the opening scene of the play, Act I, Scene 1 "When shall we three meet again?" etc.

The principle of the investigation was to reconsider the content of the scene and therefore try to gain fresh insight into the role of the three sisters and their relationship to each other. It is a scene for which many of us hold preconceived views. Four different ideas emerged, two which through their game-like quality brought out something of the element of irresponsibility with which the witches promote Macbeth's role in the play; a second emphasized their disparate unity through the contemporary analogy of the 'Pop Group'; the third, a hitch-hiking fantasy brought out very strongly the attitude to time which is fundamental to the play. These hitch-hikers were unable to 'thumb a lift', to cause time to wait for a few minutes. Several points emerged which were both useful in discussion relative to the play as a whole and contributed to work which took place on what became the second illustration.

This again involved the three witches, but this time in the situation where they meet Macbeth in Act I, Scene 3 "All hail Macbeth". Here again the group responses brought out aspects of the text which might have been hidden under other modes of scrutiny. One group of witches behaved as babies — who in this situation in the play is infantile? Is it Macbeth in his response to them or the witches in their dependence upon supernatural signs for their motivation? Is it the perception of this infantile aspect of Macbeth's nature which enables us to understand his increasingly irrational behaviour during the course of the play? Are we concerned with reality, with fantasy, with nightmare, with dream? So the questioning continues, and continued for the group when they worked together creating a kind of 'Nightmare Collage' of their responses to the scene. This promoted greater concentration on atmosphere and mood and also a tremendous sense of dispersal of personal energy which began to promote some understanding of Banquo's lines

> "The earth hath bubbles as the water has,
> And these are of them. Whither are they
> vanished?"

After all, what is a spirit to the Elizabethan mind other than a form which can change its identity? To a culture deeply embedded in necromantic belief none of the witches' behaviour is strange. For twentieth century students who do not subscribe to the drug cult, it is a fairly difficult belief to accept. And so there must have been some development or extension of thought in the students, who themselves made the relationships which brought them forward in the text to look at Banquo's lines. The third illustration showed an exploration in terms of sound, of Lennox' speech "The Night has been unruly", Act II, Scene 3. This gave an example of the exploration of the imagery of the speech, an attempt to create the environment which Lennox describes. It also brought out a mood which was destructive and exceedingly powerful; the emotions generated here had something of the turmoil which is the crux of the play. One of the students, later, in the discussion, stated how difficult it had been to comprehend Macbeth's ability to commit murder. This speech, which Shakespeare uses in order to make a verbal painting of the atmosphere of Macbeth's initial crime, has something of the nature of the crime within its structure. An exploration of this nature, therefore, can contribute to the development of understanding of the whole play. At this stage the problem of style was considered — what sort of style adds to your response to the text? Do any elements of style arise from your response? Is it comic? Is it tragic? Is it naturalistic? etc. These questions do not invite a simple solution and in this illustration we saw short examples which demonstrated some of the problems of discovering a style. One group was working in a way that might be described verbally as a 'Nightmare Cartoon'. Could this perhaps be a viewpoint which might be followed through relative to the whole play?

Again, questions, and in the final illustration we saw work where the students, having searched through the whole text, had tried themselves to find an illustration of the central theme of the play, reality and illusion.

John Hodgson concluded the demonstration as follows:

> "What matters is where the work took us, in thinking and in trying
> to look through the play and discover these themes, the inter-
> weaving themes, their recurrence. We might decide now to
> write our essays, to have a few seminars, to put together some

of our experiences in a kind of Marowitz collage. Really the most important thing at this moment is what we have put into it, what we have been able to get out of it, how we have extended our skills and made all our abilities work together."

Looking back at the diagram you will see that the illustrations in fact showed us something of the second half of the spiral. The first half, the providing of the environment which would sharpen the students to respond to the text and to begin to investigate it, had gone before, in order that the illustrations might emerge. The response of the students was no myth, it was a growing changing reality. It would, however, be a myth to expect the same pattern to work with any other group of people, any other text, any other source material. Because, as one of the students pointed out, they had a share in the process, therefore the results were unique to that group. Also, no other text would entail the identical method of exploration. What we have to work with are principles and when they are clearly and simply stated, our problem should become less immense. Where drama is concerned then, there can never be **one** blueprint for an approach, indeed for **the** approach. There is no such thing. For every situation, we need to look again at the principles upon which we base our work and plan from there. These principles quite clearly involve stimulating people through the means that we have at our disposal, those aspects of literature and behaviour which are dramatic. Stimulating, however, is not enough: recognition is vital as is ensuring that a person is continually being extended, mentally, physically and emotionally.

* * * * * * *

Perhaps it is now possible for us to look at the final question posed on the 'Conference Brief' and to consider what we feel the answer to be. There are bound to be problems of communication if we begin to discuss this problem as was apparent from all the reports of the Seminar Leaders, so perhaps it is a matter which we can all put to the test, in our own teaching and working environments, so that it can be evaluated at a later date. It would be an example of mythical behaviour on my behalf if I tried to give a short answer now.

Ritual behaviour is essentially cyclic and so it seems apt to conclude with the remark which Geoffrey Hodson made in his summing up:

Is this the end?   There is no end.

Vivien Bridson

Drama Education for What?

NOTE

The Conference staff and seminar leaders included James Arnott, Martin
Banham, Gavin Bolton, George Brandt, Nat Brenner, Roger Chapman,
Brian Clark, Muriel Crane, John Fernald, John Harris, Nicholas Hern,
John Hodgson, Geoffrey Hodson, Michael Pokorny, Donald Roy, David
Scase, Peter Thomson, Harry Thompson, Simon Trussler, Clare
Venables, Michael Walton, John Williams and Nicholas Worrall.
Conference Convenor: Vivien Bridson.

The NUS Festival

Harold Hobson, theatre critic of The Sunday Times *and for years one of the leading spirits behind the National Union of Students drama festival, tells the story of its development*

When the National Union of Students executive approached the Sunday Times in 1955 for financial assistance in the sponsoring of an annual drama festival, no one guessed that the consequences would be particularly far-reaching. Certainly it was not anticipated that each year a larger number of student companies would enrol themselves in the Festival; nor that the festivals would continue for a decade and a half with ever increasing strength; nor that the idea of competition with which the festivals began would become extremely unpopular, and eventually be discarded; nor that the student companies which entered the Festival would be so savagely critical of each other; nor that the conception that, by virtue of their achievement and ability, some people know more than others, would in time be abandoned; nor that the Festivals would discover talent of so high a quality that in the early seventies it was beginning to exert a considerable influence upon the theatre as a whole.

There are many people who believe Ronald Pickup to be the most talented young actor who has appeared in the National Theatre Company. Mr Pickup played Sparky in the Leeds University production of John Arden's 'Serjeant Musgrave's Dance' which won the trophy presented by the Sunday Times at the Festival held in Leeds in 1961. Terry Hands is one of the principal formulators of Royal Shakespeare Company policy. He played Delio in the Birmingham University production of 'The Duchess of Malfi' at Oxford in 1960. Another figure of growing importance in the Royal Shakespeare Company is Buzz Goodbody. She too first attracted widespread attention at one of these Festivals, when at Cardiff in 1967 she adapted and directed Dostoevsky's 'Notes from Underground' for Sussex University. The director of the winning production in the very first Festival, held at Bristol in 1956, was Timothy West. Mr West, now one of Britain's most prominent actors, directed Wilder's 'Our Town' for Regent Street Polytechnic. Geoffrey Reeves, who subsequently worked with Peter Brook in Paris, and is potentially a talent of incalculably progressive merit, directed the St Catherine's College, Cambridge, production of Edward Albee's 'The Zoo Story' at Leeds in 1961. This production won the NUS plaque for a one-act play which was presented that year for the first time. The Festival has also had an influence on professional criticism. Michael Billington, the very important and influential drama critic of The Guardian, produced Ionesco's 'The Bald Prima Donna' for Oxford University at the Oxford Festival in 1960.

When the Sunday Times agreed to support the NUS Festival financially the task of organizing it was given to Kenneth Pearson. There is no doubt whatever that the success of the Festival, and its establishment as a flourishing branch of academic activity, was in very large measure due to Pearson. Pearson is a man who combines strength of will with great personal charm. No difficulties, no disagreements or jealousies (and these are plentiful in college societies) ever ruffle his urbane good humour. His talents as a diplomat are very striking; equally striking is the manifest enjoyment which he took in the Festivals. This enjoyment spread over the whole Festival, and amongst all its participants. It was invaluable in setting the Festivals upon a sound foundation.

From the beginning Pearson succeeded in interesting the professional theatre in the NUS Festivals. He invited prominent actors and directors to address the competing students each morning of the Festival, which usually lasted for five or six days at the turn of the year. Ralph Richardson, John Neville, Peter Hall, Peter O'Toole and many other leading members of the theatrical profession gave talks which aroused great attention, and were eagerly awaited by the students. Professor J Russell Brown and J W Lambert, Literary Editor of The Sunday Times, also spoke at these meetings with great effect.

These talks were generally preceded by a discussion among the students themselves as to the merits of the plays which they and their rivals were producing during the Festival. Pearson was again very successful in securing chairmen of distinction for these discussions. Brown, Lambert, and Michael Meyer were particularly good at keeping a firm hand on the proceedings. A firm hand was certainly necessary. The students displayed a keenness in criticizing each other, and a somewhat smug satisfaction with their own achievement that came as a surprise to those accustomed to the more charitable atmosphere of the London professional theatre.

The N.U.S. Festival

In the early days of the Festival Bristol University was very generous in offering hospitality. Two or three Festivals were held there. Twice the Festival was held in London, but London proved expensive for most of the students, and it was soon decided that the proper place for the Festival was the provinces. Oxford, Southampton, Loughborough, Aberystwyth, Exeter, Leeds, and Bradford all were the scene of one or more Festivals. By the middle of the nineteen sixties the pattern of the Festival was firmly established. Each morning there was an address from some figure prominent either in the world of the theatre or of academic life, followed or preceded by the students' own discussion of the previous day's productions. The afternoon was given over to one-act plays, for which the NUS offered a plaque; and the evening was devoted to full-length productions competing for The Sunday Times Trophy. For some years there appeared to be no reason why this formula should ever change.

But nothing lasts for ever. The first indications that an increasing number of students were not completely satisfied by the arrangements made for them came in connection with the adjudication that determined the destination each year of The Sunday Times Trophy. This adjudication was delivered by myself on the last morning of each Festival. I devised for it a method based on Acton's celebrated condemnation of Robespierre, in which, after mentioning Robespierre's many virtues, Acton dismisses him as the most hateful character in European history since Machiavelli. This trick of giving the verdict against the **apparent** weight of evidence (though not, of course, against the real but suppressed facts) was strongly criticized. On two occasions, especially, it was considered that I had been particularly unjust. The first was at Bristol in 1962, when I awarded the Trophy to Bristol University for their production of 'Camino Real', instead of to the popular choice, which was Liverpool's 'Henry IV', marked by a very rumbustious performance in the chief part by Martin Jenkins. The second followed two years later, when most people thought that an Oxford production, full of grace and charm, of Ionesco's 'Rhinoceros' was superior to the Leeds production of 'Three Sisters' to which I gave the Trophy. I have never had any doubts that Bristol were better than Liverpool, but it is very possible that the students were right about the merits of Oxford, a university of which I was more than ordinarily critical because I belong to it myself.

Largely as a result of the growing restiveness of the students at what they considered the erratic nature of my judgments, Rona Laurie and Clive Wolfe were called in as members of the adjudicating board, thus changing a dictatorship into an oligarchy. Clive Wolfe had been one of the players in the winning company in the very first Festival, and had maintained his interest in the event ever since: Miss Laurie is one of the most distinguished teachers of drama in the country. Their knowledge of the theatre is as striking as their judgment is sound, and their contribution to the adjudication was of very high value. They also have attractive and generous personalities, and they added enormously to my enjoyment of the Festivals.

The spirit of criticism however continued to gain ground. By this time the roll call of distinguished speakers at the Festival had become really impressive. In addition to those already mentioned, addresses had been given by Lindsay Anderson, Robert Bolt, Christopher Fry, William Gaskill, John Gielgud, Robert Morley, Michel St Denis, and Anthony Quayle. Each individual talk was a great success, but there was a growing feeling that the Festival contradicted the spirit of the times by being frankly élitist. In response to this the practice of a formal address was abandoned, and distinguished visitors were asked instead to give a demonstration class of acting and producing. Joan Plowright, Robert Stephens, and Nancy Meckler each did this. They were extremely efficient, and Stephens in particular was able to show the students at Exeter in 1969 how far their technique fell short of professional standards. After this these professional exercises were abandoned in their turn, and students held their own workshop workouts.

In 1968 Clive Wolfe was appointed by The Sunday Times to be the Festival's first professional Administrator, and when, for the Manchester Festival of 1970 I resigned as Adjudicator, he discovered in James Roose-Evans of the Hampstead Theatre Club a successor of quite astonishing brilliance. When I look back on all the exciting and revealing things that have happened in the Festivals, when I think of all the various talents they have revealed, when I consider its splendid record in work accomplished, I can think of nothing which even remotely rivals the bravura, even the splendour, of Roose-Evans' adjudication at the 1970 Festival. Roose-Evans set a higher standard than had been demanded before; he was witty, cool and devastating.

The students were now, in the natural evolution of events, and in accordance with the contemporary atmosphere, beginning to take a much greater control of the Festival than had been possible in previous years. What had been a benevolent despotism was developing into a modern form of democracy, and important changes were made. The movement against competition had become very strong, and it was decided not to award The Sunday Times Trophy in future. It was decided also to have no further formal adjudications.

The roll of winning companies was thus complete, and unless some

great alteration takes place in student opinion it will not be added to.
This is the list of companies which gained The Sunday Times Trophy
between its inauguration in 1956 and its abandonment in 1970:

1956 in Bristol.	The Student Players of Regent Street Polytechnic, London: Thornton Wilder's 'Our Town'
1957 in London.	Queen's University Dramatic Society, Belfast: Jean Giraudoux's 'Tiger at the Gates'
1958 in Bristol.	University College, Cardiff: Christopher Fry's 'A Sleep of Prisoners'
1959 in London.	Birmingham University Guild Theatre Group: Luigi Pirandello's 'Six Characters in Search of an Author'
1960 in Oxford.	Durham Colleges Dramatic Society: Ann Jellicoe's 'The Sport of my Mad Mother'
1961 in Leeds.	Leeds University Union Theatre Group: John Arden's 'Serjeant Musgrave's Dance'
1962 in Bristol.	Bristol University Dramatic Society: Tennessee Williams's 'Camino Real'
1963 in Loughborough.	Liverpool University Theatre Group: Henrik Ibsen's 'Brand'
1964 in Aberystwyth.	Leeds University Theatre Group: Anton Chekhov's 'Three Sisters'
1965 in Southampton.	Manchester University Theatre Group: Arthur Miller's 'The Crucible'
1966 in Bradford.	Southampton University Theatre Group: Albert Camus's 'Caligula'
1967 in Cardiff.	Leeds University Union Theatre Group: Max Frisch's 'The Chinese Wall'
1968 in Bradford.	Edinburgh University Dramatic Society: Harold Pinter's 'The Homecoming'
1969 in Exeter.	Leicester University Theatre: Kevin Laffan's 'Zoo Zoo Widdershins Zoo'
1970 in Manchester.	York University: 'The Ancient Mariner'

In 1961 the one-act section of the Festival began. The winners of
the NUS Plaque are as follows:

1961	St Catherine's College, Cambridge: Edward Albee's 'The Zoo Story'
1962	University College, Aberystwyth: Gwyn Williams's 'The View from Poppa's Head'
1963	Keele University Drama Group: Jean Genet's 'The Maids'
1964	St Luke's College, Exeter: Eugene Ionesco's 'The Chairs'
1965	Newton Park Training College: Harold Pinter's 'The Collection'
1966	Keele University Drama Group: Samuel Beckett's 'Endgame'
1967	Oxford University Experimental Theatre Club: René de Obaldia's 'Jenousia'
1968	Brighton Students' Federation Dramatic Society: Harold Pinter's 'The Room'

1969   Dryden Society, Trinity College, Cambridge: Samuel Beckett's 'Krapp's Last Tape'

1970   Leicester University Theatre: George MacEwan Green's 'From Out of a Box'

York University's production of 'The Ancient Mariner' was not only notable for being the last entry to win The Sunday Times' Trophy.   It was notable also for being the first to win it with an original work.   In the natural course of development a desire grew, both among the students and among the officials of the Festival, that the Festival should become the arena for original work. Consequently in 1970 it was resolved that only original work should be accepted for the Festival. It is too early yet to say whether anything of permanent value will result from this. From the present trend of events it seems unlikely that a new young author will be discovered to be compared with the discoveries made by the Festival in other fields. The tendency of the Festival seems to be to present works which are the composite result of company creation rather than of individual dramatists. The productions which have so far been presented under the new rule have been full of vigour, and show that students pay close attention to Grotowski, the Living Theatre, Ed Berman, and Pop art. The future is full of hope, but it is as yet too early to start banging the drums in celebration of the arrival of a new genius, either individual or collective.

Everyone concerned in The Sunday Times-National Union of Students Festival is justified in looking back upon its achievements with pride; and in the years to come they may be even greater than in the past.

Harold Hobson

The Seventeenth National Student Festival, Bradford 1972

Geoffrey Axworthy, Director of the Sherman Theatre in the University College, Cardiff, and past Principal of the Central School of Speech and Drama, assesses the 'new-style' Bradford NUS Festival

Harold Hobson has described the evolution of the Festival he has been closely connected with for seventeen years. I have been asked to bring the record up to date with an account of the 1972 Festival at Bradford. Obviously it would be pointless to 'review' the productions, in 'Sunday Times' sense; the 1973 Festival at Durham will be here and gone by the time this article appears. The theatre is an ephemeral art, and writing accounts of performances the reader almost certainly did not see and which, in this case, are gone forever, reveals the predicament of the drama reviewer in its extremest form. Many readers may have no first-hand experience of this unique annual event. This article, therefore, will attempt to give a general account of how the Festival is developing, what purpose it serves, and what significance it has in the world of Drama in Education.

The Festival takes place in a different venue each year (although Bristol and Bradford have each been host three times), for six days, at New Year. An awkward time, particularly for Scots members, exiled in a land with no conception of Hogmanay (and this festival in particular has a terrible lack of frivolity). More seriously, the timing is awkward because the programme has to be selected by early December, from a very large number of entries (fifty-seven this year) in colleges all over the country. As the academic session begins in October the time for preparation of an entry is generally only six or seven weeks. This haste shows in many of the pieces offered, even those that get through to the Festival. It is not just that they lack 'polish' — a quality not highly regarded in current student theatre — but that, largely based on new scripts, that require time to work out, or on group or improvisational techniques that demand established working relationships, they have not had time to cook right through. I say this not to 'knock' the Festival but rather to put it in perspective as a marvellous get-together of people active in college drama, and a display, not of finished productions, but of 'work-in-progress'. An outsider might ask why students do not spend more of the time between festivals planning and preparing their entry for January. The reasons are many and varied. The student's time is short between finding his feet in the world of college theatre and being swallowed up by other demands — like final year exams. In many colleges there is little continuity from year to year; particularly in universities where drama is entirely extracurricular. The most 'finished' entries are, as one would expect, from groups for whom drama forms part of the curriculum.

Harold Hobson does not mention how representation at the Festival has changed over the years. He lists the winning entries over the past fourteen years — almost exclusively university theatre groups. 1964 is the date of the first win by a training college. With the abandonment of competition drama schools became eligible in 1972. A good half of the 1972 entries (and final showings) were from non-university colleges. Since the NUS is now active in upper schools it may not be long before we see entries from that source as well.

To my mind the most noticeable contrast of recent festivals has been between the precise, disciplined modes of expression exhibited, for example, by several generations of students from Rolle College Exmouth, building on two years of creative drama work at Dartington; and the performances by groups which have little to draw on but their own devices. In earlier times such groups had the discipline of the author and his text to work within. Now this approach has fallen out of fashion: today's groups, living on ill-digested scraps from the tables of Grotowski and others, often without effective leadership, explore their souls and bodies in isolation. In consequence there has been a strong demand in recent festivals for 'daily workshops', sessions in which these groups could find out how others worked. The success of the Festival in meeting this demand has been variable. Experienced practitioners of group work, like Nancy Meckler of the Freehold Company, were naturally most able to meet the demand. The 1972 Festival had much less to offer in this field than previous years, although, for those who stayed to the end, John Broome, of the Royal Shakespeare Company, risked and achieved the impossible on the final morning, by conducting a two-hour movement and dance session with over a hundred participants.

The 'straight' scripted production, the decline of which has been

noticeable at NUS Festivals for many years, almost reached extinction
at Bradford. The only example to reach the Festival was the production
of John Spurling's 'Macrune's Guevara', significantly by a professionally-
orientated group from Manchester University Drama Department and the
Polytechnic Theatre School. Other uses of text in such as the forty-five
minute version of 'Woyzeck' by the Northern Counties College of Education or the musical version of 'The Bacchae' by Bingley College of
Education were radically adapted from their originals. Ancient myths
and the classics were the dominant sources this year. St Bartholomew's
Hospital, for instance, presented a most entertaining case-history,
modern, of that unfortunate pair, Damon and Pythias. Essex University
liberally employed all current forms of popular entertainment to bridge
the gap between Greek Tragedy and ourselves in 'Prometheus Rebound',
and got away with it miraculously at times. One group even reworked
the Open Theatre's reworking of Van Itallie's reworking of Genesis —
'The Serpent'. Even Keele's 'Fallacy', a traumatic ritual in which the
audience approached with bared feet and hushed reverence, and was
roughly violated by the entire company, derived, I am solemnly assured,
from the Oedipus myth. Well, it may have. The titles of two of the pre-
arranged discussions reflected the above trends. 'The Tribal Origins
of Today's Experimental Theatre', led by Barry Edwards; and 'Who
Needs a Playwright?' led by playwright Trevor Griffiths. Barry Edwards'
own 'Electric Sunrise' — which employed movement, vocal and instru-
mental sounds — though one of the best worked out pieces of the Festival
nevertheless seemed a great deal less 'experimental' than, say, Stravin-
sky's 'Rite of Spring' staged half a century ago. Of the many shows at
the Festival which freely adapted traditional material through a company
rather than an author, none seemed to me more impressive and moving
than the performance in Bradford Wool Exchange entitled 'A Naming
Ceremony for Christmas' by a professional fringe company, The Welfare
State. A re-enactment of the Feast of Fools, lit by burning circles of
fire and an itinerant fire-eater, costumed in an extraordinary collection
of rubbish (or more politely objets trouves), it was nevertheless pure
theatre magic. Partly through the involvement and mystery created by
the setting, partly through the intensity of the performances, this piece
had for me a reality denied to many pieces with more 'immediate'
themes.

This remark applies particularly to another large group of plays at
Bradford labelled 'Political Theatre'. Bradford has a reputation for
this genre, and specimens of it — memorably Albert Hunt's 'John Ford's
Cuban Missile Crisis' have been well received at previous festivals.

The 1972 festival mounted a large political theatre fringe, including three pieces by an energetic group — The General Will ('The Rupert Show', 'The Moshe Dayan Extravaganza', 'The National Interest'). Their themes were, respectively, Mary Whitehouse and all that, the Israeli-Arab conflict, and Industrial Relations. Only The 'National Interest', which gave a run-down of the new Industrial Relations Bill that was really amusing and thought-provoking, really worked for me. The other two, and the contributions of Bradford Art College, 'Harold Wilson Sinks the Bismark' and 'The Destruction of Dresden', offered nothing that the mind could bite on — an 'Aunt Sally Theatre' of cheap laughs. This was particularly true of 'Dresden' in which Air Marshal Harris was caricatured as an angry Punch, and the terrible drama of that event 'dramatized' by the tearing up of cardboard boxes, or presented in undigested chunks read from a paperback. One does not have to believe that the bombing of Dresden was a justifiable event to feel strongly that such a presentation is a gratuitous insult to both the living and the dead. More acceptable was the send up of the American Moon Landing staged by Al Beach and Mick Banks in the very moon-landscaped environs of Bradford University, using a Bedford van, and an incredible collection of space gadgetry, including fire irons, and egg beaters; and their hilarious final show 'Closing Ceremony' which offered an hilarious image of the week's gropings with a mountain of old clothes in the centre of the Great Hall, into which Pantomime Dames dived head first in search of bargains. This, and York University's 'Hudson's Amazing Money-Making Steam-Driven Railway Pantomime', provided more entertaining satire than the earlier items intended for discussion at the Political Theatre symposium. This spent an inordinate amount of time discussing the merits of Cardiff University's 'Welcome to the Degree Factory' which, though a genuine piece of student protest theatre, was only very marginally 'political'.

The surprise event of the Festival was the Drama Chorus of Macalester College, St Paul, Minnesota. Fifty bright-eyed, smartly dressed students presented a concert of poems, sketches, songs and dances. Those who predicted a disastrous reception for such a predictably 'square' entertainment were wrong. It was the hit of the Festival, and deservedly so. Like Rolle College's 'Interred Side by Side', it was an achievement that had been worked for.

The enormous scale of the Festival — twenty-six plays in six days — meant that a great many halls had to be pressed into service, many of them creating great staging and acting problems. The Great Hall of the University rendered insignificant performances that probably had

233

much greater impact in the more intimate and better equipped spaces in which they were directed originally. This is one of the hazards the Festival has not really coped with as it might, by providing advance information on the available stages. Although the Festival's technical crews achieve miracles of improvisation working through the night, productions which attempt to make elaborate use of lighting and staging are at risk. 'The Audition' by West Midland College of Education, was one of the few to use the stage in a way that expressed the subject. In 'Woyzeck' on the other hand, largely performed on a scaffolding 'climbing frame', the staging seemed imposed on the subject. Bingley College, being close by, got around the difficulty by staging their 'Rock Euripides' in their own well-equipped studio. The Hudson Pantomime had one major advantage, well exploited by the director and his company, in being presented, late night, in the convivial atmosphere of the Bradford Playhouse, rather than in the cavernous Great Hall, or the chilling flatness of Margaret MacMillan College.

As more and more purpose-built university and college theatres become available, in which good lighting and staging can be used as the exciting elements of theatre they are, groups are likely to become more and more impatient of the limitations forced on them by these dreadful examples of 'educational stages'. They will question the assumption that amateur means can overcome acoustics and sightlines that would defeat the most accomplished performers. Hopefully, when they come to positions of responsibility, they may build better college theatres and drama spaces.

I have tried, in a little space, to give an account of an immensely diverse and diverting week of theatre, of a festival that is, considering the problems and the resources available, extremely well organized, and most exciting of all unpredictable. After each Festival I look forward to the next. The terms of reference — if not the actual selection — are getting more and more open. Perhaps next year, weary of improvisation and weak scripts, the trend will be back to texts; or perhaps a renewal of interest in — dare one say — acting? Performances at Bradford, on the whole, depended more on exploitation of self, or on caricature, than on transformation, which is the true root of acting. The experience of the Festival Fringe for me was to see Sheffield Vanguard's premiere of another John Spurling play 'Shades of Heathcliffe', which was very finely acted.

Festival journalism, produced by voluntary critics between midnight and breakfast, this year left much to be desired. This is the time when criticism can really count — when the event is simmering in the mind.

This year's discussions, rather aimlessly conducted in unfocused halls, seemed weak and irrelevant. Perhaps the terms of reference were too remote. Perhaps the only vital subject for an NUS Festival is Student Theatre. The Festival offers an image of what, at this time, it seems to be. But is the image a true one, or the creation of the selectors? Is there really, in this country, a distinctive thing one can call Student Theatre? If so, what is it like, how does it work, where is it going, what does it need? Who, and what is it for?

Geoffrey Axworthy

ASSITEJ in North America

The 1972 Conference of the International Children's Theatre Association (ASSITEJ) was held in Montreal and Albany, NY.
Joyce Doolittle and Richard Courtney present this report of proceedings

The international Children's Theatre movement (ASSITEJ) held its fourth congress this last June in North America. Co-hosted by Canada (June 14-18) and the United States (June 18-25), five hundred delegates from all over the world assembled to watch professional companies from Russia, Roumania, the United States, and both English- and French-speaking Canada, as well as listen to addresses, and to conduct ASSITEJ business.

It was suitable to assemble first in bi-lingual Montreal, a modern, active and artistic city. Delegates had the opportunity to visit the galleries, theatres, concert-halls and restaurants that make this city famous. As later in the United States, the Moscow Central Theatre for Children, the Ion Creanga Theatre of Bucharest, Les Jeunes Comediens du Theatre du Nouveau Monde (Montreal) and The Children's Theatre Company of the Minneapolis Institute of Arts (USA) all performed — and the Roumanian actor, Ion Lucien, was the toast of the Congress! In addition, the Globe Theatre (Regina), La Nouvelle Compagnie (Montreal), Young People's Theatre (Toronto), and Playhouse Holiday (Vancouver) were officially invited to perform in Montreal only. Every afternoon from 4.0-6.0 pm came Communic-Action — a kind of 'fringe' activity, with many events at the same time open to delegates. Some of the most exciting were Company One (Victoria, BC), the participation workshops of Dr Giselle Barret (of the French-speaking University of Montreal), and the Pompledale Players, a participational group from Calgary. Daily there were films on children's drama and theatre being shown, and there were two major addresses on the Congress theme: 'Creativity in Children and Young People, and the Role of Theatre for Children in This Process', by Frau Ilse Rodenberg (director of the

Theatre of Friendship in East Berlin), and by Professor Richard Courtney (The University of Calgary). There were receptions and dinners hosted by the Mayor of Montreal, the Province of Alberta, and by The Secretary of State of Canada.

On the 18th June, delegates crossed the border by bus, and after a picnic lunch at Ausable Chasm, arrived at the State University of New York in Albany where, for six more days, delegates enjoyed daily performances, films and social events on the splendid Edward Durrell Stone designed campus, with its five new theatres placed at the disposal of the congress. A special feature of the New York sessions was daily critiques of the previous day's performances by professional newspaper critics, including representation from The Saturday Review, The Christian Science Monitor and The Critical Digest, followed by comments and questions from the floor. US theatrical companies represented in Albany only included: The Georgia Tour Play, The Atlanta Children's Theatre, The Little Theatre of the Deaf and the hit of the Albany sessions, The Eisenhower High School from Minnesota with their brilliant but tender play 'The Capture of Sarah Quincy'.

At meetings of the General Assembly of ASSITEJ Nat Eek, chairman of the US Centre of ASSITEJ was elected President of the world organization; Joyce Doolittle, chairman of the Canadian Centre of ASSITEJ was elected Vice-President; Ion Lucien was appointed Treasurer. Continuing on the International Bureau of ASSITEJ are: Vladimar Adamek, Ilse Rodenberg, Vice-Presidents; Rose Marie Moudoues was reappointed Secretary General. Further ASSITEJ business included a resolution to establish a committee to study the relationship of creative drama to ASSITEJ proposed by Gerald Tyler of the British Centre, which was defeated, and a motion to include Spanish as a fourth official language, which was tabled and sent to the bureau for further study.

On Sunday, June 25th, a stalwart band of Europeans and Canadians left Albany for a 'foreigners only' 3-day excursion to New York City, which included a visit to 'La Mama' Theatre, a tour of the Lincoln Centre and a performance of 'Follies'. At a reception hosted by the USA International Theatre Institute Rosamond Gilder voiced a view shared by many delegates — that the Fourth General Assembly of ASSITEJ marked a watershed in the history of theatre for young audiences.

When ASSITEJ next meets in Brussels in 1974, it will be with increased strength and self-knowledge. The 14-day North American Congress was the longest, most complex and best attended in the history of the organization.

Joyce Doolittle
Richard Courtney

Postscript to ASSITEJ

Joyce Doolittle and Richard Courtney refer in their report from ASSITEJ
to the proposal from Gerald Tyler concerning the relationship between
creative drama and ASSITEJ. Gerald Tyler writes to 'Drama in Education' that "this year's efforts towards that goal have in themselves been
dramatic" and contributes the statement he submitted to the President
of ASSITEJ. We feel that important issues are raised here:

WHAT IS CREATIVE DRAMATICS

Creative Dramatics is a general term for improvisation, situation drama,
playmaking, role playing and all those forms of informal drama which
rely upon individual or group spontaneity. It is inherent in those parts
of Children's play, and its extensions, which seem to have elements of
drama within them. As far as it concerns children it consists of happenings and situations which are child made and which do not demand to be
seen or assessed.

These quasi-dramatic manifestations can involve speech, movement,
dance and sound, even involve dressing up and the use of properties or
may call for a special locale or playspace. Yet it is something done by
the players themselves with no thought of, or concession to, an audience.
Nevertheless it does demand the operation of the intellect, the will and
the emotion and what arises can be expanded into objective, constructive
play. Creative dramatics forms the rough stuff of theatre where the
participants can find out much about other people and themselves and in
its practice much can be learned about the drama as a whole. In the hands
of a sympathetic and skilful teacher it can lead to an appreciation of
dramatic form and dramatic presentation and also to the writing of plays.
Creative dramatics can be enriched by contact with all the arts; especially by seeing dramatic presentations. It is deepened by contact with
life itself.

The practice of creative dramatics can sometimes touch upon unex-
pressed feelings and emotions within the participant and so help him to
play out problems which lie within his thoughts and behaviour but which
do not always easily find vocal expression. Creative dramatics can
arrive quite spontaneously and ideas, thoughts and emotions can be
played out in dance, puppetry or in a dramatic situation. It is the function of education to guide those inborn instincts to play so that when the
time seems ripe they may be deepened into meaningful objective dramatic play. This, in turn, will help to develop the conscious drama of
older children into something which is more truly part of theatre.

It should be stated that creative dramatics is not confined to children's work but is something which also belongs to that experimental, mental-play area of the imagination which is part of the adult world. It is something which the actor often uses privately when working out a characterization or a situation in a play. It is something which some producers use when an actor finds it difficult to understand, or express himself in, a section of a play. It is something we all use in coming to terms with life situations.

If adults write or act for children then it would seem essential that they should understand something of this aspect of drama and allow it to influence their work.

This shadowy area between personal play and the theatre is what we understand by the term Creative Dramatics and it is this which we recommend as a proper study for ASSITEJ within its constitutional aims.

Gerald Tyler

NADA at Bangor

A report on the conference of the National Association of Drama Advisers

The National Association of Drama Advisers held an open course/conference at the University of North Wales, Bangor, from 21-27 September 1972. Its aims were to give the 75 course members (drama advisers, head teachers and teachers) 'learning through experience situations' related to the needs of the early-school leaver now conscripted into schools for an extra school year; to relate our often stated aims as educationists (especially those concerned with drama in education) to the practical implications of those aims not only within the school, but also within society at large; and, through practical work, to point to the decisions that have to be made in terms of curriculum planning and school organization, if such aims are to be realized.

The course was conceived as an organic whole, there being three phases which, while being separate in content, had an organizational style reflecting the theme of the course. Phase I consisted of six consecutive sessions conceived in the style of a traditional school timetable. Each session had merit on its own, for all course members were able to experience the expertise of each tutor before dividing into groups with only one of the tutors, but, by implication, such timetable organization ignored the developing interests of students and emphasized the pigeon-holing of experience and the lack of opportunity for carry-over from one session to the next. Phase II involved the course members in work in groups. Each group related to the tutor's specialism (visual arts, drama, writing, and environmental resources) but a large period of time (15 hours) allowed students to pursue particular interests to some depth. All groups had a stimulus pack of material as a starter for personal or group enquiry. Phase III again involved work in groups. This time, through a simulation exercise as staff of a school, course members had to solve the problems of constraints of staff and facilities upon the type of humanities programme experienced in the freer condition of Phase II. There were twelve hours for this section of the work. There were also three additional lectures concerned with the broad theme of the conference.

The Conference went through an uneasy period towards the end of Phase I — some of which the tutors had expected. There was a feeling amongst some members that the pressure of the 'traditional timetable' was frustrating and too intense and disjointed (a situation reflected in many schools); others felt that points of view had been overstated, that they were well aware of problems of school organization and ethos and were more anxious to find answers than to re-state the problem. Others found the sessions of immense value in themselves as learning situations. Areas covered in this phase were:

a) principles of education
b) a reassessment of value judgements related to 'creative writing'
c) a programmed event involving the visual arts within a dramatic framework
d) an insight into the use of museum and natural resources
e) a consideration of the implications of selection, streaming etc by course members taking a Verbal Reasoning Test in the prescribed conditions
f) a consideration of musical styles in relation to anthropological circumstances.

There was a release of tension and joy in the work as Phase II began and we observed some creative work embracing the arts and the humanities of great interest and expression. This involved the use of writing, tape, film, research, the visual arts, drama, and music. The involvement of course members developed considerably during this phase.

The role-playing in the simulated schools of Phase III had an uncanny reality to it. Staff-room meetings in particular dealt in a direct way with personal relationships between staff, staff and head, and staff and pupils, and there was a genuine involvement in the crucial debates of curriculum planning and organization related to the way we establish learning situations for young adults within certain unchangeable constraints.

Two of the visiting lecturers made a lasting impression. The sincerity, commitment, and humility of John Ordd caused most of the Conference to look very closely at their own roles within education — particularly the validity and honesty of them in the context of the claims we often make for drama in education. There were severe implications in John's session for the climate of schools and the values they should encourage.

Bert Parnaby, in his first public statement since taking over national responsibility for drama from John Allen, gave a committed statement on the future of drama in education, making a plea for a breadth of vision in our application of the various patterns of drama and urging an acute assessment of our work in drama and always related to an equally acute assessment of the assumptions and aims of education itself.

This too brief report is a personal response to the course. It does not necessarily represent the views of the National Association of Drama Advisers or, necessarily, of other course members.

David Morton

Note: David Morton, Course Director, was assisted by the following:
Tutors: Derek Bilton, Museum Service Organizer, Notts; Eric Bolton, Inspector of Schools, Croydon; John Butt, Curriculum Development Adviser, Devon; Alan Gummerson, Senior Lecturer, Art Education, Leeds Polytechnic.
Lecturers: Bernard Baxter, Longbenton High School, Northumberland; Jack Featherstone, HMI; Michael Haralambos, University of Minnesota; Peter Oliver, Director, Oval House, London; John Ordd, Liverpool Free Centre; Bert Parnaby, HMI.

5. Ideas
Projects
Materials

Growth of Theatre Schools Departments

The work of the Schools Department in any theatre should be the most exciting and creative of all the departments. In schools' work theatre is stripped down to its essential form: it takes a problem, explains the issues, demonstrates clearly the facts and leaves the audience to consider its verdict. Theatre is for life – it makes for a better life because at best it clarifies the world a little and enables us to make choices, to take sides; it should never demand acceptance of specific beliefs but offer up the facts as we see them. It is very easy, faced with a large building, an even larger financial responsibility, tax-payers' money, the problem of programming and day-to-day adminis-tration, to lose sight of the main ideal. Schools companies are small units. Because they are faced daily with students all too eager to receive knowledge, their moral responsibility is continually before them – one hopes the administrative problems can be taken off their back by the main house so that they can serve as a spearhead to our work.

The growth of Schools Departments has been comparatively recent. For myself I first became involved at the Royal Court Theatre – our audiences were low, it seemed to me that something must be done to ensure that an audience was prepared for the coming years. I became involved in this work on the 'bottoms on seats for ten years' time' principle. However, I was quickly changed by the work itself – one of the early projects I set up was to take a hundred children at the end of the Summer Term for two weeks, half from London Secondary and Comprehensive Schools, half from Grammar Schools. The show was to be theirs. There were no plans, only a date booked at the Royal Court, a fortnight to work in – and the kids. I threw into the melting pot exercises which lead to developing various techniques, possible ways of demonstrating facts, and they decided what they wanted to say and how to say it. The most frequent complaint over the two weeks concerned school, 'we are taught what to think, not how'. I became increasingly aware that theatre was a wonderful educational tool and began to understand why I often heard myself saying, 'I've learnt all I know from theatre'. A group might decide they wanted to say something about Biafra – and in the first instance this would be expressed as a generalized 'isn't it all awful'. However, if you put something on the stage you have to think (1) what are the facts (this means research, experts in to talk to them, etc) (2) what do we really want to say (3) what technique is best – a masked play about suffering, a fairy story about the ludicrous political situation, or both? How, too, can every-one's opinions in the group be incorporated – how was the boy who wanted to sing and say 'I don't really give a damn about Biafra' to be incorporated? The whole effort led to clear definition of thought and an expression of their beliefs at that moment in time for their mums and dads who were to make up a large part of the audience. Clarity of thought, the right of everyone to express his opinion and the necessity for everyone to have an opinion were the watchwords of the fortnight. The barriers in classes and ages were broken down; there was only a problem to be solved. It wasn't therapy, as much dance drama is: it was an exploration of life.

The political connotations of this work, which seemed to me as natural as breathing, were soon presented to me: questions in the Houses of Parliament, about 100 students who stood up and said what they thought. The work of any Theatre in Education team, the work of any Drama Adviser, will eventually lead to the development of critical and aware minds. Theatre techniques seem to me to be the most valuable educational tool available today – but do we want critical minds? It is so much easier to teach what than how to think – it is much safer unless we are all willing to put every organization up to constant critical analysis. I am only too well aware, as I write, of the problems of the teacher. I myself taught for two years and remem-ber very clearly the sense of exhaustion on Fridays, the tension of school life and the seeming impossibility of getting through any day without, at some time, falling back on the authoritarian line of 'now all shut up' – even in a theatre it is difficult to stand up each day and say what I believe may be wrong, what I think now may be useless — let's face the moment as it comes – but in theatre this attitude is essential. Theatre and education are inseparable – for me, plays which entertain always teach. I similarly think that what is taught should always entertain. The Northcott Theatre is concerned to make theatre a necessary part of life. It is natural therefore to work in the schools. I often think that as the theatre was used by the Church to clarify in physical terms the Latin text, that life today is all Greek to me, and that I am privileged to spend my life clarifying my own thoughts and, I hope, helping other people to do the same.

Jane Howell

Don't Play with Porcupines: the Young People's Theatre of the New York City Center

On a recent Saturday afternoon in the large basement space of the New York City Center which has been converted for use by the Young People's Theatre, fifteen children, under the guidance of Artistic Director Marjorie Sigley and Stage Manager Charles Suggs, were playing grown-ups at the dinner table. Each of the 'adults' gave advice to the children in the audience about things not to do in life. Most of the admonitions were typical: "Don't play with matches" and "Don't put your feet on the couch". However, when the time came for one small girl to speak, she warned the children: "Don't play with porcupines!"

The phrase became the theme for the remainder of a unique afternoon in theatre for children. The City Center project, at times referred to as 'Instant Theatre', takes aspects of children's theatre and creative dramatics and combines them into unusual, productive, and sometimes highly amusing afternoons of theatre.

Good children's theatre can provide standards for the child's own work in creative or informal dramatics, while creative dramatics may give the child a greater appreciation of theatre as an art form after he has had the opportunity to explore the various elements of play production. Why not combine the two concepts so a child may both observe good children's theatre and have the opportunity to create his own? Why not have a short children's theatre production and then have the adult actors serve as leaders while the children create their own plays? This innovative approach is the foundation upon which the City Center's Young People's Theatre is built.

In a recent issue devoted to children's theatre in New York City, Cue Magazine characterized the City Center project:

> A new entrant in the children's theatre field is the City Center's Children's Theatre... Participation theatre calling for play-clothes and playful ideas, this year old troupe gives the children the chance to become part of a theatrical workshop. A large poster proclaims: 'You can be anybody; anything; anywhere; at any time' – and that's what it is all about. *

---

* Dorothy Moses Schultz, 'Children's Theatre', Cue Magazine, March 11, 1972, page 10

The basic structure of each production is divided into three parts. During the first the actors present a story or idea to the children in the audience. During part two the actors divide into pairs and each pair takes a group of children into a small rehearsal space and the children develop their own version of the story or idea. Finally, they return and each group performs for the remaining groups and the adults in the audience. This basic structure can best be illustrated by a description of 'The Time Machine', which the Stage Manager has called, "In many ways our best production". *

As the audience entered the theatre down one flight of stairs, they passed displays of costumes from previous productions, and photographs of the current offerings. At precisely 2.0 pm the doors opened and the children were informed that a very important experiment was being conducted inside; for this reason everyone was asked to enter quietly. It seemed that we would all be waiting for 'The Professor' to return from a secret journey. After this, the children were given coloured tickets as they entered the theatre; each colour indicated the section in which he would sit, and the group with which he would later be given the opportunity to improvise his own play. The audience was divided into five groups, each sitting on a large oilcloth mat in front of the stage area. The stage itself was dimly lit and contained several tables and chairs and a 'Time Machine' at stage centre. Futuristic walls reminiscent of string sculptures bordered either side of the playing area. Coloured lights revolved and cast their shadows against the back wall.

The actors entered one at a time as we did; they were also waiting for the Professor to return. As the audience was seated and the house lights dimmed, one of the Professor's aides entered and explained that the Professor had not yet returned from his trip in time, but was expected back any minute. A discussion followed which identified the eight waiting actors as portraying doctors, lawyers, the town mayor, a newspaper reporter, and other members of the community. They were as confused as the audience concerning the whereabouts of the Professor.

Suddenly, as the Time Machine glowed, the Professor magically appeared from his trip into time. He explained that there was so much to see in time that he was only able to glimpse a small bit of it. The cast discussed going forward in time, backward in time, slow motion,

---

* Charles Suggs II, private interview held at New York City Center, March, 1972

fast motion, instant replay, and other aspects of time. They decided
that with the help of the young people they would explore a period of
time that the Professor had not yet been able to visit. Each group was
conducted to a section of the large basement space by two of the actors,
and part two of the programme began. Adults in the audience were
given a forty-five-minute coffee break.

During part two the children developed a situation concerning some
aspect of time, which they later presented to the remaining members
of the audience. Some groups began by partaking in exercises dealing
with slow and fast motion. The group I observed was led by an actor
and an actress who had the children sit in a large circle and think about
all that they had just heard about 'time'. After a few moments, each
member of the group was asked to tell what he had seen in his mind.
Most of the children thought forward in time, so it was decided to explore a situation of the future. The most articulate group member was
a boy who had a rather well-developed fantasy concerning a conflict
between a monster computer and some townspeople. He elaborated on
the story at the urging of the actors, and the group began to put the
situation together as a play. Left alone for five minutes, the children
quickly evolved portions of the story into dramatic form. It remained
for the actors to codify the plot into a series of incidents so that the
children would all be aware of what was to happen next. A brief rehearsal was led by the actors before the Professor called, or as he
termed it 'phased' the five groups back in. They returned in an orderly fashion.

A brief discussion with the actor/leaders of this particular group
revealed that they were only able to leave the group alone if they found
a rather articulate individual who could organize the story. If not,
much more supervision would be necessary. The children of this
group divided themselves into computer monsters and townspeople:
boys playing the monsters and girls the townspeople. The actress
helped the girls define and refine their portion of the story; the actor
worked with the boys. This boy-girl division was evident in every
group that afternoon.

The performances in the final phase of the production ranged from
quite good to mediocre. The first group was the hastily assembled
collection of younger children who had attended with their big brothers
and sisters. This group was led by Miss Sigley in an exercise which
necessitated their becoming babies again. As they grew into imaginary adults, the advice of one little girl provided the title for this
paper. It was interesting that with this group, as well as nearly

every other group, the actors were able to call each child by his first name.

As the other groups performed, at times the actors provided narration in order to make the story clear for both the child actors and the audience. In every case the actors indicated both the beginning and ending of the story. In the group I watched, the children remembered about one-half to two-thirds of the material which had been rehearsed, but that which was retained was performed surprisingly well. At the end of the entire performance, the actor in charge thanked everyone for attending and invited the children back for subsequent performances. Both parents and children were delighted with the entire experience and made comments such as, "It was fun!" and "Mommy, when can we come back?"

In order more fully to understand the process involved in creating this type of theatre, I observed a final dress rehearsal of 'Mateus', a production designed for older children aged 12-15. As with 'The Time Machine', the workshop was divided into three parts. The rehearsal was of the opening presentation which brought to life a Polish tale by Janos Korchak. The story tells of a young prince who becomes King and is suddenly confronted with the problems of ruling a country. Later these problems are turned over to the audience as they explore the various divisions of a governmental cabinet such as education, finance, defence, and health. The audience is then charged with the responsibility of presenting recommendations for policy in these various areas. Speaking of an earlier version of this same play, The New Yorker magazine noted that the young people:

> ... advised the king in the play to devise "fines for any company who throws their garbage into the river", to make "strict laws against drug pushers" ... "and to help young people get into the hospital without paying so much money and having to wait while the child sits there and half dies." *

The problems that young King Mateus experienced closely parallel the problems facing the great powers of the world today. He had a war which had been continuing for sometime, and many economic problems relating to inflation. One weakness in this script resulted from an inherent weakness in this type of theatre: it is difficult for an actor to create a villain in the initial presentation and then come off stage to work freely with the children in creating their own section of the play. The audience cannot ignore the role that the actor has just portrayed, especially if the character has been pictured as inherently bad or evil.

---

* 'Close to Somebody', The New Yorker, October 23, 1971, page 36

In order to avoid this problem, the City Center productions often have no clear antagonists. In 'Mateus' the cabinet members are considered corrupt officials, but somehow reform by the end of the play. An attempt was made to make the unseen Sad King who ruled the neighbouring country the antagonist, but this function became unclear when he offered unconditional peace to King Mateus who immediately rejected it. Even with this problem, 'Mateus' was a stimulating vehicle for 'Instant Theatre'. 'The Time Machine' and later productions such as 'The 5 W's', by employing a series of geometric figures or concepts such as time, do away altogether with the necessity for an antagonist. The problem could also be circumvented by not assigning a group of children to work with the actor-villain.

The rehearsal itself was efficient and businesslike. This particular show, unlike some, was scripted and careful attention was given to cues, pace, timing, and lighting. One major role was rehearsed by more than one actor, for reasons which were not clear, although a look at cast lists shows that there have been occasional changes during the first season of operation. Music cues by an accomplished pianist were carefully integrated into the production to provide background and mood for various segments of the play, including some which were reminiscent of Charlie Chaplin films. The piano even serves as a subtle control during performances, helping to gain and retain attention.

The creator of the workshop is Marjorie Sigley. Miss Sigley, or 'Sigi' as she prefers to be called, has operated a children's theatre at the Round House in England for the Royal Shakespeare Company. She comes from Buxton, England, and received her education in that country. She attended Goldsmith's College, London University, and her first job as a director was with the Mermaid Theatre. From 1960-1964 she directed a theatre department in a secondary modern school in London. She originally came to this country to teach improvisation at the HB Acting Studio, where she still teaches in addition to her work at City Center. In an interview Miss Sigley's comments about children's theatre in the United States cut to the heart of the problems in the art form:

"Children's theatre in America is looked upon as a business. All of the touring packages must present plays that will make money or the company will cease to exist. Another even more important factor is that the actor's priorities are not in the proper perspective in this country. Children's theatre is a job to take between plays for adults. Little, if any in-depth study goes into plays for children. The material which is normally presented for children is usually poorly written and staged.. There is little to inspire the actor to place importance in the performance for children." *

She certainly was not suggesting that the actor who performs for children should not also perform for adults. She noted that on her last visit to London she saw Eric Porter and Dorothy Tutin perform in a refurbished favourite, 'Peter Pan'. She pointed out that these actors, as well as others, prepare their roles with, "... the same dedication as they approach adult performances of any of the famous Shakespearian roles."

Miss Sigley noted: "Few children in this country want to be children. They are pushed to act grown-up from such an early age that there is almost no time to be a child." This view is reflected in the name change at City Center from Children's Theatre to Young People's Theatre. The project is designed for the youth of today because they help create it. The audiences come from all economic and social levels. The theatre is funded in part by the Rockefeller Foundation and the New York State Council on the Arts, as well as being declared a constituent company with other City Center divisions such as the Ballet and Opera.

Admirable as the company is, there are certain drawbacks to the operation. The most evident is the great number of productions. In April, 1972, the company was performing two productions – one for younger and one for the older children. In Easter week a special show was performed, and on the following Saturday two more shows were scheduled to begin. A look at the full schedule for the year reveals that there were twelve different productions from September through to early May. Even though the company of ten professional actors is employed full-time, this is an enormous demand, especially when it is remembered that the productions are created largely through improvisation. Although the theatre is developing an audience that returns frequently and therefore needs many productions, the schedule is excessive, and the fatigue is evident at times in tired performances and unclear improvisations.

The performances by the actors seem too long in almost every case – all are forty minutes or over – and most of the presentations have very little action, an essential ingredient for this type of theatre. A more reasonable schedule would aid more careful refining of ideas for the initial presentations. 'King, Simon, and Co.', the special

---

* Marjorie Sigley, personal interview held at New York City Center, April, 1972

Easter presentation, was the first I had seen to employ settings to any great extent. A reversible house and a huge book with pages of nursery rhymes were integral parts of this production. The problem with these set-pieces was that they were fashioned out of inexpensive corrugated cardboard. They looked as if children had hastily cut them out, rather than a professional scenic artist. If the attempt is to bring quality theatre to the children, all elements should be of quality, including the settings.

The company's future plans call for a workshop in which children will attend every day for a week and create an entire play, including sets and costumes constructed from simple materials. However valid an aspiration this may be, I would hope that the unique 'instant' quality of the City Center project is not lost. With its group of professional actors, its uses of improvisational techniques, its successful transformation of audience into performers, and its sense of group creativity, this company provides New York City youngsters with a theatre that is truly their own, in which they may take an active part at every performance. This unique opportunity should not be lost in the search for future expansion.

Michael W Gamble

Children's Theatre in Belfast

On the 10th July, 1971 eight people – mainly students or ex-students from Bretton Hall College of Education – got together to begin discussing, writing and rehearsing material to be used in a street theatre experiment in Belfast.

None of them had had direct experience of street theatre, but had been influenced by ideas emanating from Ed Berman's enterprises in London, from the Leeds group, Interplay, and from Theatre in Education companies in England. Just three days later they were in Belfast exploring the possible areas in which they would stage the project.

The idea was to involve children on both sides of the religious / cultural divide – separately at first. So for eight days – four on each side of the peace-line that runs between the Shankhill and the Falls Road – the Belfast Street Theatre Summer 71 Company presented four participatory plays based on the Finn MacCool legends.

The children made their own costumes and props in the mornings. They began the afternoons with games related to the drama. Each play lasted about ninety minutes and on each successive day the children's participation increased, so that by the end some of them were able to play name-roles within the story. The children also made their own instruments for the street band and, from the second day, were able to join the Company on its parades through the streets, as well as provide a 'score' for the dramascapes.

The Company went to Belfast with the intention of bringing the children of both 'sides' together for one final production. However, on arrival, they felt that any breaching of the peace-line itself would have been impossible at that time. Somehow 'neutral' territory had to be found – away from the troubled areas.

The Botanical Gardens – a large park not far from the city centre – provided the perfect answer. And so, with children from the Protestant Shankhill Road and Sandy Row and the Catholic Falls Road and Divis Street, the whole park was used – including the bandstand and the rock-garden maze – in a free-wheeling, colourful and musical spectacle, the focus of the drama shifting from area to area in the manner of a silent-movie chase. 'Yellow Submarine' was staged only once, but it brought some two hundred children together in an atmosphere free of tension and anxiety.

Following the project, Fred Lancaster, an actor/teacher, Judith Wild, a drama teacher, and Nancy MacKeith, an actress and social worker, obtained a grant from the Ministry of Community Relations to establish a children's theatre/community arts centre in Belfast, housed in St Andrew's Church, Hope Street.

Fred Lancaster

'The Knight of the Burning Pestle' at York

Since we are the first Special Drama students at Hull University, our first-year course has been on an experimental basis from an educational standpoint, nothing more so than this Summer term project.

Basically the project consisted, or rather culminated in a performance of Francis Beaumont's play 'The Knight of the Burning Pestle'. It was in fact an attempt to examine theatre history from a practical point of view, and although it was an academic concept in itself one hoped for a revaluation of the attitudes towards Jacobethan Drama which have gradually been built up by drama historians and theoreticians.

The production of the play was accompanied with research work (by each of the eight students involved) into specialized topics, such as Jacobethan staging, acting style, social position of the players etc. Each student brought to group discussions, improvisations and finally more formal rehearsals a fund of academic research with which to mould production ideas.

Two performances were eventually staged, one in the Elizabethan courtyard of St Williams College, York, and one in the stable courtyard of Burton Constable Hall, with varying degrees of success.

The first major problem which will be obvious to everyone is the difficulty in bringing together the academic approach with any vital performance. This approach was necessary, however, because we were not just producing a play, but attempting to understand the problems and advantages of what had been considered the 'Golden Age' of English Drama, and this inevitably required the springboard of academicism.

Discussions with the group showed that certain insights into Jacobethan production were gained, if only basic things such as performing in the open air, the small size of the acting area, and the amorphous nature of the audience. However, once on stage, confronted with an audience, a great deal of consciousness of our purpose in performing was lost as we overcame nervousness and groped for lines. Added to this was the consciousness that whatever we were doing was being assessed for the inevitable qualifying examination.

Of the plays to choose from, Beaumont's 'The Knight of the Burning Pestle' is an extremely esoteric play, mocking a society which is no longer that of our audience. Though it failed in its day because of its scathing satire on the middle class audience, any such satire, intrinsic to the play, was lost upon a modern audience.

Perhaps the most rewarding experience from our point of view was our dress rehearsal at Burton Constable when a party of Junior School children watched us. Uninhibited by the normal behaviour of a twentieth century audience they sat on the stage, chatted with the actors and roared their approval or booed at the bits which they did not like. Could this be interpreted as the behaviour of a Jacobethan audience? Such a point is arguable and it should be noted that the children only really reacted to the obvious knockabout humour, the giant barber being their favourite character.

A criticism of our particular exercise was that the individual areas of knowledge researched into were not shared enough by the group and we were each seemingly left stranded with our own particular topic, with very little knowledge of what the rest were doing.

Despite such criticism, a basic point which may seem irrelevant to all those dedicated students dragging their way through higher education was that such an approach to academic work made the course far more interesting and seemed to give far more stimulus to us to read around, through and beneath the subject.

Having said this, I think it necessary to point out that such a process as that mentioned above is not as revolutionary as it seems. It seems to me to be a very different (and most interesting) means to a very similar end. It seems to be an intellectualization of 'theatre' in the same way as a 'dead', absolutely academic approach. Admittedly the audience seemed to enjoy it but on the whole they were made up of the students and academic staff of the University. Had the play been produced with the twentieth century audience most in mind perhaps the audience would have got more from it? The validity (I use the term with care) of such a production seems to have been mainly to the student/performers. Such a production may have been wrong theatrically but it was not wrong educationally, as we were, from the outset, studying theatre history from a practical angle and not practising theatre.

Bob Carlton
Student, Hull University

An Experiment at Ibadan

The School of Drama, University of Ibadan was opened in 1963 and one of its aims was to produce specialist teachers of educational drama capable of not only laying the foundation for a dynamic theatre tradition in the country, but also teaching drama as a school subject. Drama was not a subject in the school curriculum and neither its place in the school nor its role in education was understood. Amidst the acute prejudice that drama is simply a design for entertainment, recalling the usual end of the year 'school concert' or that drama is useful for teaching infants through play, recalling Caldwell Cook's 'Play Way' method, the task was not at all easy. The education authorities had neither shown interest in recognising our diploma as conferring qualified teacher status nor the necessary encouragement that could urge us to go on. Teaching practice was an important aspect of the two-year diploma course, but it became difficult to arrange. There was as much comment on the lack of scope provided in the present school curriculum for the development of educational drama, as there was an intense ignorance of the essential correctives that the use of drama in the school could provide if planned effectively within the status quo. The school time-table simply had no room for drama!

It was obvious that a case had to be made. The education authorities would need persuading that drama could stand on its own feet as a subject in the school curriculum. It was felt that a strategic experiment had to be planned and the agencies of education had to be involved. The campaign began with a workshop designed for primary school teachers and organized under the auspices of the Ministry of Education in Ibadan. The six-week in-service course, [1] meeting once a week for two hours each time, was based on the following syllabus:

1st Week: **The Idea of Educational Drama:**
        (a) Introductory talk on philosophy and history
        (b) Discussion on uses in school.

2nd Week: **Creative Dramatics**:
&
3rd Week: (a) Playmaking and improvisation
(b) Practical exercises.

4th Week: **The School Play**:
&
5th Week: (a) Choice and adaptation
(b) Production technique through exercises.

6th Week: **Applied Drama**:
(a) Teaching the language arts
(b) Teaching literature.

It was clear at the end of the workshop that those who benefited from it had come up with a new consciousness. They had found drama to be an excellent discipline. When the campaign had gathered momentum, requests were made to certain schools in Ibadan (primary and secondary) for the placing of our students for teaching practice. Some replied with enthusiasm, others with some scepticism. After a survey, however, the greatest need was found to be in the handling of Oral English in the primary school and in the teaching of English Literature in the secondary school. The main problem of teaching these subjects was of course found to be educational. It had to do with the way and manner in which the learner was brought to learn the subjects. We observed that both the aim of education and the significance of the learning process were treated in the abstract and therefore offered no meaningful precepts or realities to the learner. The second of these experiments is described here.

ENGLISH LITERATURE IN THE SECONDARY SCHOOL

In designing the experiment for the teaching of English Literature through drama for the secondary school, we faced new problems. We needed an approach that would persuade the authorities that drama is not a waste of time, that it would still provide the readiness necessary for the formal examinations in Literature at the end and that literary appreciation is not the 'sine qua non' of the practice of criticism. The basic assumption of the drama approach was explained at a week-end workshop organized by the education authorities for teachers of English Literature in the secondary school. [2]

Assumption:

Interpretation is basic to the study of literature in the secondary school. Interpretation itself is a kind of creation and it is a most rewarding experience if the moment of interpretation is a shared creative activity. Literature is a work of art and can be better appreciated artistically and concretely. Everything that can give it life and form and significant meaning can be seen in 'performance'. It is in performance that we are able to arrive at a true understanding of the author's meaning. 'Interpretative performance' is one vital element that we have found missing in the handling of literature in the secondary school. To bring a sense of reality to literature therefore, those who handle it in the classroom must look beyond the 'examination paper'.

It is assumed that a story is at the core of many forms of art, implicit or explicit. This approach presupposes that an understanding of literature comes through the unfolding of its story core. Whether the work of art is based on a real experience or fancy or sentiment and is cast as a novel or a poem or a drama, it is an important exercise to search for the story element and once this is grasped, it casts a spell on the material. There are in any story three vital elements: plot, character and setting. These serve as the dynamics on which real appreciation of the literary piece depends. Any story has a design, good or bad. The design is a form of movement. Sometimes certain aspects of the movement may not necessarily be supplied by the author in the format he chooses. For instance, Shakespeare in 'Julius Caesar' did not begin the drama with the scene where Caesar 'thrice refused' the offer of a crown, yet 'ambition' was basic to the plot that brought about his tragic end. He leaves us to exercise the imagination and create the meaningful parts that form the vital links in the movement of the drama but which are missing in the text. Any deductions thus made are valid and such an exercise is an effective way of developing the learner's powers of imaginative composition.

It is during performance or 'acting out' of the story element that the learner is exposed to the values of literature. In the exercise he not only makes contact with the experience of others, the totality of response that he makes helps in self-development. This can be achieved by using the techniques of 'improvisation'. Improvisation is an impromptu creation which is formed from hints and suggestions gleaned from a given text or based on a 'stimulus material'. It is primarily concerned with evoking the imaginative process. Its essence is in the opportunities it offers to those who are stimulated and guided through it for invention and self-expression. During the process of an exercise in improvisation, the learner is encouraged to wonder, to question, to discuss and to evaluate his own feelings and those of others. The moment of discovery arrives when his attempt to create a play out of a story, a poem, a thought or a situation materializes in a theatrical form.

We had observed in almost all the schools we sampled that the teaching of poetry was the most uninspiring. It is the mechanics employed in its treatment that made it such a boring and an uneventful exercise. Poems by African authors, especially, were sadly neglected and one of the excuses given was that many of the poems were obscure. Teachers complained they did not have an available library of critical works on them to aid their appreciation. In a design to change attitudes to the study of poetry and create a sustained interest in it as an important branch of literature, a lesson was planned based on the technique of improvisation as an attempt to explore the creative processes through which poets and writers work.

In the experiment, two groups of Secondary Class Five students were used. They had been reading poems by African poets. The first group was given copies of three poems by Leopold Sedar Senghor: 'Totem', 'The Dead' and 'Prayer to Masks'. [3] Subjecting them to the new treatment, the class produced an improvisation-based piece, 'A Dance of Masks', which used the poems, music and dance to achieve a powerful dramatic unity.

In the other class, the poems treated were those by the Ghanian poet, G Awoonor-Williams: 'Songs of Sorrow' and 'Song of War'. Reading the poems several times over under the guidance of the group leader, the students saw the two poems in a synthesis of one profound experience – a confrontation between Africans and European missionaries about the second half of the nineteenth century. Their improvisation yielded a play titled, 'Cry Havoc' with the following scenario: [4]

Characters:	VILLAGERS (worshippers of 'Oro' cult); VICTIM (Chief Priest, later a convert to Christianity); WHITE MAN (a Missionary and Colonialist); AKU (an Old Man of the Village); and a NEIGHBOUR.
Setting:	A village near the sea. A White Man has arrived in it. He is a Missionary. The whole village is in festive mood before the interruption of White Man.
Scene I:	An 'Oro' shrine. The god is visible. The 'bull-roarer' can be heard in between evocation rites off-stage. The worshippers beat and sing excitedly. They enter led by the Chief Priest who later becomes Victim. Dressed in white, they beat bamboo sticks and dance round the god. The noise of the 'bull-roarer' continues.
	The White Man enters. He is annoyed with the people for making noise. He mimes a repeated warning directed against the Chief Priest. He walks across the shrine and, desecrating it, he pulls down the god. He orders the Chief Priest to follow him. The worshippers become irritated. They leave the stage to plan with their elders how to rescue the Chief Priest.
Scene II:	Victim returns but he has been converted. Bemoaning

his new status as a vagabond, the elders of the village
arrive. Aku and Neighbour console Victim. But the
whole village is in affliction due to the White Man's dese-
cration. There is wailing and weeping off-stage. A
coffin is brought on stage carried by two men. Victim
discovers the dead man to be his aged father. While a
ritual burial of the dead is in progress, White Man enters.
He is annoyed to find Victim performing pagan rites. He
disregards the corpse and upsets the occasion. In a state
of frenzy, he compels Victim to follow him at once. The
people struggle with White Man to retain Victim. Victim
is taken away forcibly. Aku, the old man, is pushed and
falls down. The people are greatly agitated. They swear
to extirpate White Man. They rush out leaving Aku who
picks himself up slowly and says wistfully, "I shall sleep
in white calico. War has come upon the sons of men.
And I shall sleep in white calico. Let the boys go forward. "
The war-boys enter, ready to march forward and cried,
"Let the white man's guns boom ... We are fighting them
to die. We shall die on the battle field. " They march out
with their bows and arrows, cutlasses and machets,
carrying the coffin.

Scene III: The scene opens into a dark empty stage. There is noise
of war off-stage. The white man's guns boom but the sea
rumbles noisily in sympathy. Shots of cannons are heard
but there is also thunder and lightning. The stage is
slowly covered in smoke amidst wailing and weeping of
women and children. End.

By involving the class in interpretative performance, the dynamics
of the drama were used in transforming the poems into a theatrical
experience of great significance. Having been stimulated into flights
of the imagination through the illumination offered by the poems, the
students created their own plays, their own theatre. The 'stimulus-
response' method employed in the act of improvisation enabled them to
discover in each poem the locale or setting, character and plot, structure and language significance. The author's meaning was searched
for through a creative involvement and an artistic activity. The
important achievement of this approach was found to be in the self-
understanding which enabled the students to evaluate and share in
some original experiences such as probably prompted the author in the
first instance. Exploring through the words of the text and the poetic
form, the students saw the vision which these evoked: Words create
impressions, sometimes particular, sometimes general. In order to
get at the right interpretation both the effect of the words within the
context of the literary work as well as some unspoken reflections which
gave the motivation for the underlying plot of the play, were critically
examined.

The decision to follow up the play that emerged through the exercise and set it within the frame of the theatre, extended the scope of

the lesson into a new dimension. The use of movement, sound and colour not only gave the creative activity a symbolic and dynamic significance, it also developed a discussion on aesthetics.

Conclusion:

We had set out to teach poetry but had arrived at developing creativity. Teachers waste so much useful time when they spend a good part of the lesson periods for Literature on reading the selected text mainly as an exercise in literary appreciation. Surely developing reading skills and critical appreciation are useful. It is the duty of the teacher of Literature to help his learner to acquire the necessary skills involved in critical thinking and to develop basic competence in comprehension. But the teacher of drama has a different aim which is as valid. Through guidance, he conditions the learner to become sensitive, flexible, original and coherent; through imaginative illumination, he helps him to develop a balanced perspective on life. Teaching drama goes beyond the basic search for information and rational comprehension of facts and ideas.

Our experiment was a strategy aimed at drawing attention to the place and role of Drama as a subject in the school. We studiedly utilized the opportunity offered us to teach English language and literature by actually teaching drama. We taught drama not as literature as it is generally presumed but as an art. Drama in the school curriculum is a creative art. To teach creativity is the aim of educational drama – a subject which reaches its own fulfilment through the resources of the other arts.

Joel Adedeji

NOTES

1. The course was held at the British Council Centre Ibadan, from November 15th to December 20th, 1965. Twenty teachers attended. The author of this article was in charge of the workshop.
2. Following the paper read to the meeting of teachers of English Literature in the secondary school arranged by the Inspectorate Division of the Ministry of Education, Western Nigeria at Akure in May 1966, the author used the opportunity of the workshop to demonstrate the new approach he was advocating.
3. Miss Esohe Omoregie, a second year Educational Drama student, handled the class and brought the exercise up for a staged performance before an excited audience.
4. J A Oyeyinka, a second year Educational Drama student, was the leader of this group. The improvisation was also staged by the students as a group activity.

Chikwakwa, Zambia

Chikwakwa Theatre was the brainchild of Mr Michael Etherton, lecturer in Theatre and Drama at the University of Zambia, and took shape through a series of self-help work parties during 1969. University staff and students, together with some townsfolk, enthusiastically took part in the work parties and by the dry weather of 1970, the Theatre was ready for use. The guiding considerations as regards the actual theatre construction were: it was to be as cheap as possible, using local materials; it was not necessarily meant to be permanent; and it must be capable of being reproduced in rural areas.

Chikwakwa Theatre is an open air theatre by design, a deliberate attempt to make a pastoral image for Zambian theatre. Lighting is provided by open fires, gas lamps and paraffin lanterns. The theatre is located in Chamba Valley not far from Kaunda Square and about 4 kilometres from the University Campus. The location of the theatre was influenced by the kind of audience that was envisaged; the theatre was to be directed to those sections of the community not likely to have much contact with the University. It was also meant to serve as a centre of non-theatre activities, eg. Art Workshops, Poetry, Traditional Zambian music etc.

Chikwakwa Theatre is dedicated to the development of a truly Zambian theatre for the people through existing cultural and social conditions. Zambia is experiencing a slowly unfolding social revolution which requires that kind of theatre entertainment that externalizes, emphasizes and comments upon the various sorts of situations, which are being experienced by Zambians in all walks of life.

The Chikwakwa concept of drama does not regard a play solely as literary art. English words and poetry are not enough. There must be a multiple use of language, so that a play can be transformed into life by being spoken and experienced by actors and audience in the most suitable language or languages.

The emergence of the nascent Zambian theatre should not only address itself to the people, but it must use the language of the people, eg. Zambian township English, main Zambian languages, etc.

Improvisation should be used at times as it maintains and allows for a great fluidity between actors and audience which builds up the play as it proceeds, but its heavy reliance on the talents of the actors is its chief disadvantage.

Integration of Zambian music and dances and the use of Zambian languages in Chikwakwa productions necessitates a good deal of transposition of foreign cultural elements into the Zambian setting, or the provincial setting, as the case may be. Transposition of theatre pieces (from one country to another, from one culture to another, from one period to another) enables the participants to appreciate much more profoundly the relationships of the plays to the cultures which engendered them. It is hoped that would-be Zambian writers and producers, as well as actors, will begin to appreciate cultural elements in plays that require adaptation and those elements which express something universal.

Through the careful transposition of a play making it express aspects of Zambian life or universal human situations, the audience is able to respond to known situations, songs and conversations. The audience's enthusiasm soon inspires the actors and creates a very relaxed audience-actor relationship.

The use of Zambian songs and dances during the course of the action can serve a number of related purposes: to underline to the audience some particular aspect of the plot; to provide continuity between scene changes; to attempt to achieve, if possible, a total marriage of the verbal plays with music and dancing; to dig up, through a modern approach to the study of traditional performing arts, ancient dances and songs, and by taking the postures, gestures, movements, rhythms of traditional dances and songs, create new dances and songs; to underline the fact that no dance or song in Zambia was traditionally just for entertainment, but were originally part of community life and their structure and characteristics today originated with their historical function in initiation, rain making, etc.

Everyone talks of making the school's curriculum and all school activities relevant to the needs and aspirations of the community, and it seems that Drama would be one of the best approaches. There should be no division between the existing traditional dance troupes and dramatic societies, and much more contact with the surrounding community is required.

Youngson Simukoko

The Special Nursery: Exploration in Creative Play for Young Severely Handicapped Children

The Special Nursery was the brain child of the MOH for the area, a cathedral city in the South of England, who initially conceived it as providing relief for mothers of handicapped pre-school children. The Special Education Department offered two members of staff, a remedial teacher and myself, who were invited to the first planning meeting. The Health Department were to supply a qualified nursery nurse, premises in a local welfare clinic and any equipment that came within their scope. We emphasized that this was an ideal opportunity for stimulating creative play and that the group should not be treated just as a creche. There was a large and very willing band of voluntary helpers who would bring children in their cars and stay to help if they wanted. We had a generous equipment allowance from Special Education.

The group was to meet two mornings a week and some children, depending on family pressures, came both mornings. We had a maximum of twelve children from eighteen months to four years, with a wide range of handicap, mental, physical, multiple and several queries.

My teacher colleague had worked in the same ESN school where I was drama and movement therapist, and she had a wide experience of junior and senior ESN children. My experience was with maladjusted children, adult psychiatric groups and adolescent mentally and physically handicapped. Neither of us had worked with such a young group before. With the anticipation of the new venture, difficulties seemed minimal and we settled into a flexible routine of free play until orange juice time, then more structured small group work, finishing up with music and movement and singing. The presence of voluntary helpers made for a high staff ratio and could mean total group participation, despite degree of handicap. This was important for instance in marching and dancing games, when a non-mobile child could be supported by a helper. Nobody was ever left out and the normal children of helpers made a very valuable contribution.

There was some tension from nursing staff when the room or children became grubby or paint-spattered. It was noticeable, too, that visitors from health departments inspected the sluice or the nappy routine, while educationalists made lists of our equipment and joined in Ring-a-Roses.

We suffered a major setback when the health office informed us we were not allowed to visit parents, as this was the Health Visitor's job. We had visited all parents when the group was formed and again three months later to chat over the activities at the nursery, especially those in which their child succeeded. Parents asked for ideas to do at home. We found that many felt not only guilty but helpless too. We explained our meetings to the Health Office, but they were adamant. Quietly, we arranged to meet parents at other people's houses and said nothing.

We had a difficult patch when my colleague left and I wanted more scope to develop intensive and individual work. Some of the helpers were frustrated and felt they were in a rut.

I consulted a music therapist colleague, Julienne Brown, with whom I already worked in a psychiatric social centre. We had wanted the chance to work with young children and find areas where we could collaborate as therapists, as well as developing music and drama in its own right. We drew up a programme for the morning's activities: group music and movement on arrival as children settled down; small group work in specific play activities; then after organge juice, Julienne and I were to absent ourselves in two small adjoining rooms for individual sessions while voluntary staff continued group work; then we all came together for singing.

The authority agreed and we called a full staff meeting to outline the plan and to discuss **why** we wanted to try certain activities, so that there was no feeling of secrecy. For instance, movement can help develop body awareness, coordination and control; music could stimulate sensory motor responses and pre-speech sounds and both could establish non-verbal communication.

We made a wallchart of things children had already achieved and ideas for progress. While we were doing private sessions, the voluntary helpers began to come into their own, feeling freer to try out their ideas.

One child who was sightless, with a misshapen head, came to us at two years: he would just lie and sleep, cry or suck a bottle. Julienne found he responded to rhythmic music. This response she stimulated and developed, soon realizing that he had a musical intelligence higher than that of a normal child of two. She built on this to mobilize him,

266

and to stimulate speech sounds and singing. Then one of the very patient voluntary helpers followed this through by teaching him to walk by following her singing round the room.

I worked with a very intelligent 'Hole-in-heart' boy of about four, very backward in motor development and with no confidence. His mother was terrified he would fall and would caution him before he moved. I worked from safe lying and sitting positions, rocking and swaying until he would allow himself to be totally supported by me. This was his breakthrough and he progressed to 'flying' and throwing. He became not only confident but daring and would now be the first round the obstacle track which was for staff and children to go through and under and over before going home. Children exercised their muscles as adults got stuck and had to be pulled or pushed through!

We were presented with a large play mattress with humps and bumps and covered with different fabrics and textures. This was valuable for stimulating touch, as was what we did in painting, pastry, and movement. We did a large foot collage — children and staff. In the case of children who had to be carried, we dunked their feet in a washing-up bowl of paint and held them on the paper.

We had to encourage the voluntary helpers to talk with the children, even if a reply was not possible; they had tended to feel there was no point.

Having exhausted most singing games we decided to write our own, specifically designed for this group. The 'Singing Clock', for instance, brought in grading of sound and grading of movement from grandfather clocks to wrist watches. We used a lot of contrasts in movement and sound — how big and how small; how loud and how soft — essential for attempting concept formation later.

The work was very demanding and much time was spent outside the clinic writing material, assessing and planning. There were times when we despaired of communicating with other staff, let alone difficult children; especially if children were taken out of sessions for testing at critical moments or handicaps were chatted over at coffee within earshot of the group. There were intolerances on both sides.

Looking back, it was one of the most valuable two years in my work, showing how team therapy can work, and how very important is interdisciplinary understanding and cooperation, particularly between health and education. Most important, it showed just how much could be successfully attempted with such severe handicaps. We felt it would be ideal to start even younger.

Sue Jennings

Books

CONFLICT IN DRAMA/PLAYS FOR EDUCATION. John Hodgson (Ed) Methuen. Volume 1 THE PERSONAL CONFLICT (1972); Volume 2 THE SOCIAL CONFLICT (1972)

These paperback volumes bring together plays exploring a single theme, whilst as a series of three (Volume 3 CONFLICTS IN DOCUMENTARIES is still in preparation) they will cover a range of conflict expressed in drama. With notes by John Hodgson and (in Volume 2) Audrey Coldron, these collections form compact, disciplined, and exciting areas of investigation and experience.

DESIGNING A SCHOOL PLAY. P Chilver and E Jones. Batsford

We can only recommend this as the most elementary introduction to the subject, at best a useful book for children wanting to find out about putting on a play. On the one hand the skills referred to are too complex and beyond those normally available in a school, while on the other hand there is no real discussion of the point of designing anything at all. The principles of good design are discernible and teachable, but this book comes nowhere near to introducing the real concerns of sensitive and artistically valid design.

DRAMATIC INVOLVEMENT. G Gould. Blackwell

At the present moment many an English teacher finds himself straining to do some sort of work in drama; often this implies 'something to do with a scripted play'. Such a teacher will welcome Gould's collection of extracts from plays for the relevance of its themes and the quality of its selections.

Following a clear and consistent scheme the book has four sections: 'Imprisonment'; 'Victims of War'; 'Boy meets Girl'; 'Pupils and Teachers'.

Each extract is followed by discussion based upon the text presented, and by suggestions for improvisations and 'interpretation', known here as 'Exploration through Drama', with a final section of suggested written work.

For the man with little time and the need for a textbook, this may well be an ideal choice. The passages are well chosen and avoid being patronizing and the suggestions for follow-up work are sensible and helpful. I suspect that it will be the inexperienced teacher that will find the book of most use. Experienced teachers, and pupils for that matter, might find it a little too directed and 'closed' in its ideas. For example, the suggestions for improvisation are closely structured which could mean that the pupils will be guided into 'acceptable' experiences rather than to discovering things for themselves. But this is a welcome addition to the list of available textbooks for drama in schools.

DRAMA WORKCARDS (for Primary Schools). Donald Lightwood. Blackie

These cards successfully fulfil their purpose, which is to provide practical drama activities for children working in small groups. They are
in three sets of twenty-two durable cards of a sensible size, each set
representing a stage in a simple progression from Mime and Movement;
Stories for Acting to Play Making. The material and activities suggested by the cards should be interesting and appropriate to Primary school
children. They give a focus and direction to the drama activities while
allowing plenty of scope for the children's imaginations. A whole lesson
could be taken up by a group working at the activities on one card. Each
set contains the same notes for the teacher which offer particularly sensible advice on how to use the cards and help the children with the drama.

GRUB STREET OPERA (THE). Fielding, Ed. Edgar V Roberts.
Arnold (1968)

This text in the Regents Restoration Drama Series is a scholarly edition
of an under-estimated satirical play. Just the thing for livening up a
lesson on English Eighteenth Century politics!

HISTORY OF THE ENGLISH TOY THEATRE (THE). George Speaight.
Studio Vista (1969)

This is an updated version of Speaight's 'Juvenile Drama', published in
1946. Studio Vista's very handsome volume does justice to the charm
of the subject and the knowledge of the author.

IMPROVISATION. John Hodgson and Ernest Richards. Methuen.
(1966. Paperback 1967)

This has been a most influential book since it was published six years
ago. Hodgson and Richards, both actively concerned with the effective
use of drama in education, bring their experience and ideas together in
a book that not only explores the value of improvisation in theory, but
also substantiates the theory with a wealth of practice. It is an essential handbook for drama teachers at all levels, and like all good hand-
books is as much stimulant as guide.

KENNET SHAKESPEARE SERIES (THE). General Editor M Davis.
Arnold

For a decade teachers of Shakespeare have enjoyed using this series in
class. Wisely edited,this series is the work of teachers and academics
and has achieved a happy blend of the positive value of both practical
and sound scholarship.
   These editions of the plays are specially helpful for introducing
pupils to Shakespeare. They offer a good text, well-illustrated with
black and white drawings based upon performances in television and
cinema, as well as on the stage, and well presented in an attractive
cover.
   The introductions are brief but clear and instructive, while the
notes to the actual text are set on a facing page, which saves a considerable amount of thumbing.
   A well-proved success, this series may well prove habit forming
for those children who first meet Shakespeare on these pages.

LANDMARKS. Derek Stanford. Thomas Nelson and Son Ltd

'Landmarks' is an anthology of fourteen substantial extracts from English,
American and Continental plays arranged chronologically to provide an
introduction to the development of the main movements in English Drama
since the Second World War. The selection of authors and plays, which
is composed primarily of examples from 'new and experimental forms

of drama', is predictable, eg 'Look Back in Anger', 'Waiting for Godot', 'The Caretaker'. 'The Theatre of Cruelty' is not represented as the author believes it does not come across adequately through the printed word. It is, however, described in the introduction to the book which gives a broad, straightforward survey of the developments in Post-war drama. Each extract is prefaced by a short critical commentary which offers more detailed information about the author and the significance of the play. No mention is made in the introduction of the influence of Brecht, and there is nothing from the work of John Arden.

LEGEND AND DRAMA 1 and 2. Philip Payne. Ginn and Co Ltd

These attractively illustrated books provide a selection of short legends and stories from many ages and countries for Secondary School children to dramatize in small groups through mime or speech. The stories are well chosen for their dramatic potential, and the bias of the book is towards developing the children's skills in acting and production. Considerable assistance is given by the author to both teacher and child in his notes which accompany each story. These notes provide a cast list, a breakdown of the story into scenes, exercises for improvisation and significant acting points. More detailed suggestions for the teacher are available in a pamphlet 'Unscripted Drama' which may be bought with the books.

LET'S DO A MUSICAL. Peter A Spencer. Studio Vista Ltd

This book offers a considerable amount of invaluable, detailed, practical advice and information about the inception of an Operatic Society and the production of a musical. Each chapter describes the successive stages involved in mounting a production from the choice of musical to the arrangements for the first night. The text, which is written in a direct, lively style, is well supported by many bold, attractive illustrations.

NEW THEATRE FORMS. Stephen Joseph. Pitman

Published in 1968 this is a highly readable introduction to the study of modern developments in the design and building of theatres. Embodying Stephen Joseph's own theories based upon his unceasing involvement in 'Theatre in the Round', this volume is essential reading for anyone seriously concerned with the art of staging plays.

Well illustrated, full of commonsense and sound advice, it is a book that deserves to be prescribed reading for many students.

Stephen Joseph was a man of the theatre with a sharp understanding of the theories behind dramatic experiment; this exploration of theatre forms is a document that does honour to an important man whose influence will be with us for some time.

PLAYBILL ONE, PLAYBILL TWO, PLAYBILL THREE. All edited by Alan Durband. Hutchinson's Educational. (1969)

Each of these three paperbacks contains five short plays, and it is a delight to find such lively replacements for the old-fashioned kind of one-act play that was the bane of theatre in education. One either used these shabby pieces, which seemed to be based on the judgement 'No professionals do short plays, so one needn't be too particular on behalf of amateurs', or else one was reduced to trying to take a meaningful extract from a good full-length play. Fortunately, professionals do perform short plays nowadays, and amateurs (at least serious amateurs) are no longer content with hack writing.

The three books are numbered in order of difficulty for actors and directors, but the standard of the plays in PLAYBILL ONE is certainly as high as the standard in PLAYBILL THREE.

In PLAYBILL ONE, Alan Ayckbourn's 'Ernie's Incredible Illucina-
tions' is a good lunatic romp. David Campton's 'The Right Place' is a
lively morality, if a bit obvious. David Cregan's 'Arthur' should
delight actors, director and audience, whether young or old. Donald
Howarth's 'School Play' is a most successful example of drama of the
absurd and of menace. Only Beverley Cross's 'The Crickets Sing' has
a faded air about it.

In PLAYBILL TWO, David Shellan's 'Perfection City' is a good
joke with a serious point. Ann Jellicoe's 'The Rising Generation' was
both commissioned and rejected by the Girl Guides' Association. Drama
teachers will be most grateful to Mr Durband for picking up what the
Association threw out. David Perry's 'As Good as New' is a good example of the macabre fun that young people take to much more easily
than their elders. Tom Stoppard's 'A Separate Peace' is both funny and
moving, a sensitive study of the eternal conflict between human beings
and systems. Stewart Conn's 'Fancy Seeing You, Then' is the poor relation in this collection. It seems to be a long build-up to a big let-down.

In PLAYBILL THREE, John Mortimer's 'A Choice of Kings' is a
history play with credible human beings as characters (Beverley Cross's
'The Crickets Sing' seems paltry beside it). Ray Jenkins's 'Boy Dudgeon'
is a most effective study of a young delinquent. Alan Plater's 'Excursion', originally written for radio, is a piece about football fans. It
would be effective in performance by voices alone, or could form the
basis of a fine exercise in full production. Alan Gosling's 'A Dead
Liberty' is a convincing play about people who can't cope. Ronald Dun-
can's 'The Gift' is a verse play, but the verse-form seems to get in the
way of rather than to add to the overall effect of this amusing, yet sad
little play.

I doubt whether there are many collections of short plays of which
one can say that such a high proportion of their contents is so thoroughly
to be recommended.

STRATFORD-UPON-AVON STUDIES. 3 EARLY SHAKESPEARE (first
published 1961: reprinted with modifications 1967); 4 CONTEMPORARY
THEATRE (first published 1962: reprinted with corrections 1968);
9 ELIZABETHAN THEATRE (1966). Edward Arnold

The Stratford-upon-Avon Series is by now well known to teachers of
drama. On the whole the blind purchase of any of its volumes is not a
great risk. You get your money's worth. The present three volumes
contain several essays that will be found both attractive and illumina-
ting by people with special interests in particular playwrights and particular plays, and a few essays that are devoted to more general dramatic and theatrical matters. 'The Profession of Playwright' by R A
Foakes, in Volume 3, is a lively, succinct and hightly informative
account of the Elizabethan theatre; and in the same volume John Russell
Brown's 'The Realization of Shylock' is an interesting contribution to a
problem that has bedevilled 'The Merchant of Venice' for more than a
couple of centuries. Not all of the essays in these volumes are without
flaw. Kenneth Muir in 'Verse and Prose' seems to take a sledgehammer
to crack a nut, and in the same collection (Volume 4) J L Styan begins
his piece on 'Television Drama' with the remarkable claim, "The primary element of live theatre missing from television is that of dramatic
space...." Is it not true that the primary element of live theatre missing from television is presence? Still, if the publisher's price-sticker
(ominously pre-decimal) is accurate, 'Contemporary Theatre' is worth
25/-, although a touch of the Esslin would give it a very desirable fillip.

TECHNIQUES OF THE STAGE FIGHT. William Hobbs
DESIGNING AND MAKING STAGE SCENERY. Michael Warre
Studio Vista

In different ways both these books tell the same story, that of sheer professional know-how. William Hobbs' book is a thorough, exciting and
challenging handbook to the arranging of fights. Michael Warre's is the
equivalent for design and the making of scenery.
   But first to deal with Hobbs' excellent account of the way that the
blood is made to flow as an artistic event. Here we have that comfort-
ing book the clear and readable setting out of one man's way of tackling
a specific task. Reading the book gives many insights into techniques
and skills while indicating the great care that must accompany any
attempt to portray violence in a convincing manner. At once a guide,
a theoretical introduction and collection of anecdotes this is probably
the best single 'buy' in its field. Useful for the beginner and relevant
for the practised.
   In the same series by Studio Vista is Michael Warre's DESIGNING
AND MAKING STAGE SCENERY, again a readable account with some
good ideas. While providing a potted history of design this book is a
useful introduction with some splendid illustrations. The section on
'painting' scenery offers the best example of the way that both these
books by 'men in the trade' should be taken seriously by teachers. For
in describing the painting of scenery Michael Warre indicates the 'real'
way of doing it as opposed to the short cuts that we all hurriedly seek.
For in truth short cuts are exactly what they are called — they often
miss out an important part of the journey. Warre's advice is practical
and detailed while his outline of the aims of good design and methods of
working is lively and informative.
   Both these books claim space on the shelves of any library where
the performing of plays is part of the institution's programme.

USE OF IMAGINATION (THE). William Walsh. Penguin (Peregrine)

Though Professor Walsh is primarily concerned with the literary mind,
his study will be found of importance in the field of drama, making as
it does a plea for the positive and creative use of the imagination. The
early chapters on 'Coleridge and the Age of Childhood' and 'Wordsworth
and the Growth of the Mind' are particularly pertinent.

USES OF DRAMA (THE). John Hodgson (Ed). Methuen (UP)

This is a selection of essays and commentaries brought together by
John Hodgson to give 'a background to acting as a social and educational
force'. There is a wide range of comment, from Aristotle to Jean-
Louis Barrault, each introduced and interrelated by the editor. The
result is always interesting and often provocative. It is sometimes a
weird experience to find one comment from Stanislavski and another
from a very contemporary practitioner sharing equal billing! It puts
both into a new perspective.

WHAT IS THE PLAY? Richard A Cassell and Henry Knepler.
Scott, Foresman and Company

This is a large American theatre-teaching manual, which includes
twelve full length plays, fourteen critical essays, a bibliography relating to the playwrights studied, and notes, comments and questions
from the editors. It is necessarily selective, but — as in the many
similar publications from the States — one gets a lot of words for the
money. Perhaps better suited to the course system of American
higher education than to a European pattern, where the collection would
serve no complete purpose.

Index

273

Dunlop, Helen, 65
Durham, 230
   University, 227

East Berlin, 237
Eccles, David, 23
Edinburgh University, 227
'Education & children's emotions',
   53
Edwards, Barry, 232
Eek, Nat, 237
Eisenhower High School, 237
Eliot, T S, 184, 200, 201
Elliot, Dr Craig, 67
Ellis, John, 61
English Speaking Board, 3
Equity, 187
Essex University, 232
Etherton, Michael, 263
Ethiopia, 166
Exeter, 225-227
   University Drama Dept., 10
'Experiences in groups', 182

Faulkes, Margaret, 65, 66
Featherstone, Jack, 242
Fernald, John, 207-210 221
'Figures of speech & figures of
   thought', 109
Fogerty, Elsie, 60
Freehold Company, 231
Freud, 91, 108
Froebel, 85
Fry, Christopher, 184, 226

Gardiner, Charles, 153-164
Garfield, Leon, 113
Gaskill, William, 226
General Will, The, 233
General Wingate School, 165-172
Georgia Tour Play, 237
Giddens, A, 86, 98
Gielgud, John, 226
Gilbert, John, 186
Gilbert and Sullivan, 136, 185
Gilder, Rosamund, 237
Globe Theatre, Sask., 66
Goldsmiths College, 250
   Curriculum Laboratory, 43
Goodbody, Buzz, 223
Government College, Ibadan, 165
Goya, 21
'Greater London Arts', vi, 115
Greene, Graham, 184
Gregory, R D, 51
Griffiths, R, 90, 98
Griffiths, Trevor, 232
Grotowsky, 201, 203, 228, 231
Guardian, The, 224
Gulbenkian Centre, 195

Gummerson, Alan, 159, 242
Guthrie, Tyrone, 185, 186

Haaga, Agnes, 65
Hall, Peter, 224
Hammond, Barbara, 98
Hammond, J L, 98
Hampstead Theatre Club, 226
Hands, Terry, 223
Haralambos, Michael, 242
Hartlieb, Samuel, 47
Harris, John, 221
H B Acting Studio, 250
Hauptmann, G, 200
Heath, Edward, 29
HMOCS, 167
Heathcote, Dorothy, 58, 63
Hern, Nicholas, 221
Herron, R E, 85, 98
Hobson, Harold, 231
Hodgson, John, 188-192, 197,
   211-216, 219, 220, 221
Hodson, Geoffrey, 220, 221
Holbrook, David, 37
Holiday Playhouse, 66, 236
Holme, Anthea, 86, 87, 98
Hooper, Dr, 155
Huizinga, Johan, 96, 97, 99
Hull
   Arts Centre, 205
   University Drama Dept.,
      193-195, 205, 211, 255
Hunt, Albert, 232

Ibadan
   British Council Centre, 262
   Ministry of Education, 257
   University School of Drama,
      257
Ibsen, Henrik, 122, 186, 200
'Imagination', 62
Improvisation, 33, 34, 35, 39,
   40, 42, 53, 58, 59, 88, 112,
   113, 114, 121-124, 129, 131,
   136, 140, 142, 161, 185,
   234, 238, 246-252, 259, 260,
   261, 264
Institute of Contemporary Arts,
   107, 109
Institute of Education, 108
Intake School, 153, 156-164
International Theatre Institute,
   237
Interplay, 253
Ion Creanga Theatret, 236
Isaac Newton School, 139
Isaacs, Susan, 89, 98

James Report, 25-26, 190
Japanese No Theatre, 10

275